CRAFTS DESIGN

CRAFTS

WADSWORTH

SPENCER MOSELEY

PAULINE JOHNSON

HAZEL KOENIG

DESIGN

AN ILLUSTRATED GUIDE

PUBLISHING COMPANY, INC.
BELMONT, CALIFORNIA

CRAFTS DESIGN: AN ILLUSTRATED GUIDE by Spencer Moseley,
Pauline Johnson, and Hazel Koenig, University of Washington

16 17 18 — 75 74

PREFACE

This book is an introduction to crafts design. The crafts have long been considered minor arts, although history reveals that artisans of the past made no such distinctions among the arts. There is no craft area that has not been considered at one time or by some culture as a medium suitable for expressing the highest and most complex art values. Feeling and design can be worked into any material.

This book has been planned to give an appreciation of the crafts and to illustrate crafts techniques in simple-to-follow, well-illustrated steps. Design quality is stressed throughout as a fundamental part of good craftsmanship. Many illustrations have been included to show the wide range of cultures and periods of crafts design and to provide examples of techniques and forms. Primitive and folk art are included along with historic and contemporary art. A bibliography is presented for the reader who wishes to continue his study or to explore any medium in greater detail. We hope beginners in crafts design and all those interested in increasing their knowledge and appreciation of the crafts will find this book a useful source of information, instruction, and ideas.

The book opens with an introduction to design and then treats, in turn, the craft areas of paper, bookbinding, weaving, decorated fabrics, leather, clay, mosaics, and enameling. Each area is divided into two parts: first, an appreciation of the craft and, second, an explanation of technical processes. The technical steps have been simplified wherever possible to aid the beginner in his first attempts. Additional steps are included at the end of each section.

Writing this book has brought us much enjoyment, widened our appreciation, and given us new pleasure from the crafts. We will be pleased if it brings some measure of this enjoyment and discovery to our readers.

We wish to express appreciation to the many people who have so generously contributed to this book. We are especially indebted to the following: *Paper:* John Henri Engesser, Zurich, Switzerland. *Bookbinding:* Edgar Mansfield, President of the Bookbinders Guild, London. *Weaving:* Virginia Harvey. *Decorated Textiles:* Lowell Hovis. *Leather:* Steven Fuller. *Clay:* Peter Voulkos, Robert Sperry, Louis Hafermehl, Howard Duell, and John and Gretchen Fassbinder. *Enameling:* Ramona Solberg.

We are grateful to Mildred Sherwood, Art Librarian at the University of Washington, Dr. Richard E. Fuller, Director, and Joan Fechter Photographic Records, of the Seattle Art Museum, for their help with resource material and illustrations. We wish to thank Elizabeth Bayley Willis, expert on handcrafts and small industries who worked for the United Nations Technical Assistance Program in India and Morocco, who so generously allowed us to photograph items from her collection. We are indebted to the Photographic Unit of Audio-Visual Services at the University of Washington and appreciate the fine work and cooperation of William Eng, Whitie Marten, and Kay Owen.

We are also indebted to the American Crayon Company who provided the photographs on pages 226-230, and to the children's Creative Art classes at the University of Washington for many of the photographs of children's work.

And special credit is deserved by Joan Hanson, Laurel White, Paul Nelson, Aileen Moseley, and Vernon Koenig, all of whose hands contributed to the book in many ways.

S. M.
P. J.

Seattle, Washington

H. K.

Polish: *Paper Cutout.* One-fold symmetrical design. Courtesy, Embassy of Polish People's Republic.

CONTENTS

ONE   DESIGN   4

TWO   PAPER   26

THREE   BOOKBINDING   88

FOUR   WEAVING   124

FIVE   DECORATED TEXTILES   210

SIX   LEATHER   256

SEVEN   CLAY   294

EIGHT   MOSAICS   362

NINE   ENAMELING   386

           ADDITIONAL SUGGESTIONS
           FOR CRAFTS   428

           BIBLIOGRAPHY   434

CRAFTS DESIGN

Katherine Westphal: *Nymph and Satyr*. 1956. Red clay body, black, white, yellow, blue glaze, 11½" high.

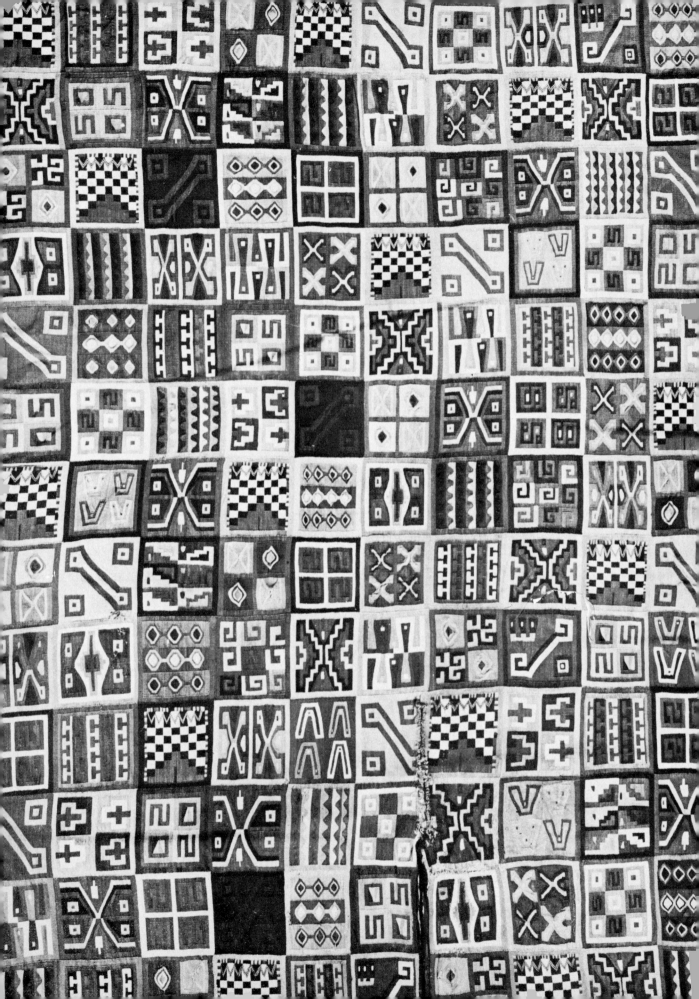

DESIGN

Inca period, Ica style (Peru): *Poncho.* Interlocked tapestry, 72″ x 30¼″.
National Gallery of Art, Washington, D. C. Robert Woods Bliss Collection,
Loan.

DESIGN

THE IMPORTANCE OF DESIGN

Good design is the basis for quality in all the arts. No amount of technical skill can offer the same satisfaction we find in a well-designed work of art. Technical proficiency is the means the artist or craftsman must develop in order to express his individual talents as a designer. There is no excuse for poor craftsmanship. The design quality provides the rich experience of the art itself, whether it be in the unpretentious work of a folk artist, a primitive craftsman, a child, or in the work of a world-renowned painter, sculptor, weaver, potter, jeweler, or designer. The character and individuality of any work spring from the unique feelings within the artist or craftsman who made it. These feelings are expressed with color, value, line, and texture, with shapes and forms, and with subject matter. Learning a craft requires developing the ability and the technical means to express these feelings sensitively and selectively. Visual order and good workmanship are inseparable qualities of fine crafts design.

MATERIALS AND TECHNIQUES

The materials and techniques the craftsman uses greatly influence the forms he makes. The obvious differences between works made of clay, weaving materials, and mosaic tesserae indicate that each material to a large degree determines the nature of the finished product. Each material has limitations and possibilities for the designer. The requirements of good design and good workmanship require the artist to become famil-iar with his material and to explore its limitations and possibilities. A sensitive craftsman thinks and designs in terms of his material, taking advantage of the special design opportunities the material offers. When the craftsman's work is finished, it should retain the qualities of the material of which it was made.

FORM AND FUNCTION

Many craft objects are designed to serve some special function. To ensure a successful design the craftsman should study the requirements of the function and incorporate them into his work so that it will satisfy its purpose. A pot meant to be used as a pitcher should be a convenient size for its purpose, and not too heavy to be easily lifted; it should have a good pouring spout that does not drip, a handle that is strong and easy to grasp, and a mouth wide enough to fill and empty without difficulty. These requirements of function provide the designer with the basic form for the work he is about to make. Beyond these requirements he is free to invent as he wishes, as long as his variations do not impair the function in any way. Even if a work is not designed for actual use, the implied function provides an abstract basis for form.

APPLIED DESIGN

Structural design results from shaping the material according to its limitations and from meeting functional needs. When the structural design is complete, additional decoration, called

Pacific Islands, Polynesian: *Tapa Cloth*. Design stamped on cloth made from bark. Courtesy, The Peabody Museum of Salem.

Virginia Weisel: *Cream Pitcher*. 1960. Stoneware, height 3½″. An example of design based on function.

San Blas Indian (Panama): *Detail of Blouse*. 1944. Appliqué cloth, 33″ x 22½″. Collection of Mr. and Mrs. Louis Hafermehl. An example of applied design.

applied design, can be added to give further richness to the form. The structural design of fabric, for example, may result in plain cloth that can be given applied design by printing, stenciling, stitchery, or appliqué. These techniques do not alter the basic structure of the material, but are simply means for surface decoration. Applied design should always be planned to suit the material and the shape. When carefully conceived, it can enhance the basic form and strengthen its visual qualities. At its best, applied design is a part of the form, so related to the structural design that it seems inseparable from the work itself. If poorly conceived or carelessly done, applied design can easily destroy the quality of an otherwise well-made and beautifully planned work.

THE ELEMENTS OF DESIGN

It is easier for the designer to plan his work if he is aware of the various elements of design and the ways they can be used to build form. Design analysis, using the elements, can aid the artist in developing design and in appreciating the work of others. Frequently, the artist finds it necessary to examine his work, one element at a time, to judge the needs of his design. Although the elements may be considered singly, in the final work they must each lose their separate identities and fuse into the total form.

The Basic Elements
 Material and space
The Measurable Elements
 1. Color
  a. Hue
  b. Value
  c. Intensity
 2. Dark and light
 3. Actual texture

 4. Size and mass
The Derived Elements
 1. Line
 2. Plane
 3. Shape
 4. Visual texture

The basic elements of all the visual arts are material and space—the material of which the work is made, and the space it occupies or creates as part of the form. Each material has qualities that can be measured. These are color, which can be broken down into hue, value, and intensity; dark and light; actual texture, which can be sensed by touch; and size or mass, which describes the amount and weight of the material. By the use of the measurable qualities the artist can derive line, plane, shape, and visual texture.

MATERIAL AND SPACE

Material and space are basic to all visual art, because no work can exist without them. We sometimes refer to them as *positive* and *negative* space. The space occupied by the material is the positive space. Its size, shape, contours, and relationships should be carefully considered by the designer. In addition to the positive space, the material can enclose, outline, or suggest voids that also become part of the design. These negative spaces must be carefully considered as integral parts of the design. Many designers concentrate most of their attention on the negative shapes because they are so important and so easily overlooked. Even a solid mass of material, when beautifully composed, affects the space around it. The sensitive designer is aware of the way material both fills and creates space, and he tries to make a relationship between the positive and negative aspects of his form.

When working with either positive or negative shapes, the artist finds the concept of form easier to grasp if he considers the volumes as geometric solids. Most forms in nature or in art can be thought of as cones, cubes, cylinders,

Detail of *The Death of Holfernes.*

Italian (Venetian): *The Death of Holfernes.* Needlepoint panel, 60″ x 6″.
Courtesy of the Metropolitan Museum of Art. Gift by subscription, 1909.
An example of design with positive and negative space.

pyramids, spheres, or oviforms. The shapes, both solid and void, that are combined in a work should be related to one another, whether they are negative or positive, large or small, kept as separate identities or fused into a single form with transitions and modifications.

The pot by the Swiss-American potter Paul Bonifas has an especially well-planned positive and negative space relationship. Note the variety of sizes—small, medium, and large—formed by the solids and the voids. The body of the pot encloses the largest space, which is echoed by the voids in the handles. These three negative spaces, each enclosed by a wall of material, contrast with the incompletely enclosed space between the body and the foot. All the spaces are planned so that they relate to each other and to the material that defines them.

In the fragment of a Coptic textile another aspect of positive and negative space has been used to form the design. On a two-dimensional surface, the spaces between shapes are referred

Paul Bonifas: *Pot.* 1937. Designed in clay, cast in bronze, height 8″. Collection of Mrs. Wells, Geneva, Switzerland.

DESIGN   7

Coptic: *Panel*. Fifth century. Tapestry weave, 9" circle. Seattle Art Museum, Eugene Fuller Memorial Collection.

to as negative shapes. Note that the value areas, which create the positive and negative relationships, could be reversed and the design would still maintain its strength. There is a carefully organized relationship between the shapes and the voids between them. The variety of contours and sizes of these voids gives a vigorous interest to the design.

DARK AND LIGHT

The use of dark and light is perhaps the most fundamental means of design building. A strong dark and light structure is basic to good design. Even works that have no value changes, such as a pot with no surface decoration, affect us visually because of the way the light falls over the surface, revealing the form. Dark and light are often closely associated with the color and texture of the material. Artists and designers like to squint at their work to check the dark-light organization, because squinting cuts out or diminishes the sensation of color and the surface detail, permitting the dark-light pattern to stand out clearly.

Dark-light design can be as simple as black and white, or it may be a complex organization of many values—blacks, whites, and grays. The steps between black and white are sometimes called *half tones*. Dark-light patterns can be made with clearly defined edges between values, or the areas may shade imperceptibly from dark to light with shading or modeling. Whichever method is used, the areas of dark and light should be harmoniously related.

Design can be made in many ways with dark and light. The designer can plan his work as light pattern on a dark ground, as dark pattern on a light ground, as equal areas of dark and light, or as a combination of these. Try to visualize the dark-light pattern with the values reversed to see if the negative areas have been properly considered.

Alternation, or counterchange, is a means of achieving dark-light balance used by designers since the beginnings of art. A checkerboard is an example of a simple dark-light alternation pattern, with an even distribution of dark and light. This even distribution gives a strong sense of balance and order, and suggests careful consideration of both positive and negative shapes.

Japanese: *Decorative Paper*. Twentieth century. Blockprint on paper. Black and white design.

Norwegian: *Fiddler and Two Dancing Maidens, Deer, and Birds*. (Detail). Tapestry, entire work 51" x 47". Oslo Museum of Applied Arts, Trondheim. Courtesy of the Smithsonian Institution. Design of many values of dark and light.

Stripe Patterns, (a) dark on light, (b) light on dark, (c) equal area.

Checkerboard pattern, an example of design with dark and light.

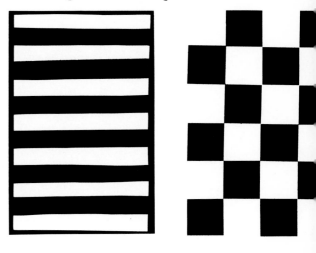

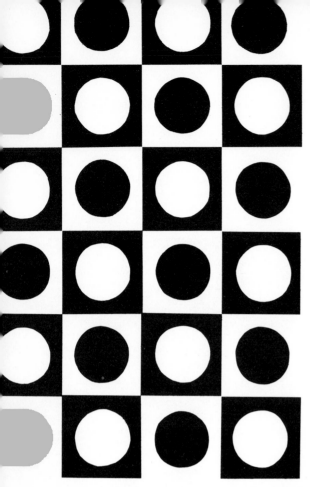

Checkerboard pattern with circles, an example of dark and light alternation (or counterchange).

The areas of a checkerboard-like pattern can be varied by introducing shapes, either geometric or derived from subject matter, into the units of the pattern. The same shape can be repeated over the surface, alternating dark on light and light on dark to create an equal-area distribution.

Further variety can be obtained by making an alternation pattern within an area. The space may be divided many times, either symmetrically or asymmetrically, and retain an equal-area distribution. These designed areas can be used alone as the basis for unit area designs, or they may become the motifs in allover repeat patterns. Half tone or gray areas may be introduced for variety.

Whatever the method of dividing the space with dark and light, the value areas should balance and have a satisfying variety and organization within the boundaries of the entire area. The principle of dark-light balance applies equally to all art, from a design cut in an eraser for stamping a decorated paper to the complex underlying dark-light structure of a world-famous painting.

A variant of the checkerboard pattern.

Checkerboard pattern with circles, using alternation within each unit.

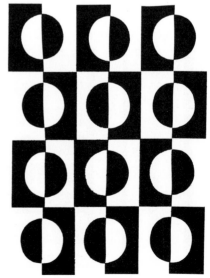

India: *Fabric Design*. Twentieth century. Woven cotton, double cloth. Alternation checkerboard pattern with geometric motif. Courtesy of Elizabeth Bayley Willis.

Pre-Columbian Peru (Inca): *Square*. Alpaca and sticks of wood, 7½" x 6⅞". Seattle Art Museum. Gift of Mr. Nasli Heeramaneck.

Glen F. Kaufman: *Window Hanging*. 1959. Cotton, linen, plastic, and wool, 72" x 36". Courtesy of the American Craftsmen's Council.

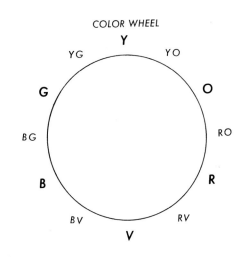

COLOR

PROPERTIES OF COLOR

Color has three measurable qualities: *hue, value,* and *intensity. Hue* is determined by the lengths of light waves and their locations in the spectrum. The names of the colors—red, yellow, green, blue, and violet—refer to their hues. *Value* is determined by the darkness or lightness of a color. Yellows are naturally lighter in value than blues, reds, or violets. Colors may be modified by mixing them with black or white to change their inherent values. *Intensity* refers to brightness of the color. Pure colors are brighter than colors mixed with blacks, grays, or whites, or with their complements. Such mixing grays the color, or reduces its intensity. The designer must learn to distinguish between these three properties and to use them in design building.

PIGMENTS

In times past, man had to rely on earth, vegetable, or animal colors for the pigments he used in his arts and crafts. Earth materials provided whites from chalk, and yellows and reds from ochre earths containing iron. Precious and semi-precious stones were ground for some of the intense blues, greens, and other rare hues. Lapis lazuli, for example, provided an intense, rich blue, but since it was expensive, its use was limited. Other pigments were made from vegetable matter, usually boiled in water to extract the juices that provided the color. Sap green was obtained from a plant prepared in this manner. Other colorants were derived from animal sources—violets from sea snails, blacks from charred bones. Colors derived from these sources were generally low in intensity. Bright hues were seldom used because of their cost and rarity. In recent times color science has brought about a revolution in color. Dyes and chemical pigments of great brilliance and permanence can now be easily made and are universally available at reasonable cost. Today's artists have a selection of hues that earlier artists could not have even imagined. In part, the history of the visual arts is the history of the development of pigments.

THE COLOR WHEEL

With the color wheel, made by bending the spectrum into a closed circle, we can see how colors are mixed. The *primary* colors, from which all the other colors can be made, are red, yellow, and blue. The *secondary* colors are made by mixing pairs of primary colors. Red and yellow, when mixed in equal portions, make orange; blue and yellow make green; and red and blue make violet. The *tertiary* colors are found on the color wheel between each primary and its nearest secondary color. Red-orange, yellow-green, and blue-violet are tertiary colors. This color wheel is used for mixing pigments. There are other color theories, such as the Ostwald and the Munsell, which may be explored for further color study.

NEUTRALS

Neutrals are also regarded as colors by the designer, but they are not found on the color wheel. They are the achromatic (from Greek— *a* meaning "not," and *chroma* meaning "color") colors. Neutrals are black, white, and the many grays produced by mixing black and white.

When neutrals have a little color added, they are called *near-neutrals*.

COLOR MIXING

There are two main categories of color mixing: mixing a color with another color or colors, and mixing a color with a neutral. Colors mixed with hues near them on the color wheel produce a variation in hue. Red mixed with orange, for example, results in red-orange. When a color is mixed with a color from the opposite side of the color wheel, the result is a grayed color. Red mixed with green, for example, results in a grayed near-neutral. Colors across from each other on the color wheel—such as red and green, or yellow and violet—are called *complements*. When complements are mixed, a grayed color always results.

Colors mixed with neutrals produce near-neutrals, or *tints, tones,* and *shades.* Colors mixed with white produce tints. Pink, for example, is a tint of red. Colors mixed with black produce shades. Brown is a shade of red-orange. Colors can also be mixed with the many values of gray to produce tones. Mixing with a neutral always lowers the intensity of a color. Even white reduces the intensity of colors mixed with it. Colors may be made lighter or darker in value if they are mixed with lighter or darker neutrals. If the designer wishes to gray a color without changing its value, he can mix it with a gray of the same value as the color.

BROKEN COLOR

Broken color designates colors mixed by placing small units or spots of color next to one another without mixing them. Since this method of color mixing was one of the principles of impressionism, it is sometimes known as *impressionist color.* But long before the impressionists, early mosaic designers and stained-glass artisans understood this principle of color mixture and used it often for its unequaled design effects. *Broken color* mixing can be used to mix

any colors the designer wishes. The result is more lively and intense than other color-mixing methods. Bits of red and blue, for instance, when placed side by side to fill an area, mix in the eye to create an iridescent violet that could not be achieved by direct mixing.

COLOR COMBINATIONS

Colors can be combined in many ways. Some color combinations—such as monochromatic and complementary color harmonies—are almost traditional. Other combinations are dictated by current fashion, or selected at random by the choice of the designer or the needs of the design. The designer must be free to select colors that will best serve his needs and satisfy his inventive nature. The combinations described below may serve as an introduction to combining colors, and their use may suggest other possibilities to the designer.

Monochromatic colors. In a design executed in monochromatic (*mono*—one, *chroma*—color) color, only one color is used. Variations are made with tints, tones, and shades, which vary the intensity and the value but not the hue.

Complementary colors, those opposite each other on the color wheel, also can be varied with tints, tones, and shades.

Triadic colors are any three colors equidistant on the color wheel, such as red, yellow, and blue, or green, orange, and violet. These too may be modified by mixing with neutrals.

Related colors are made by mixing a color or a neutral with each of the other colors used. For example, when some yellow is mixed with red, with orange, and with gray, each of the resultant color mixtures will contain yellow. The yellow, then, has produced related colors. Neutrals used as the basis for a related color combination create an especially unified effect.

Warm and cool colors. Warm colors such as reds, oranges, and yellows can be alternated with cool colors such as blues and greens, much as darks and lights are used, to create a sense of balance and unity. If the contrast between the warms and cools is strong enough, no change of value is necessary. However, value change may also be used for added interest and variety.

Vibrating colors are complementary colors of equal value and intensity. When they are juxtaposed, a vibration, one of the most exciting results of color combination, is established. Reds and greens provide a stronger sense of vibration than most other combinations. Even grayed colors can be made to vibrate if the values are close.

Limited color combinations are made by selecting a specific number of colors, such as earth colors and black and white, or yellow, red, and green, as the sole basis for the design. By limiting his color selection the designer forces himself to explore the possibilities of color mixing within a limited palette.

Prejudiced colors are color combinations that are not acceptable according to the dictates of current style or popular taste. Such color combinations as blue and green; red, orange, pink, and magenta; and black and brown have been commonly rejected by the uninitiated, although there is no real basis for this prejudice. Designers must learn that *all colors go equally well together.* Since such combinations are largely neglected, they offer the designer fresh, new arrangements to explore.

DOMINANCE, SUBORDINATION, AND ACCENT

An old rule that may help the beginner plan color combinations is based on *dominance, subordination,* and *accent:* Allow one color to be dominant, use a second color in a subordinate role, and add accents of a third color or colors. The color values may be modified to fit the light-dark pattern. This rule may be used to plan the color combination for a design but, like all rules in art, it may be broken.

NATURALISTIC AND DESIGNED COLOR

Beginning designers in our time have to fight the tradition of realism that developed in eighteenth- and nineteenth-century painting. Good design has its own color requirements, which are often unrelated to the colors associated with or observed in subject matter. Because many design motifs are based on subject matter, beginners feel constrained to use the colors dictated by the subject, often with disastrous results. A good designer knows he has complete freedom in color selection. He chooses his colors because he needs them or likes them, not because they are forced upon him by his subject matter. Naturalistic colors can be the basis of a color selection for a work of art, but they need not be followed if they do not fit the design. A sensitive designer often finds in nature color combinations that excite his imagination. He may use the colors in a motif entirely different from their source, or he may adapt the subject matter where the colors originated so that it suits his design needs.

DESIGN MOTIFS

Designs may be derived from three sources: the materials, organization, and subject matter. Usually all three work together to produce the final design idea.

Materials offer an unending source of inspiration for the imaginative designer. The colors, values, textures, and other qualities of materials may all suggest design possibilities. The discovery of a new treatment of material or the acquisition of a new color may cause the designer to want to find a way to use it in a design. A new red may please and excite the artist so much that he will start a work just so he can use it. The material that is being used will enforce its own restrictions on the design. The same motif done in mosaic, enamel, weaving, or ceramics will appear quite different because of the materials.

Geometric Motifs. An important source for design motifs is found in the use of lines and shapes that have no subject-matter connotations. These are sometimes called geometric motifs, although a ruler and compass are not necessary to make them. Such shapes as crosses, triangles, circles, spirals, dots, lines, zigzags, stripes, and checks are time-honored design materials. There are so many possible combinations and variations of these simple geometric forms that, although they have been used by designers for thousands of years, they still offer fresh and original ideas for motifs. Geometric motifs can be made with any of the elements. Lines, values, colors, and textures can be used singly or together in designing the motif.

Subject-Matter Motifs. The forms of nature and man-made objects have always been a source of design motifs. Subject matter offers a means for enriching design beyond the shapes, colors, and textures of the subjects themselves, for every motif derived from subject matter has connotations that add meaning to the design. The best subject matter in this sense is that found near at hand. Things from the artist's own environment are more filled with meaning than are exotic forms. The great artisans of all times have felt no necessity for going beyond their immediate experience and environment for design motifs.

A knowledge of the elements is convenient for designing motifs from subject matter. The subject can be analyzed in terms of line, contour, color, value, and texture. Then from these attributes the artist selects those that are most interesting or necessary for his design. Many subjects can be expressed in line alone; the contour may be used and treated as a value area; or several elements may be combined. Subject matter is the springboard for the design motif, and should never be allowed to dictate the artist's purpose.

Another way to use subject matter is to begin by experimenting with geometric motifs and then turning them into subject-matter motifs. Lines,

Bird motifs in different materials.
Ceramic. Peruvian: *Double Spout Water Jar.* Sixth century. Pottery, height 7". Minneapolis Institute of Arts.

Printed textile. Detail of block-printed textile from India. Courtesy of Elizabeth Bayley Willis.

Bird motifs (continued)
Stitchery. Detail of embroidered textile from India. Courtesy of Elizabeth Bayley Willis.

Detail from Polish paper cutout, an example of a geometric motif.

for example, can be made into stripe patterns of all kinds. Then these stripe patterns can be shaped to resemble subject matter. Dots, triangles, circles, and other geometric patterns offer a wide range of material that lends itself readily to invention. Combined with color, value, and texture, such inventions provide an endless source of motifs.

DESIGN ORGANIZATION

Once the materials and the motifs have been selected, the designer is ready to plan the design organization. Two major considerations of organization must be kept in mind throughout the designing process. They are the part-to-part and the part-to-whole relationships. The part-to-part relationship is the way the parts of the design—the shapes, colors, lines, textures, and contours—work with one another to create a satisfying continuity and maintain a feeling of eventfulness. The part-to-whole relationship is the way the separate parts relate to the total form. No mat-

ter how well several parts work together, if they do not fit the space they occupy the result is unsatisfactory. No detail of the design that is not digested into the total form should be retained. No matter how well some part works with adjacent parts in terms of color, texture, or line, or how well it suggests some attribute of the motif, if it does not function in the part-to-whole relationship it should be replaced with something that does. This is one of the most difficult design ideas for the beginner to grasp.

PART-TO-PART RELATIONSHIPS

Unity and continuity between the parts of a design can be furthered by careful consideration of the positive and negative spaces. In a good design both must be considered equally important. The skilled designer focuses his attention on the spaces between the positive shapes, and tries to make them interesting, varied, and complete unto themselves. Reversing the darks and lights will often indicate whether or not the negative shapes have been adequately treated. In three-dimensional forms, the designer must concentrate on the voids and attempt to make them integral parts of the design. This is difficult to do because the attention is so easily centered on the positive shapes.

As the eye moves across or around the design, the relationship of sizes, colors, textures, and shapes should be carefully considered. Each area should suggest or demand the treatment of adjacent areas beyond the dictates of the subject matter. The designer is free to take any liberties with subject matter that he feels are essential to the unity of his design. In the illustrated design the changes in value, color, size, and negative and positive shape keep interest alive but fit so well together that the surface continuity is easily maintained.

PART-TO-WHOLE RELATIONSHIPS

In addition to forming a satisfying relationship with adjacent parts, each portion of the design must be unshakably bound to the total form. Every motif must fit the space it occupies and relate to the basic structural design. In order to perform these two requirements, subject matter and other motifs must often be significantly altered. Each kind of space has its own requirements. A circle demands different treatment than a square, rectangle, triangle, or cruciform shape does. The sensitive designer is very aware of the space to be filled. By repeating the basic lines of the space within the design itself, he can make the motif seem an integral part of the form. Notice the differences in the basic shapes and see how the designers have filled the spaces and fitted the motifs to the shapes.

Two variations on a spiral motif.
(a) Chinese (Kansu Province): *Burial Jar, Kansu Amphora Type.* Neolithic, c. 2200 B.C. High-fired earthenware, 14⅛" high. Seattle Art Museum, Eugene Fuller Memorial Collection.

(b) American Indian (New Madrid County, Missouri): *Bottle with Spiral Decoration.* c. thirteenth century. Earthenware, 9⅛" high. Seattle Art Museum, Eugene Fuller Memorial Collection.

Design for a circular shape. Detail from interior of Greek *black-figured Kylix*; painted by Xenokles. Third quarter of sixth century B.C. Painted earthenware, 4″ high; diam. 7″. Seattle Art Museum, Norman Davis Collection.

Design for a circular shape. Persian (Rhages): Bowl. c. 1200 A.D. Glazed pottery, 8″ diameter. Courtesy of the Metropolitan Museum of Art, Rogers Fund, 1916.

Three-dimensional shapes must be treated differently from two-dimensional shapes. Only a part of the form is visible at one time, and the design must be planned with this in mind. As the eye moves around the form, each part must relate to the next and maintain a continuity. If one side of a pot is treated too differently from the other, the result will be unsatisfactory. A three-dimensional work should appear to be the same work on both sides, and the design should lead the eye easily and naturally around the form.

In the Greek *amphora* (opposite page), the design was planned to fit the form of the pot. Note that the basic volumes—the neck, body, and foot—have been treated differently to accentuate the different underlying geometric shapes. The bold figurative design on the body emphasizes the curving, bulging contour, while the more vertical and horizontal pattern on the neck perfectly restates and supports the basic cylindrical form. The attachment of the handles is also pointed up by the design. Throughout the design the forms of the pot—the subtle, rhythmic curve of the body and the handles, the circular mouth and foot, and the essential vertical feeling of the

whole—are echoed and re-echoed, creating a satisfying feeling of unity.

UNITY AND VARIETY

Two essential qualities of good design are *unity* and *variety*. Without unity no design exists no matter how interesting the parts may be. Without variety we have dullness and boredom, which are abhorred in art. Unity is the result of a sense of rightness achieved by a harmony of parts. It can be obtained most easily through repetition of shape, color, line, value, or texture. The simple repetition of a stripe or other motif quickly unifies a surface. Stripes may even be varied greatly without losing the feeling of unity. The quality of solidity that comes with such ordered repetition is seldom monotonous. In simple and complex forms, as in the Greek *amphora* on the opposite page, the repetition of forms derived from the structural design unifies the whole.

Variety does not necessitate a great number of changes. Simplicity and variety are not opposites. Even the regular stripe pattern shown has sufficient variety to hold our interest. However,

Left: Melanesian: *Kapkap.* Tortoise shell, 5¾" diameter. Seattle Art Museum, Eugene Fuller Memorial Collection.

Right: Greek: Black-figured *Amphora.* Sixth century B.C. Painted earthenware, height 16¼". Seattle Art Museum, Eugene Fuller Memorial Collection.

Lower left: Stripe Pattern, *Woven Textile from India.* Twentieth century. Courtesy of Elizabeth Bayley Willis.

Lower right: Geometric and Subject Matter Motifs Arranged in Stripes. Woven textile from India. Courtesy of Elizabeth Bayley Willis.

if the designer feels a lack of variety he can easily gain more without destroying the unity. Merely by varying the thickness, color, value, or texture of the stripes, the designer can produce an endless variety. Regular or random changes in the pattern afford delightful variations on the basic repetition. Skilled designers learn to achieve variety with such simple means.

Most design is unified through the repetition of some underlying pattern such as the stripe. Subject-matter or geometric motifs can be easily grouped in a striped or checkerboard pattern. Sometimes these underlying pattern structures are bold and obvious, but often they are less easily seen. Repetition need not be monotonous to be effective.

PLANNING THE DESIGN

MATERIALS AND FUNCTION

When planning a design, the designer must first consider the material to be used. The choice of material is determined by the function of the finished piece. For example, a weaver might select wool yarns to make a length of suiting, a scarf, or a baby blanket, and cotton for place mats. The weaver would then have to decide upon the weight of the fabric, the color, the pattern, and whether the finished piece is to have any additional decoration. After selecting the material, the craftsman should experiment to become familiar with its qualities and possibilities before planning and deciding upon a final design.

A potter would have to decide upon a clay and the piece he plans to make, and then design the piece so that it meets functional requirements.

CHOOSING THE BASIC ELEMENTS FOR THE DESIGN

Once the material has been selected and the requirements of the structural design and function have been satisfied, the applied design must fit the purpose and form of the piece. The designer must decide upon a design plan, whether to use a single unit design or an allover pattern. He must decide what design elements to use and how to use them; he must decide whether to plan a design with a predominance of line, of dark and light shapes, or of rich color interest, or with any combination of elements. If one element in a design is held constant, a wide disparity of other parts is possible if they do not distract from the basic unifying element. Many different colors might be used if they fit a value pattern, many values of one or two colors could be combined, or many different motifs might be unified by a single line quality.

MEDIA FOR DESIGN STUDIES

The material to be used might also influence the choice of medium to be used in making preliminary studies for the design. Cut paper might suggest a plan for a stencil design, or a brush and paint might be used to plan a brushed glaze or engobe design on a pot. These limits do not have to be observed, however, for a good cut-paper design might be translated into the basis for many other decorating techniques and not be confined to stencils. Paint, charcoal, crayons, pencils, and inks provide excellent means in planning designs to be used with other media. The first plan might be done in dark and light, or in dark, medium, and light, with paint or charcoal, and then translated into corresponding colors. Several designs might be made for a single purpose and the most pleasing one selected, or a new design made from a combination of the most satisfying parts.

RELATING THE DESIGN TO THE SHAPE

A good design is well adapted to the surface to which it is applied. To be well integrated, it must enrich and emphasize the structural qualities of the surface and form and not subtract from them. A three-dimensional piece has requirements to fulfill that a flat surface does not. On a cylinder, for example, only one-third of the design is visible at one time, and the designer must take this into consideration.

Predominant elements of a three-dimensional form are emphasized by a repetition of the elements in the applied design. The horizontal or vertical quality of a piece might be enhanced by a repetition of horizontal or vertical stripes, and predominant shapes of a pot might be repeated in a design applied to it.

Specific design areas can help differentiate the parts of a structure and can emphasize these parts. To illustrate, one design area might emphasize the basic shape of the top of a compote, another the stem, and another the base. Many Greek vases and the enameled *King's Cup* are designed in this way.

TO EXPAND THE DESIGN EXPERIENCE

The Elements of Design. The designer who becomes familiar with and understands the elements of design so that he is able to use them easily and spontaneously to create satisfying designs derives a great deal of pleasure from his efforts. As he adds to his experience he increases his range of satisfactions.

Study of Other Designs. The designer learns by observing and analyzing good design in the work of other artists, in the art of other cultures, in natural forms, and in any other suitable source material. He must develop a sensitivity to form and color in everything he sees.

Collecting good pictorial examples and arranging them in a file is very helpful in ex-

Jean (Hans) Arp and Sophie Taeuber-Arp: *Duo Collage.* 1918. Paper on cardboard, 33⅞" x 26". Collection of Mr. and Mrs. Burton G. Tremaine, Meriden, Connecticut.

panding design resources. A slide collection is excellent for study, as are good books. Collecting and living with well-designed objects offers an opportunity to increase sensitivity. Sketching or tracing fine examples from nature or man-made objects trains the hand and the eye and enhances the design vocabulary.

Interest in Materials. A designer derives great pleasure from discovering new materials and new ways to use familiar materials. Sometimes the most commonplace materials can become unusual and elegant finished designs if they are used imaginatively.

Henry Takemoto: *Decorated Pot, Papaikou V.* 1959. Ceramic, 26″ x 30″ x 30″. Courtesy of the American Craftsmen's Council.

Upper right: Anni Albers: *Silk Tapestry.* 1948. Woven tapestry. Busch-Reisinger Museum, Harvard University.

Lower right: The House of the Architect Alexander Girard. Santa Fe, New Mexico. Objects from the architect's collection of folk arts and crafts.

Jean (Hans) Arp: *Squares Arranged According to the Laws of Chance.* 1916-1917. Collage of colored papers, 19⅛″ x 13⅝″. Courtesy of the Museum of Modern Art.

PAPER

Hans Christian Andersen: *Cutting*. Presented to Mrs. Melchoir in 1874. Cut
paper. Courtesy of Hans Christian Andersen's House. Odense, Denmark.

PAPER

Paper has been used as an expressive art medium for many centuries and has become identified with the artistic productions of such cultures as those of China, Mexico, Poland, and Japan. In fact, Japan has sometimes been called a "paper country" because of the extent to which paper has been used efficiently and artistically as a means of solving problems of economy. Although this material as we know it was invented in China around 200 B.C., it was not known in Europe until nearly one thousand years later when it was introduced to the West by Arabs, who had acquired the papermaking process in their conquests in the Orient. At first it was used only as a writing material (supplementing the traditional papyrus, which was doubtless the earliest paper, and from which the word *paper* is derived). As such, it was an important factor in the development and production of the book, especially after the invention of the printing press. However, its uses have been expanded during the years to include innumerable functions that serve both aesthetic and utilitarian needs.

At first all paper was made by hand, each sheet individually. Early European papers were made entirely from a pulp of rags. In the Orient, materials such as bamboo, straw, jute, maize leaves, and esparto grass were made into paper pulp. A species of mulberry osier was grown in Japan, especially for its bark to be used in papermaking. Some very fine and enduring papers were developed during the time of the Renaissance and were used by Botticelli, Raphael, and other masters of that period.

The idea of using wood for making paper occurred to a French naturalist named Reamer in 1719 when he observed the formation of the nest of a wasp. Yet wood pulp was not used for this purpose until over one hundred years later. A machine for making paper was invented in 1789.

With the equipment and technology available today, papers are produced to serve all needs. The variety of papers produced is most extensive; there are thousands of different kinds. They may be classed generally as news and printing papers, writing papers, wrapping and package papers, and miscellaneous types such as tissues, blotters, and cardboards. They vary in texture and color from delicate tissues and brilliant cellophane to rugged cardboards. They may be shiny, smooth, thin, opaque, rough, transparent, rigid, or flexible, depending upon the purpose for which they are to be used. Some papers have been given a white coating for fine book work. Coated papers also come in colors. These attributes make them delightful and exciting to work with, and challenging to the imagination.

When kept flat, paper may be used as a medium upon which to produce patterns of stamped impressions or painted designs, or it may be modified by cutting away parts. It has also been used for collage and découpage compositions by many painters.

Decorated papers may serve various pur-

Six-panel *Wave Screen,* blue and gold on paper. Attributed to Korin (1658-1716). Japanese, Edo period. 48¼" high. Seattle Art Museum, Eugene Fuller Memorial Collection.

Mexican: *Paper Cutout.* Colored tissue paper. Courtesy of Esther Gingrich.

Polish: *Paper Cutout.* Shapes cut from green, purple, yellow and pink papers. Courtesy, Embassy of Polish People's Republic.

Polish: *Paper Cutout.* Shapes cut from red, yellow and purple papers. Courtesy, Embassy of Polish People's Republic.

German: *Christmas Decorations.* Gold-coated paper, 3″–4″ high. Courtesy of James McGrath.

Mary Jane Rice: *Valentine Paper Flags.* 1954. Paper with printed and cutout decorations. Courtesy of the American Crayon Company.

Polish: *Paper Cutout*. Shapes cut from black paper. Courtesy, Embassy of Polish People's Republic.

United States: *Wallpaper*, about 1820. From a house in Guilford, Connecticut. Printed from woodblocks. Courtesy of the Cooper Union Museum.

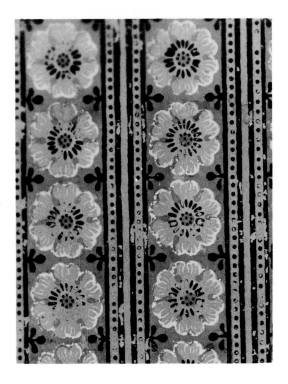

poses such as for wall coverings, screens for room dividers, and wrapping papers. French wallpapers, on which patterns were produced by the wood-block process, were popular in colonial America. The Japanese, too, developed the art of the block print, which was used to print designs on paper for shoji screens used for room dividers, and on papers for wrapping packages or covering books. Papers made by the fold-and-dye process were also used for these purposes.

Paper cutouts have been made famous by Polish peasants who have carried on this tradition for many centuries. These symmetrical designs are known for their individual style and great vitality. Sometimes the paper is folded once, as in the most popular type from the Kurpie region, with areas removed by sharp-pointed tools. Other forms are made from squares or circles that are folded several times, and out of which are cut intricately patterned shapes, similar to the examples shown. The darks and lights produced, by the cutout and the closed areas, are carefully interrelated so that positive and negative spaces are well balanced. Although there is variety in character and size of the shapes, similarity is produced by a repetition of angles and curves that bring about unity.

The Pultusk specimens of Polish paper cuts are considerably different from the Kurpie examples. They are appliquéd with varicolored glossy papers similar to the beautiful rooster with the overlay of cut shapes. The Pultusk designs are classified according to certain types, and each has its own folk name. These types include ribbons or banners, circles or stars, stylized little trees, multicolored shapes, single figures of men, and figured compositions.

Similar in construction to the Polish cuts, although different in form, are the symmetrical paper fetish figures that represent one of the ancient traditional arts of the Otomi Indians in Mexico. The human and mythical figures that

Polish: *Paper Cutout*. One-fold symmetrical design. Courtesy, Embassy of Polish People's Republic.

Polish (Kurpie Region): *Paper Cutout*. One-fold symmetrical design. Courtesy, Embassy of Polish People's Republic.

Polish: *Bird*. Appliqué of cut paper shapes. Courtesy, Embassy of Polish People's Republic.

Mexican, Otomi Indian: *Fetish Figure* (facsimile). Design cut from folded bark paper. Courtesy of *Print* Magazine.

characterize their designs are related to curing ceremonies conducted by the *brujos* or witch doctors who rule the "magic" life of the people. The designs are cut from folded paper made from the bark of trees, and are rich in contour outline. The figure shown here is bold and primitive in design and organized on a strong vertical-horizontal plan. Angles, curves, and shapes are repeated in a balanced relationship.

Other paper cuts in Mexico are found in the perforated colorful banners stamped in tissue papers that are strung across the streets to float in the breeze as religious processions pass by. These papers, which are fragile and temporary, are usually destroyed soon after their function has been served.

The art of collage—in which flat pieces of paper are arranged in a composition and pasted to a canvas or paper backing, or in which selected papers are used in relationship to painted areas on a canvas—was introduced in modern times by the French painter Braque, who sometimes used pieces of imitation wood-grained paper to simulate real objects on a canvas. Similarly, such painters as Picasso, Gris, Arp, and Miró have used collage methods—gluing corrugated papers, printed newspapers, and even photographs to the surfaces of their works.

In his later years Matisse employed the art of découpage—cutting shapes of varied and expressive contours from colored papers and mounting them in pictorial arrangements. He used these colorful forms as decorations on walls, in books, and as the basis for designs for church windows and vestments.

Many painters have found paper of assistance in planning compositions, by using it to experiment with arrangements that later are executed in paint on canvas.

Paper can be folded to make three-dimensional structures, and by this means a great many art forms have been produced. These are often very sculptural in conception, for paper can be

Juan Gris: *Still Life, the Table.* 1914. Collage, paper and gouache on canvas, 23½" x 17½". Philadelphia Museum of Art.

Henri Matisse: Papier Découpé. Black shape on red background. 19¾" x 15¾". Courtesy of Berggruen & Cie., Paris.

Henri Matisse: *Maquette* for *Nuit de Noël*. 1952. Gouache on cut and pasted paper, 53⅜" x 20⅝". Collection, Museum of Modern Art. Gift of Time, Inc.

Lampshade. Scored paper, height 28″. Courtesy, University of Washington Press.

Japanese: *Birds and Boxes.* Traditional Japanese paper folds. Courtesy of the American Crayon Company.

shaped so that abstract qualities are revealed through the planes that comprise the geometric forms. The little paper decorations from Germany were folded from gold paper and made to place on the Christmas tree. Artists like Picasso have created sculptural compositions with the use of stiff papers and cardboards.

Comparable to the folk art of Poland in the creation of paper cutouts is the ancient, traditional paper-folding art of Japan, known as *origami* (*ori,* "to fold"; *gami,* "paper"). In this art form, the paper is folded to represent animals, birds, people, and numerous other subjects. These are made from square sheets of paper, generally without cutting, pasting, or attaching other parts. Minute folded-paper beetles that nestle in the palm of the hand appear almost lifelike; frogs will hop when pressed at the rear; and birds will seem to fly—their wings move when the tail is pulled.

Origami is a national art form in Japan, and the techniques of folding are taught to the children in Japanese schools as part of the cultural heritage. Paper folding is also taught in the schools of Spain and Argentina. A number of books explaining these techniques are available in Oriental shops and bookstores. Special origami papers may be obtained in exquisite colors.

Modern three-dimensional sculpture in paper originated in Poland, where artists developed distinctive styles by means of complex folds, scoring, cutting, and pasting. Out of this has grown a form of decoration used rather widely in advertising and window display.

The beautiful folded-paper light shades that are used effectively in contemporary settings come from Sweden and Denmark, where families have carried the principles of sculptural design into the media of paper and successfully created new forms for lamps.

Papier-mâché is a French term meaning "paper pulp." It refers to objects modeled from paper, saturated in water and paste, by methods

Japanese: *Toys: Frog, Dog, Badger, and Bear*. Twentieth century. Papier-mâché with painted decoration. 2" high.

Chinese (Taiwan): *Mythological Figure*. Papier-mâché decorated with cotton and fabric, on a wood base. Height 11". Courtesy, *Craft Horizons*.

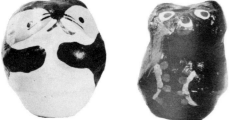

Burmese: *Covered Bowl in the Shape of a Bird*. Twentieth century. Papier-mâché, lacquer, and gilt with painted decoration, 2½" x 3½".

Japanese: *Folk Toy*. Contemporary. Papier-mâché, 11" x 14½".

India. *Ganesa (Ganesh)*. Papier-mâché with gesso, painted and gilded. Courtesy of Elizabeth Bayley Willis.

Mexican: *Judas Figures.* Papier-mâché. Photograph by Erwin Lang. Courtesy of *Sunset* Magazine.

36   CRAFTS DESIGN

that can be used to produce bowls, trays, toys, and large fetish structures such as the Judas figures from Mexico. These Judas figures are used in religious processions and are later destroyed with firecrackers built into the structures. In some parts of Europe where fuel has been scarce, peasants have resorted to the making of papier-mâché bricks in press molds to burn in place of firewood.

Fascinating toys have also been made of papier-mâché. The small Mexican toy horse and rider is formed with a mold and is hollow inside. Paint is used to decorate the objects by balancing spots of color and adapting a line design to the features and costume to conform to the subject and shape.

The charming paper doll from Mexico is secured at the joints with cord. The figure has been decorated with painted areas and a detailed design on the front.

The delightful Japanese toys formed like little frogs and other animals are made of paper and balanced with a weight in the base so that they will always remain upright.

Papier-mâché can be combined with other materials: the Chinese mythological figure riding the colorful spotted animal is a combination of cotton, wood, and fabric with paper; the Japanese movable tiger has a jointed tail and hemp whiskers protruding from its head.

The piñata in the form of a rooster combines pasted papers, which form parts of the structure, with dry, cut fringe made of colorful crepe and tissue papers, which simulate feathers and provide an interesting textural surface. It was built over a framework of cardboard and wire.

The piñata is a traditional form used in Mexico. Although piñatas vary in shape according to the imagination of the designer, they are generally in the form of birds, animals, and figures designed to hold Christmas gifts and delicacies. In the traditional ceremony the piñata is suspended from the ceiling. A child is selected,

Mexican: *Piñata.* Twentieth century. Papier-mâché covered with crepe and tissue paper, height 28".

Mexican: *Jointed Doll.* Twentieth century. Papier-mâché with painted decoration. Height 9½".

Mexican: *Toy Horse and Rider.* Twentieth century. Papier-mâché, height 10".

blindfolded, and given a stick with which he attempts to break open the piñata. When this has been accomplished, sweets and gifts are showered on the eager children below.

An example of a papier-mâché object produced from a press mold is the beautiful covered dish from Burma, made in the form of a setting bird with head, tail, and wings compactly arranged and related to the total form. A stylized pattern, derived from the shape of feathers, covers the entire space and produces a suggestion of texture. This circular pattern is also carried out in other parts of the design—in the head, eyes, beak, wings, and tail—thus repeating the roundness of the basic form.

The expressive Indian Ganesa, or Ganesh, is made of papier-mâché covered with gesso, in the form of an elephant, and is painted and gilded. This benevolent god, one of the best-loved divinities in India, is revered by nearly every Hindu; as the "Lord of Obstacles," he is worshiped at the beginning of all undertakings, so that snags and hindrances may be removed. He is particularly interested in literary and educational activities, and is the patron of grammarians. Manuscripts and printed books often begin with the auspicious formula "Reverence to Lord Ganesa."

Outstanding sculptors like Elie Nadelman and Alexander Archipenko have made use of papier-mâché as a medium for serious compositions in sculpture. Nadelman spent his last years perfecting sculpture for people of small means as he wished to bring beauty into their homes. Two of his papier-mâché figures are to be carved in pink marble in large scale for the new Lincoln Center of Performing Arts.

Another exciting use for papier-mâché is shown in the animated window decorations done for a Christmas display in a department store in Zurich, Switzerland. They are the creation of John Henri Engesser, a talented and imaginative designer who combines a number of materials with the papier-mâché and develops complex mechanisms enabling the various groups and figures to move in synchronization with accompanying music. The examples shown are the central window from the theme "Scenes from Life in Medieval Castles," where a castle built of wood and glazed boards stands before a pale blue background. Ladies sit in the balcony and watch the performances while a banquet is in progress, troubadours play, and ladies balance on a see-saw.

John Henri Engesser: *Life in Medieval Castles,* animated window display. Switzerland. 1952. Papier-mâché, metal, wood, felt, paint. Figures 26″ high. Courtesy of *Graphis.*

Elie Nadelman: *Two Women.* c. 1934. Papier-mâché—pulverized paper and fibrous plaster filler, formed in a mold, height 14″. Courtesy of the Robert Isaacson Gallery, New York.

DECORATED PAPERS

Papers may be decorated by a number of different methods. Stamping and printing, wax resist, stencil, fold-and-dye, and painted papers are described here.

STAMPING AND PRINTING

Designs for printing may be cut from various materials such as wood, erasers, linoleum, and potatoes. Some objects with interesting shapes or textures—such as a wooden spool, a coarse sponge, an onion, a piece of bark, or a leaf—can be used without cutting. These objects can be inked and used as stamp patterns. There are various ways of inking a stamp for printing: paint may be applied with a brush; a sponge may be saturated with color and used as a pad; or printer's ink may be rolled out on a slab and the stamp pressed on the inked surface.

MATERIALS

1. Materials for the stamps—blocks of wood, spools, art gum and other erasers, sponges, linoleum blocks, carrots, potatoes, onions, or any other suitable stamping material
2. Cutting tools—knives, razor blades, gouges
3. Stamping media—water color, tempera, ink, printer's ink, or dye
4. Brushes, brayers, sponges, and pans for color mixing

POTATO PRINT

1 Cut a potato in half, across or lengthwise. Use old newspapers to cover the work space.

2 Cut a design in the surface of the potato by removing parts with a knife. Only the raised areas will print.

3 Paint the surface of one of the cut halves with any water-color paint, tempera, or ink.

4 Press the painted potato against the surface of a sheet of paper. Paint it again and make another print. Continue this process to produce an allover design. The design may be varied by changing the placement, color, or sequence of the stamps.

5 Try printing the cut potato in various arrangements.

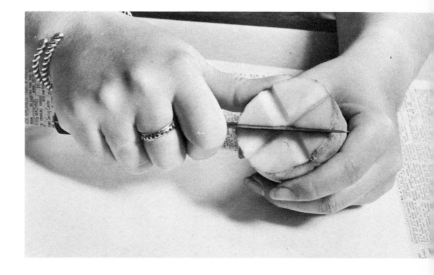

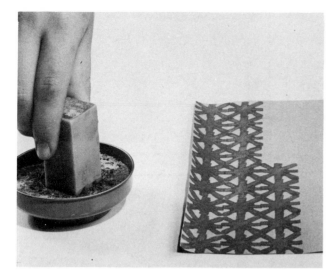

ERASER PRINT

1 Prints can be made with various kinds and sizes of erasers, including art gum erasers, soap erasers, and erasers on the ends of pencils. With a knife or razor blade, cut a design in the end or side of the eraser. Put a piece of sponge in a small container and soak it with a water paint or colored ink.

2 Press the eraser against the inked sponge and then stamp it on the paper. A pattern is formed as the design is repeated.

WAX RESIST

In making a wax resist design, wax, a water-resistant medium, is combined with a transparent water paint. The paint adheres to the portions of paper not covered by the wax.

MATERIALS

1. Resist media—colored crayons, beeswax, paraffin, liquid floor wax
2. Transparent water-color paint, or thinned-out tempera paint
3. Brush

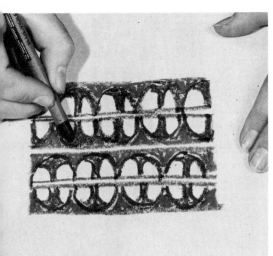

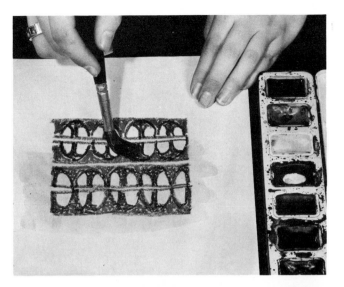

CRAYON METHOD

1 Make a design with colored crayons. To produce contrast and brilliance, press heavier in parts, and leave some areas open without color.

2 Cover the crayon design with a brush full of transparent water paint; let the particles of paint cling to the crayon surface, and in the open areas. Ink or thin tempera may also be used.

LIQUID WAX METHOD

1 For hot wax resist, cut pieces of paraffin and beeswax and melt them together in a double boiler, or in a coffee can placed in a pan of hot water. Before the wax hardens, quickly apply it to the paper with a brush. Liquid floor wax can also be used and does not require heating.

2 Water-color paint is brushed over the entire paper, but colors only the unwaxed parts. To remove the wax, cover with a piece of newspaper and press with a warm iron.

3 *For a crackled effect, apply hot wax freely to a sheet of paper and crumple it in the hands. Open the paper and apply paint with a brush, forcing it into the cracked areas.*

STENCIL

A stencil is made by cutting shapes in a piece of paper with a knife, razor blade, or scissors. A waterproof transparent stencil paper, through which the design can be seen and traced, is available commercially. Color is applied through the cut openings to the paper underneath, with a stiff stencil brush which is flat on the end.

MATERIALS

1. Stencil media—stencil paper, or any light- or medium-weight paper
2. Cutting tools—knife with sharp blade, razor blade, or scissors
3. Printing media—tempera paint, water color, printer's ink
4. Stencil brushes

1 *Cut shapes from a piece of paper with a sharp knife or razor blade.*

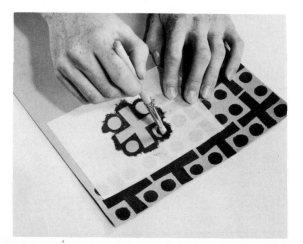

2 *Place the cut-out stencil on a sheet of paper and hold or tape it in position. Using a stiff stencil brush, apply a thick water paint or printer's ink, sparingly, with a pouncing motion. Brush from on top of the stencil edge to the inside of the design being careful not to get paint under the cut-out edges of the stencil.*

FOLD-AND-DYE

In the fold-and-dye method the design is produced by folding the paper and dipping its edges and corners into color. The paper used must be sufficiently absorbent to allow the color to spread over the surface into the fibers. The colors must flow easily; therefore, such media as water paints, inks, and dyes are used.

MATERIALS

1. Papers—silk span (available at hobby supply sources where model airplane kits are sold), Japanese rice paper, newsprint, paper toweling
2. Color media—water color, thinned tempera paint, colored ink, dye, and food coloring (available at most markets)
3. Brush, and small containers for colors

1 *Fold a sheet of suitable paper into pleats or other folded shapes. Vertical, horizontal, and diagonal folds may be used separately or combined. Dye, paint, food coloring, or inks may be used full strength or diluted. Put the color in open containers. Dip the edges and corners of the folded paper into the color. A brush may also be used to apply the color. As the color is absorbed, it spreads and forms a pattern. The paper may be refolded and redipped for more complex designs. With practice regular ordered repeat patterns can be achieved.*

2 *Fold-and-dye patterns made on silk span paper with food coloring.*

Example of a painted paper.

PAINTED PAPERS

Painted paper patterns can be planned by assembling painted squares in various combinations. One or two designs selected from a number of sketch squares may be used as units for a particular repeat pattern. Sketches may be designed and placed so that the individual units of the pattern are obvious, or so that the created pattern, when assembled, may conceal the identity of the original unit. Squares may be placed side by side, alternated with other squares, or laid out in a slip pattern arrangement.

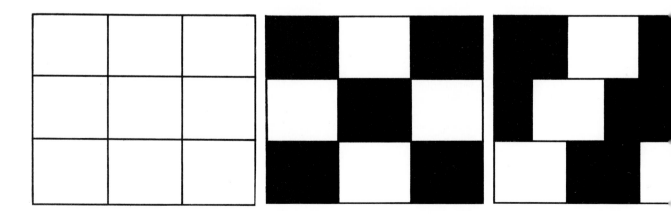

MATERIALS

1. Tempera paints
2. Brush, ruler, pencil
3. Paper, newsprint, drawing paper

1 Draw a number of 4-inch or 5-inch squares and paint them a variety of solid colors.

2 Design each square by breaking up the space with a simple motif such as an X, a cross, or a circle. For additional details use varied widths of lines, dots, additional circles, or other suitable elements. Try many variations of these simple motifs.

3 Assemble selected units so that many combinations may be observed. Select one plan for the finished paper.

4 Draw a pattern grid of 4-inch or 5-inch squares on large paper and paint the design according to the unit plan.

5 Many pattern variations may be achieved by experimenting with combinations of units, variations in colors and values of units, and alternation of design. The motif plans may be created by the use of other design elements and subject-matter variations, as was suggested in the Design section of this book.

William M. Enking: *Paper Forms.* 1953. Courtesy of *Everyday Art Magazine.*

PAPER SCULPTURE

Some basic folds and cuts for paper are presented as guides to provide a means for using it as a creative art medium. When paper is folded into three-dimensional shapes, it is transformed into geometrical structures having facets or planes that possess sculptural qualities. When it is left flat, the cut-out areas produce a pattern.

MATERIALS

1. Paper—all kinds
2. Scissors—large and small
3. Knife
4. Stapler
5. Steel square or ruler
6. Gummed tape
7. Paste and rubber cement

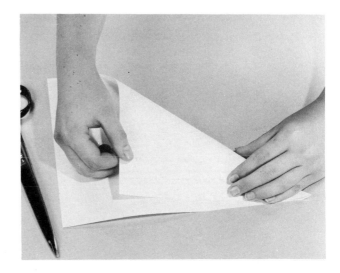

TWO-DIMENSIONAL FORMS

BASIC STEPS

1 *The square is basic to many flat and three-dimensional forms constructed of paper. To make a square without the use of a ruler, fold one of the short sides of a rectangle so that it lies parallel along the adjacent long side.*

2 *Cut off the extension of paper beyond the folded piece.*

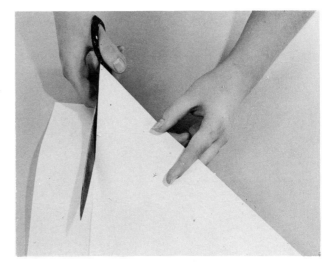

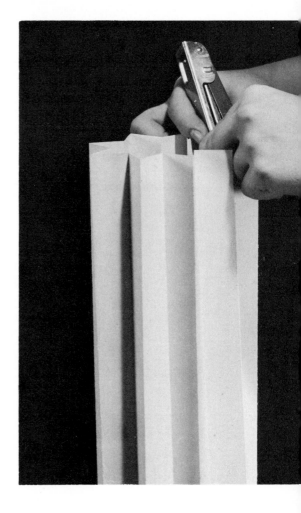

3 Pleated papers are basic to many sculpture problems. Fold a rectangle in half, then in half twice more. Crease well.

4 Open up the folded sheet and reverse the folds into accordion pleats.

5 Bring together the outside edges and fasten with staples, tape, or paste, to form a three-dimensional structure.

EXPANDED PAPER

1 *To expand a flat piece of paper, take any shape, such as a circle or a square, and make a continuous cut from the outer edge to the center.*

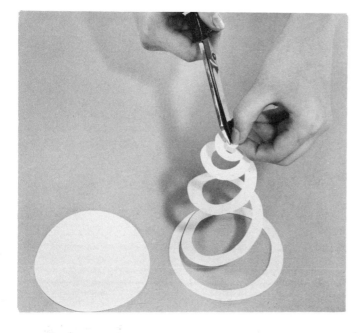

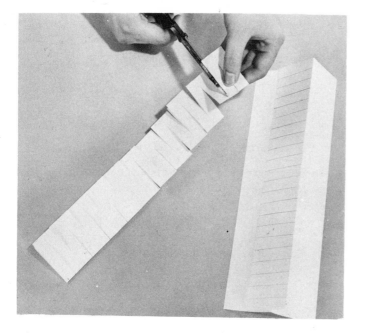

2 *Pull the shape outward and suspend it so that it can hang from a string.*

3 *Fold a rectangle lengthwise two or three times and cut in from either side alternately, stopping ¼ inch from the opposite edge.*

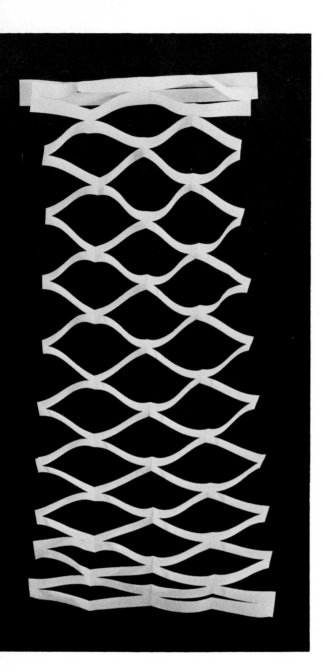

4 Unfold the paper and stretch it out to reveal the cut areas. Suspend or pin it to a flat surface.

5 Fold a square diagonally two or three times. Cut from the fold edges, first from one side and then from the other, to within ¼ inch from the opposite edge.

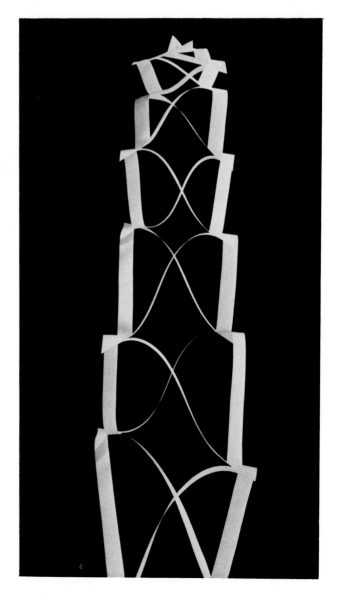

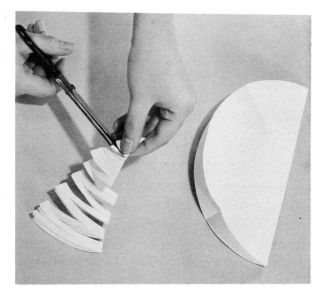

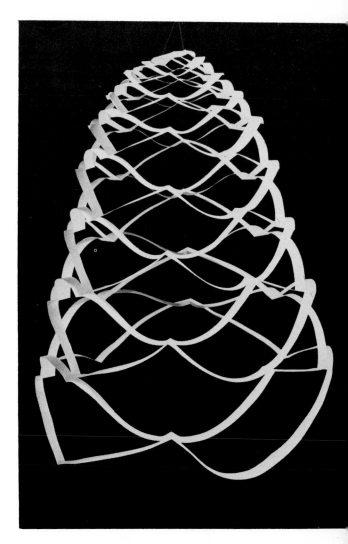

6 Cut a circle and fold it in half two or three times. Cut across the fold edges, alternating from side to side to within ¼ inch of the opposite edge.

7 Unfold the shape and stretch it out.

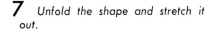

8 To make an interlocking standing structure, fold a rectangle in half the short way. Open it up and fold each outer edge to the center. Draw ½-inch spaces on one side to within ½ inch of the center fold.

9 Fold the rectangle again on the center line and cut on the marked lines from the fold edge.

10 To expand the structure, unfold the paper. Start at the upper left and crease the top strip so that it will fold back. Crease the second strip so that it will fold forward. Continue alternating to the bottom. Starting at the upper right, crease the top strip so that it will fold forward and the second backward. Continue as before. The two halves are now folded in reverse to one another.

11 To form a lantern shape, fold the paper in half. Draw a guideline along the outer edge. Measure and cut strips along the fold edge up to the guideline. Unfold the paper and fasten the outer edges together.

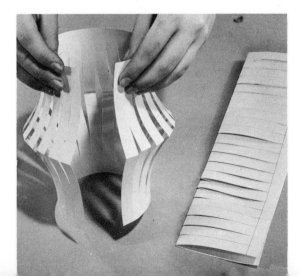

GEOMETRIC SHAPES

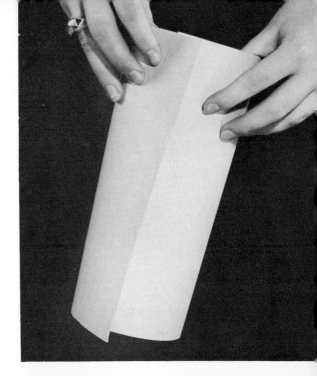

1 To make a cylinder, roll a flat sheet of paper and fasten the over-lapped edges.

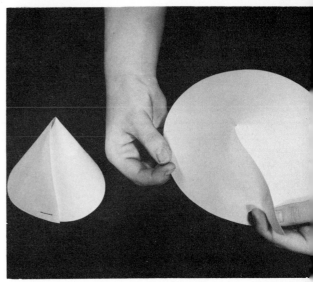

2 Three-dimensional geometric shapes can be formed from flat pieces of paper. Cut a circle. Slit it from the edge to the center along a radius. Overlap the slit edges and fasten in position. For narrower cones increase the overlap, or before overlapping remove a sector such as a semi-circle or quarter-circle.

3 To produce a three-dimensional structure with flat sheets of paper, cut two identical shapes and slit each one to the center.

4 *Interlock the slit shapes by inserting them at right angles.*

CURLING

Paper can be curled more easily with the direction of the grain. Use a pair of scissors or a ruler to stretch it and experiment to discover in which direction it curls best.

PAPER STRIPS

A great variety of paper forms can be constructed with the use of paper strips. Trimmings from paper may be accumulated to use for this purpose. Printing establishments have waste boxes filled with discarded paper trimmings from all kinds of papers. In addition to the three-dimensional forms presented here, weaving also can be done with paper strips.

1 *To produce a shape made by interlocking strips, place the ends of two strips at right angles to one another and fasten.*

2 *Start with the strip underneath and fold it straight back across the one on top. Continue folding first one strip and then the other back and forth until the paper is entirely folded. The folded strip can be used in various ways. For instance, putting the two ends together and fastening them with a staple or piece of tape, a circular structure is formed as shown in the illustration.*

3 To form a paper-strip ball, lay four strips across one another and staple them together in the center. Pick up the ends, overlap, and staple.

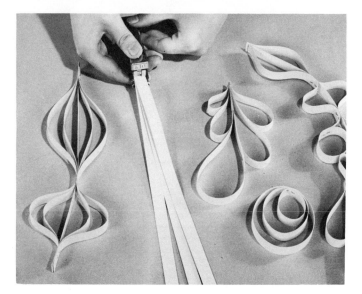

4 To make looped forms start with several strips of paper stapled at one end, using two, three, or more strips.

5 Push up the two outer strips to form loops, and staple them to the center strip. Try variations for looping such as those in the illustration.

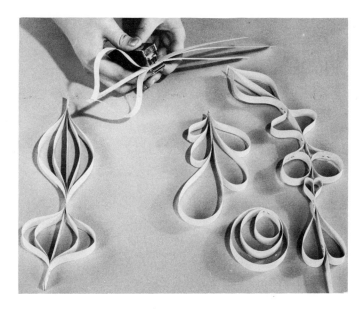

6 *Example of a composition using paper strips.*

SURFACE TEXTURES

The surface of a piece of paper may be changed by slitting parts with scissors or a sharp knife and bending them forward. This produces a textural effect.

1 *To cut slits in the paper, fold a sheet in half a number of times and make straight or curved cuts along the fold edges, varying the cuts in width and depth.*

2 *Unfold the paper and bend the cut tabs outward.*

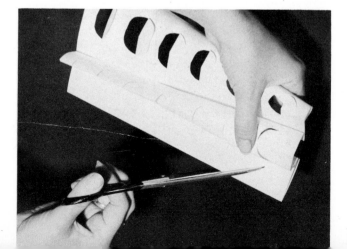

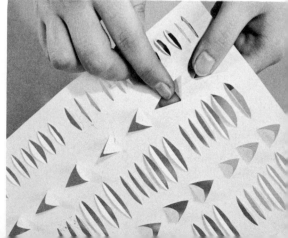

3 *An example of textured areas used as pattern, made by slitting the paper with the sharp blade of a knife or razor blade.*

CUTOUTS

A pattern is produced when areas are cut from a flat sheet of paper. The cut-out portions and the parts remaining form a dark-light de- sign, in which there is a positive and negative relationship.

1 *To produce a simple cut shape, fold the paper in half twice and cut as demonstrated in the illustration.*

2 Fold or pleat a rectangle into a strip. Try cutting various-sized shapes and contours from both edges.

3 Unfold the cut paper, wrap it around a cylinder of a contrasting color paper, and fasten. Note the dark-light pattern produced by the cut-out areas.

4 Fold a square in half along the diagonal. Fold in half twice more. Cut out a variety of shapes from the fold sides, open edge, center, and point. Open up the paper and study the results. Refold and cut to make improvements.

5 An allover pattern produced with designs cut from Japanese origami papers and mounted on circles of different colors to provide contrast.

6 For a multiple cut, fold a sheet of lightweight paper in half several times. Reverse the folds to form accordion pleats as in the illustration on page 50. Cut out shapes along the fold edges and in the center parts, using sharp-pointed scissors. Leave the bottom edge flat to form a base.

7 Unfold the paper and arrange the structure so that it will stand, or pin it against a flat background.

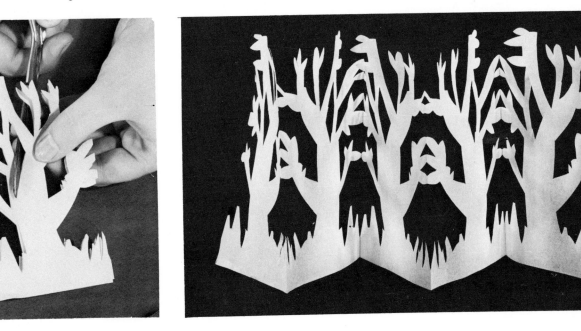

GEOMETRIC STRUCTURES

One can make geometric structures by folding a single sheet of paper or by cutting and assembling separate parts.

BALL MADE OF CIRCLES

1 Cut 20 identical circles of any desired size and color. To turn up the edges place on the circle an equilateral triangle template made of stiff paper. Mark around the template with a scissor blade or dull knife. This will score the paper so that it will fold more easily. To make the equilateral triangle, divide the circumference of a circle into six parts by using the radius of the circle as a measurement. Draw lines connecting alternate marks.

2 Assemble five circles by pasting their flaps together to form the top of the ball. Fasten together five more circles for the bottom of the ball.

3 Arrange the remaining ten circles in a strip and fasten.

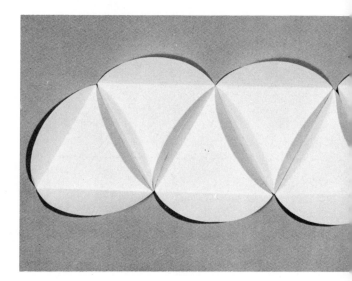

4 To assemble the ball, attach this strip to the top and bottom parts.

5 To make a flat structure instead of a rounded one, fasten together six circles instead of five. Add additional circles to the outer edge to provide variation to the contour.

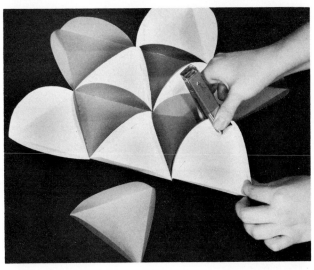

6 To vary the form of the ball, use triangles in place of circles. Cut 20 identical equilateral triangular shapes. Fold up the edges and fasten together in the same way as for the circle ball, or staple at the creases.

POLYHEDRON

One can make a polyhedron by folding a square sheet of paper into 16 equal parts.

1 Fold a square sheet of paper in half. Unfold. Fold each side in half by bringing the edge to the center fold, and crease all folds with the thumbnail to get a sharp edge.

2 Without turning the paper over, fold the square in the other direction and repeat the process. The folded paper will now be composed of 16 squares.

3 Turn the paper over. This is important. Fold the square in half on the diagonals and crease well. Fold each corner to the center, and crease.

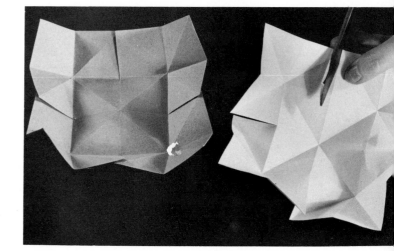

4 Do not turn the paper over. Cut a slit, the length of one crease, in the center of each of the four sides.

5 Still not turning the paper over, place one hand underneath the center portion and push. The section will then pop upward. Do the same under the central points of each of the four corners.

6 To form an inner support for the polyhedron use another square sheet of paper and repeat steps 1 through 5. The second sheet must either be the same size as the first or 1/16 inch smaller.

7 Now turn both papers over. With the hands gently force the lining paper into a ball. Do the same to the other piece of paper. Holding the two balls with the open edges toward each other, wrap the outer ball around the inner structure. Shift them until they fit together.

8 Paste down the loose points of the outer ball.

9 Examples of finished balls that have been decorated with paint and cut-out shapes. Note how the design is adapted to the shape of the structure. Design areas may also be cut in the outer paper revealing the liner through the openings. Enlarged polyhedrons may have openings cut through both the inner and outer papers. The openings may be covered with tissue paper to form a lantern.

FOLDING AND SCORING

Folding and scoring achieve similar results in making three-dimensional structures. Folding is used when the paper is light in weight. Scoring is a means for creasing heavier papers, which would crack and be uneven along the fold if not scored first. By pressure with such instruments as a knife, scissor blade, or compass point, a dent is made in the paper that permits it to fold easily.

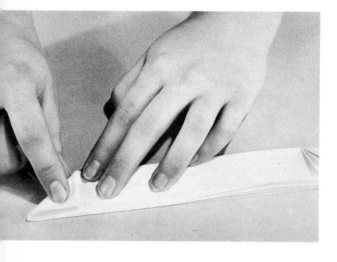

FOLDING

1 *Fold a rectangle several times. Open and refold into accordion pleats. Fold down the upper corners at each end and crease well. Fold them again backward to make the crease sharp and more pronounced. If they are folded back and forth several times to deepen the crease, the next step will be easier.*

2 *Open up the paper and hold it in one hand; use the other hand to push in the creased ends. If the paper has been creased well, this can be accomplished easily.*

3 *Various types of folds can be produced by creasing the folded paper strip in between as well as at the ends. Fold it over at right angles, or in an oblique line. Open up the paper and force it into raised and lowered creases.*

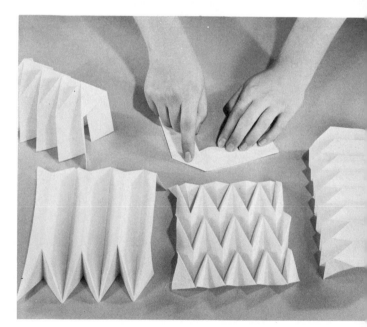

CIRCULAR FOLDED STRUCTURE

1 To make a fanlike circular structure, separately fold two sheets of paper as described in steps 1 and 2 above. Lay one on top of the other and staple them together through the center.

2 Spread out and join the edges together with staples or paste.

SCORING

1 When straight even lines are desired for scoring, indicate dimensions with pencil marks or draw light lines as guides. Score with a ruler and knife to break the paper, being careful not to cut through it.

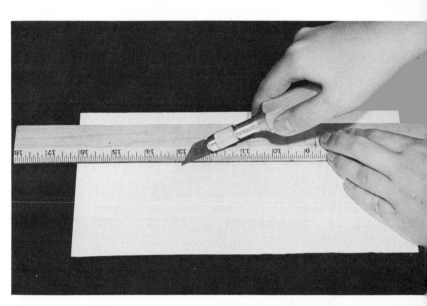

2 Single or double curves may be scored by first drawing lines and then scoring them with a scissor point or other instrument. The paper bends when scored. To make the scored circle, draw one or more lines with a compass, and score each. Cut the circle from the edge to the center along a radius. Overlap and staple the cut edges.

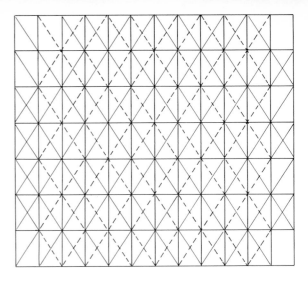

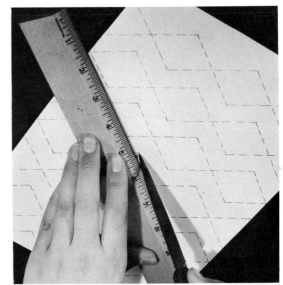

SCORED PAPER WITH SLIT PATTERN

1 Draw and score parallel lines about 1 or 2 inches apart, using a ruler and knife.

2 Turn the paper over. Draw equally spaced horizontal lines any distance apart. With the vertical scoring on the other side this makes a vertical-horizontal grid pattern. Draw in the diagonal lines to conform to the grid pattern.

3 On the diagonal grid, mark off a pattern of diamond shapes as indicated in the photograph.

4 Cut slits through the horizontals in the diamonds as indicated, with a sharp knife or razor blade.

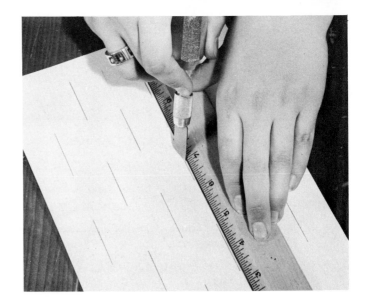

5 Push the slits open and press the folds into place. The vertical lines will all be upward and the diagonal creases will recede.

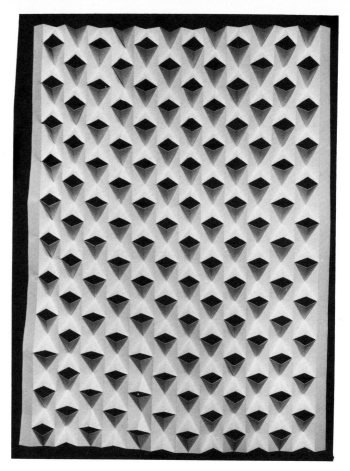

6 The finished paper. An allover design is produced, and the projecting parts of the paper give it a sculptural quality.

LIGHT SHADE

1 Use a strip of paper 1 or 2 yards in length depending upon the size desired. Mark off vertical lines at regular intervals spaced 1 inch or so apart. Draw in the diagonal lines at whatever position and length desired to complete the grid.

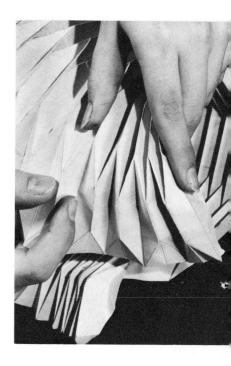

2 Score the vertical lines with a ruler and knife.

3 Score the diagonal lines. This may be done on the same or the opposite side of the paper.

4 Crease the scored lines, and collapse the structure as the paper begins to take shape, for this makes it easier to handle. The form will automatically fall into a rounded three-dimensional structure, which can be fastened together at the outer edges. Run a needle and thread through the points at the top, pull the edges together, and tie well. Do the same to the bottom edge.

5 A finished structure suspended on a thread.

PAPIER-MÂCHÉ

In paper sculpture the paper is used dry, and three-dimensional form is achieved primarily through folding. With papier-mâché it is used wet in combination with paste, becoming hard and retaining its form when dry.

Paper can be made into pulp by tearing it in small pieces, soaking it in water, and adding paste. It may be torn in strips and dipped in a paste mixture; or crushed, wet with paste, and shaped.

There are three processes for making papier-mâché structures: the paper pulp can be modeled like clay; it can be used over frameworks such as bottles, globes, fruit, boxes, newspaper coils, wire armatures, and chicken-wire screening; or it can be pressed into a mold to form a thin shell.

When papier-mâché objects are dry, their surfaces can be covered with a choice of materials and decorated with paint; a protective coat of lacquer or wax may be applied.

MATERIALS

1. Paper—newspapers, paper toweling, crepe paper, tissue paper
2. Paste—flour, starch, wallpaper paste, or commercial products
3. Objects on which to build forms—bottles, globes, assorted boxes, fruit
4. Supplements—wire, brown wrapping paper tape, chicken wire, twine

5. Surface decoration materials—paint, gesso, sand, waterglass, sawdust, sandpaper
6. Protective materials—wallpaper lacquer, clear varnish, liquid floor wax
7. Brush, spatula
8. Scissors

MAKING THE PASTE

Paste mixtures can be made by cooking flour or starch with water, or mixing wallpaper paste with water. Library paste thinned with water can also be used but is more expensive.

1 To make a cooked paste, mix 1/2 cup of flour or starch with water to a thin or runny consistency. Stir this mixture slowly into 5 cups of slightly boiling water. Cook for two or three minutes and cool. To preserve add a few drops of oil of cloves or wintergreen.

2 To make an uncooked paste, use about three parts water to one part wallpaper paste powder. Put the water in a pan and sift the paste over the surface with the hand or a spoon. Stir and let settle a few minutes before using.

PAPER PULP METHOD

To make the pulp, tear small pieces from newspaper strips and place them in a pan; cover with hot water and soak for several hours or overnight. Paper strips found in packaging may also be used for this purpose. Slick papers should be avoided because they are difficult to soften. After the torn pieces have been soaked, they should be disintegrated as much as possible by squeezing and rubbing them between the hands. The use of a hand or electric beater makes a finer pulp; however, this is not neces-sary. When the pulp is broken down, most of the water is squeezed out and paste, starch, glue, or waterglass is added. (No more should be mixed than is actually used, for when the pulp is dry the remainder will harden and be difficult to remove from the pan.) The pasted pulp is then modeled like clay or added to an armature or newspaper-shaped core. All kinds of structures like figures, puppet heads, masks, and fruits can be made in this way.

1   Tear the paper into small pieces and soak in hot water.

2   Add paste to the prepared pulp.

3   To make a fruit or similar form, wad up a piece of newspaper and tie with string or tape. For any additional parts, wrap pieces of wire with paper strips and insert in the wadded paper. Cover the form with the paste-soaked pulp and press firmly into place until it adheres to the surface.

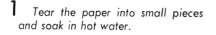

4   Sawdust can be used as a substitute for paper pulp. Mix it in the same way with either paste or glue. For a puppet head, roll a piece of cardboard (about 3 by 5 inches) to form a tube that will fit comfortably over the index finger, and secure it with tape or string. Cover part of the tube with a wadded piece of newspaper; leave the rest projecting, to use as a neck for the puppet. Use string or tape to hold the paper in place. Apply the sawdust or pulp all over the surface and then add additional amounts to model the features.

PAPER STRIP METHOD

Paper strips an inch or so in width are torn from newspapers or paper towels. Several may be torn at one time, either freely or by tearing along the edge of a ruler. Torn strips absorb the paste mixture better than cut ones. Paper tears more easily in one direction than another, and paper toweling, when torn across the grain, will stretch and be easier to fit to the form on which it is applied.

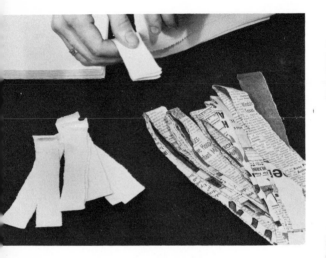

1 Tear the strips freehand or with a ruler. Use newspapers or paper toweling.

2 Dip the strips in the paste mixture.

3 To make a rhythm instrument like a maraca apply paper strips to the surface of a light globe (extra-large globes are best). Strips may be any length; however, small pieces are sometimes easier to handle. When applying the strips, shingle them so that they overlap at the edges. Apply three or four layers of strips. When the strips are dry, break the glass by striking the globe on the edge of a table to produce a rattle. Or leave a ½-inch area uncovered at the top, break it with a nail, insert beans or gravel, and cover with paper strips. Globes can also be used for puppet heads or fruit forms.

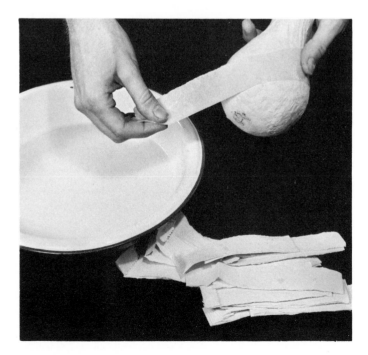

4 Painted globes with pattern applied, to be used as rhythm instruments.

5 To make a bottle figure apply pasted strips of any length, overlapping edges where possible and smoothing out bumps and wrinkles. Use several layers.

6 Add additional parts, using wire, cardboard, ice-cream sticks, tongue depressors, and wadded-up pieces of newspaper. Hold them in position with pasted strips.

PAPER 75

7 *Two examples of finished bottle figures.*

8 *Masks or wall decorations can be made by using strips over a wadded paper core, constructed over a paper plate. This animal mask has ears and whiskers made of folded layers of pasted paper.*

9 Finished examples of papier-
mâché masks.

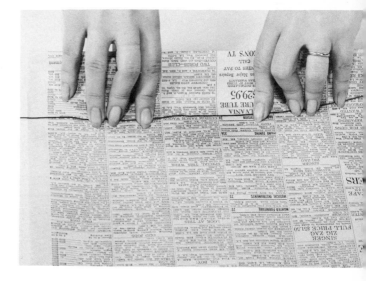

10 To make objects with newspaper coils, cut a piece of wire and lay
it on a folded section of paper.

11 *Roll up the newspaper containing the wire to form a coil. Hold in position with tape or string.*

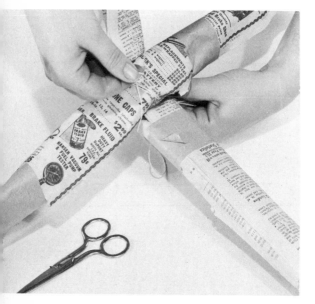

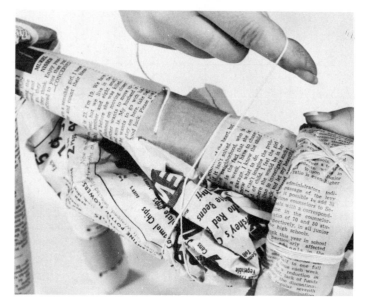

12 *To make an animal structure, use one coil for the body and bend it to form the neck and head. Tie other coils across to form the legs.*

13 *Bend the paper coils in position so that the form can stand upright. To build out the figure add crushed pieces of newspaper wherever desired and secure with string or tape.*

14 *To add additional parts like ears, wrap wire around the paper coil, secure firmly, and then cover it with several layers of pasted strips.*

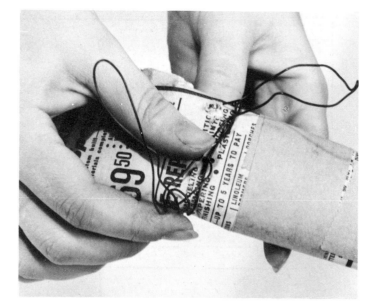

15 Cover the animal form with pasted strips of newspaper or paper toweling, overlapping the edges. Use as many layers as needed.

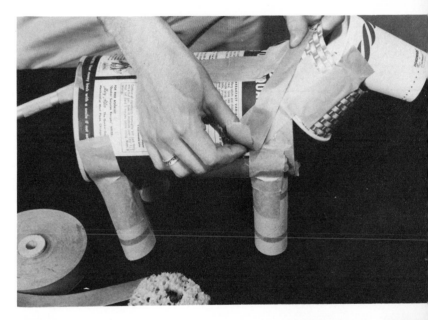

16 A framework for animal or other figure structures may be built up with boxes. Use assorted sizes and shapes, and fit them together in a balanced composition. Moisten the brown wrapping-paper tape with a wet sponge and fasten the parts in position. Avoid using slick tapes because they tend to resist pasted strips.

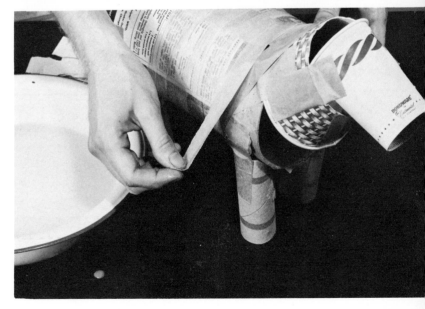

17 Cover the box structure with pasted strips, overlapping the edges and using as many strips as necessary to complete the project.

PRESS MOLD METHOD

Either strips and small pieces or paper pulp may be used in press molds. A ready-made form such as a bowl or tray, or one made of clay or plaster, may be used for this purpose. Several layers of paper are pressed into the form.

1 Grease the inside of a bowl with Vaseline, cold cream, liquid soap, or something similar to prevent the paper from adhering to the sides when it is dry and the molded form is removed. In place of the grease, pieces of waxpaper or a layer of paper strips, dipped in water only, may first be applied to the mold.

2 Tear the pasted strips to a convenient size and place over the inside surface of the mold. Overlap the strips and fit them as neatly as possible. Use three or four layers depending upon the thickness of the shell desired.

3 When it is dry, remove the paper structure from the mold. If it sticks, pry the edges loose with a knife or spatula. Torn places may be mended with additional pasted strips.

SURFACE DECORATION

The surface of the papier-mâché may be left as it is or sanded carefully to produce a smooth finish. To obtain different textures, cover it with other material like fringed crepe and tissue papers, gesso, or a sand and waterglass mixture. Paint can be used to provide decorative patterns. A protective coat of wallpaper lacquer, clear varnish, or liquid floor wax will help preserve the material.

1 For a crepe paper overlay on the surface, fasten the end of a crepe paper strip to the papier-mâché object with a pin. Wrap the form with the strip, overlapping and stretching it to fit in place, using pins wherever necessary to secure it to the structure.

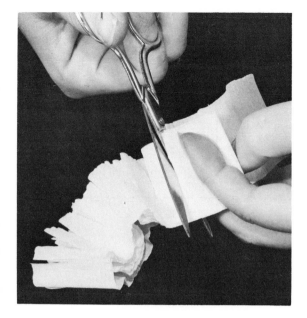 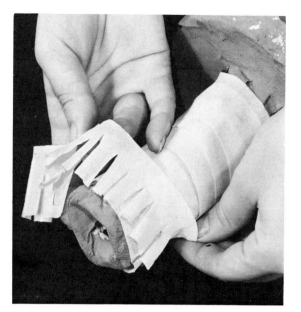

2 To add a fringed layer to the crepe-paper-covered object, lay several strips of crepe paper together, and cut a fringe along one edge. It is faster to cut through several thicknesses at one time. Cut across the grain.

3 Wrap the fringed strips around the object over the first layer of plain strips, overlapping and pinning them where needed to hold them in place.

4 Finished example covered with crepe paper.

5 To produce a smooth surface over the papier-mâché, apply a mixture of gesso with a brush. Several coats can be applied. Sand to finish.

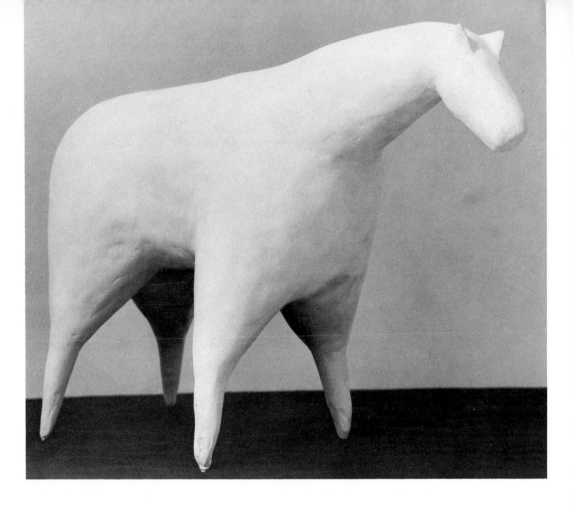

6 *Papier-mâché animal sculpture covered with gesso.*

7 To produce a rough texture, mix sand with waterglass to a heavy pastelike consistency and apply to the object with a spatula or tongue depressor.

8 To decorate the surface with a pattern, paint the papier-mâché with an opaque tempera color. When the paint is dry, add lines and areas of color, contrasting lights with darks. Painted lines can be grouped to simulate textures and produce allover patterns.

82 **CRAFTS DESIGN**

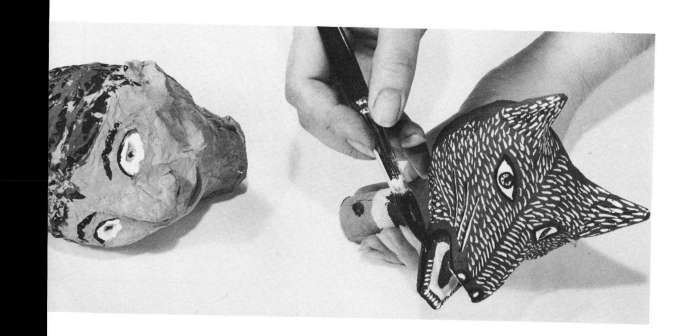

9   *Finished painted animal sculpture.*

ADDITIONAL SUGGESTIONS FOR PAPER

Papers found in general school supplies can serve many purposes; however, it is desirable to try other kinds as well. Teachers should save interesting pieces of gaily colored and textured papers, even very small ones, so that they will be available when needed.

Design learnings need to be emphasized in working with paper. When cutting out shapes, students should think of the total effect such shapes produce, their relationship to one another, and their contribution to the entire pattern. They can, for instance, cut shapes out of light-tone papers and place them against darker papers to study the forms and see whether there is a well-related balance of light areas with dark, and whether the negative spaces are of equal interest to positive ones. Only by continuously experimenting and applying the elements and principles of design can students improve their own designs.

In three-dimensional structures, whether of paper sculpture or papier-mâché, representational factors should be subordinate to design. Emphasis should always be on the *form* experience and the sculptural qualities. Students can be made aware of form through such geometric shapes as the cone, the cylinder, and the cube. They can study the effects of light falling on the planes that compose the surfaces of these volumes.

In exploring ways of working with paper,

students should first practice some of the basic folding, cutting, curling, and scoring techniques, and learn ways to fasten the pieces together. As they become familiar with the properties of the paper and how to handle it, they should be encouraged to try their own compositions—keeping in mind that good design rather than novelty is the aim.

The opportunity to decorate paper should not be overlooked, for either paint or bits of colored papers applied with paste can sometimes add a great deal to the total effect. Studying pattern by making all kinds of decorative papers as well as paper cutouts will be of assistance in applying design to paper structures.

SUGGESTED PROJECTS

Students may wish to apply their ideas to making valentines, cutting snowflake patterns, or cutting out imaginative masks from folded sheets of paper. Flat paper cutouts may be used in wall decorations, bulletin boards, or window displays. Many exciting things can be done with papers in decorating for Christmas and other festival days. Even the simple paper chains that the youngest child can make are effective when they are made of colored and metallic papers and hung in parallel rows to cover a wall. Angels made from cones and other shapes never fail to delight.

Paper strips or pulp can be used over various

foundations such as cardboard tubes and cartons, light globes, and bottles of all sorts, which may be removed when the object is dry, to form a shell, or retained as part of the structure. Wire frames may also be used when figures need to be bent into shapes. Bulky figures of considerable size may be built over large cartons or wood structures, as is often done for commercial window displays. These may be used to make a Santa Claus, angels, or a Halloween witch for school affairs. The young child can build a form by stuffing a paper sack with crushed sheets of newspapers, leaving enough of the bag free to be pulled together and tied with a string. He then can wad up pieces of paper and attach them to the paper sack with pasted paper strips or brown paper tape to shape an animal or person. Older students may wish to build masks over clay forms, wire frames, or structures made of cardboard obtained from boxes and other sources.

Attractive beads can be made with papier-mâché. The pulp may be modeled into round, oblong, or cube-like shapes. When dry, they can be painted and strung with a needle and strong thread. The needle will penetrate the paper pulp, or an awl or ice pick may be used for making holes. The application of shellac, varnish, or clear nail polish will provide a protective coat.

South of Milwaukee. Collage of cut and pasted paper. Child, age 10. Studio San Damiano, Milwaukee, Wisconsin. Sister Mary Thomasita, U.S.F., instructor.

BOOKBINDING

Byzantine: *The Archangel Michael*. Eleventh century. Enameled book cover.
Venice, San Marco Treasury. Alinari.

BOOKBINDING

Although bookbinding as we know it today did not begin until around 200 B.C., the history of the book extends back to the time of the early Sumerians who invented a pure form of written language about 3500 B.C. The Sumerian written language was unusually beautiful and decorative in style, being formed of wedge-shaped characters chiseled in stone or impressed in damp clay with a stylus. The Sumerians, and later the Babylonians and Assyrians, produced thousands of clay tablets about three inches square and covered with inscriptions. These might be considered the first books, and they were assembled in what we would call libraries.

The Egyptians wrote on sheets of papyrus made from the papyrus plant, a reed that grew along the banks of the Nile. The outer parts of the stalk were laid parallel in a row and a second layer was placed across them at right angles. These were beaten and pounded until they were welded together to form a flat writing surface. A form of ink and a pen made of reed were used for writing. Several of the sheets were fastened together to form a roll, and a number of rolls might be needed to complete a book.

One of the most famous of the early Egyptian manuscripts was the Book of the Dead, which contained chapters dealing with funeral ritual and the Egyptian beliefs regarding life after death. Perhaps the oldest book in the world still in existence is a volume called the *Papyrus Prisse*, dating back to about 2500 B.C. It is composed of eighteen pages in Egyptian hieratic writing, and is now kept in the Louvre at Paris.

The Romans kept their records of transactions, as well as codes of law and contracts, on *diptychs*, composed of two or more writing tablets of wood similar to our old-fashioned slates, hinged together with leather thongs. The insides were coated with wax upon which impressions were made with a stylus.

Papyrus continued to be used until paper was introduced in the twelfth century A.D., but around the second century B.C. parchment began to replace papyrus as a writing material. It was made from the skins of various animals and prepared by cleaning and rubbing smooth, so that a flat, even surface was available for writing. A fine parchment made of calfskin was called *vellum*. Well-prepared parchment was prized by the medieval bookbinders and illuminators. Since vellum was fairly costly, old manuscripts or spoiled pages were frequently scraped down to remove the previous texts and used again for new material. Texts written on reclaimed parchment are called *palimpsests*. The term *vellum* has come to have a different connotation in present-day binding and is often used in connection with a specially prepared cover cloth for binding books.

The writing on the early scrolls took the form of columns about the width of one of our book pages. This form made the scroll more convenient to read as it was unrolled while held horizontally. Later, instead of being rolled, the scrolls were folded with the creases coming at the

Japanese: *Deer Scroll.* Seventeenth century. Painting by Nonomura Sotatsu. Calligraphy by Honnami Koetsu. Ink, gold, and silver on paper. 12½″ high. 30′ 3¾″ long (half of the original scroll). Seattle Art Museum. Gift of the late Mrs. Donald E. Frederick.

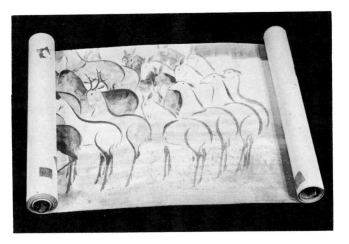

Babylonian: *Clay Tablet.* 744–669 B.C. The British Museum.

Hebrew: *Scroll, The Book of the Law.* Fifteenth century. The British Museum.

Siamese: *Sutra.* Nineteenth century. 55 palm leaves with wooden covers, 22″ x 2¼″. Seattle Art Museum, Eugene Fuller Memorial Collection.

BOOKBINDING   **89**

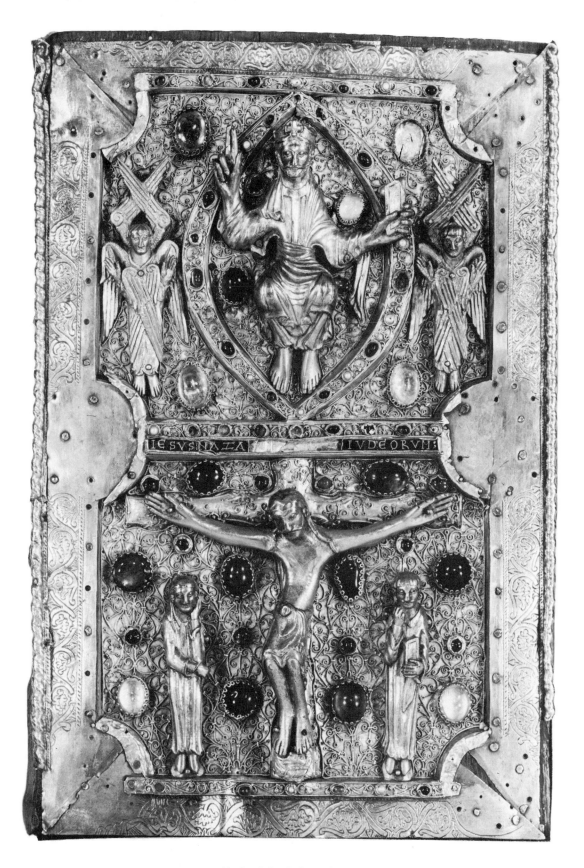

England: *Book Cover for the Four Gospels.* c. 1040. Silver ornamented with jewels. The Pierpont Morgan Library.

spaces between the columns into reverse sections, forming accordion pleats. It was not long before holes were punched at the margin end of these flattened sections and they were tied together with string. Next they were sewn on leather thongs or cords, and the form began to resemble the book as we know it today. Thin boards of wood were placed on the top and bottom of these assembled sections to protect the pages and keep them flat. Eventually the cords or bands on which the pages were sewn were fastened to the boards by being laced into the covers.

As the art of binding developed, the back of the book was covered with leather to conceal the cords, and soon the leather was extended over the entire surface of the boards. Covers were fairly plain at first, but as skills developed and talents were released the bindings became more and more elaborate. Binders in one country competed with those in other countries to produce the most beautiful books of which they were capable.

Originally, books were produced and bound almost entirely in monasteries by monks especially trained to do this time-consuming and careful work. The monks had special places called *scriptoria* set aside for copying, and the precious manuscripts were well guarded lest they should become damaged or lost. Pride was taken in the design and decoration of the parchment pages, and thus the art of illumination was born. This art involved the use of elaborate borders and initial letters painted with gold and colors, as well as illustrations in the form of miniature paintings depicting the life of Christ and events connected with the Apostles. The pages were sensitively spaced, with margin and

Persian: *Book Cover*. Seventeenth–eighteenth century. Leather, 11⅝″ x 18⅛″. Seattle Art Museum, Eugene Fuller Memorial Collection.

Persian: *Kufic Page*. Seljuk Dynasty, c. eleventh century. Vellum, 12″ x 13½″. Seattle Art Museum, Eugene Fuller Memorial Collection.

India, Rajput: *Rhada Inviting Krishna to her Pavilion*. Sheet from a book. c. 1634. Paper, 7¼″ x 5½″. Seattle Art Museum, Eugene Fuller Memorial Collection.

text carefully related. These books were mostly religious in nature—primarily the four Gospels of the New Testament, or prayer books containing devotional material.

Cover bindings became extremely important by the fourth century. As the art advanced, jewels, enamels, precious metals, and carved ivory were introduced, and covers became very ornamental and elaborate. In a later period, gold tooling and various decorative stamps were used for impressing patterns.

The Byzantine emperors displayed books of massive size, upon their completion, by carrying them in public processions. These books were richly colored in leathers of red, blue, or yellow, and gorgeously decorated by silversmiths who used beaten gold and silver on the leathers. Bindings were expensive because manuscripts were rare and costly.

Some of the best work was done in Irish monasteries, where there was much creative activity during the fifth, sixth, and seventh centuries. Many of the bindings produced then were quite plain; however, the *Book of Kells,* named for the

Kells Monastery, has been considered by many authorities to be the most beautiful book in the world. With its well-designed and illuminated pages, handsomely lettered text, and richly conceived binding, this book is truly an imaginative and inspired work of art. It contains the four Gospels, handwritten in Latin on vellum. The ornamented borders, initial letters, and fill-ins are rich in pattern and in the use of gold and color. Illustrations showing incidents in the life of Christ and portraits of the Evangelists are part of the page embellishment. Facsimiles of this book are available in libraries, so that it is possible for anyone to see and study it. The original, however, is kept in the library of Trinity College in Dublin, Ireland.

Manuscripts referred to as the *Book of Hours* became popular in Europe, especially in France. These books contained calendars, with emblems or scenes suited to each month, and included prayers and lessons from the Gospels.

Two great discoveries—the invention of paper and of printing—did more than anything else to advance world culture and the art of the

French: *Book of Hours.* Fifteenth century. Courtesy, University of Washington Library.

Irish: *Elaborate Initial Letter from the Book of Kells*. Eighth century. Trinity College, Dublin, Ireland. From publication by Urs Graf Verlag Gmbh, Switzerland. Courtesy of Phillip Duschnes. By permission of the Board of Trinity College, Dublin.

School of Paris: *Page from an Antiphonary.* Initial containing scene of the Pentecost. Fourteenth century. 18¼" x 12¼". Seattle Art Museum, Eugene Fuller Memorial Collection.

German: *Page from Gutenberg Bible.* 1450–1456. Courtesy, University of Washington Library.

book. Until this time, the knowledge confined in books was available only to wealthy patrons, heads of state, and church officials. Wealthy Romans secured literate slaves to copy books for their personal libraries; but most people were denied the general use of this wonderful material. Although there were libraries in ancient Egypt, Greece, and other parts of the early world, they contained only a limited number of books since all books had to be produced tediously by hand.

Paper was invented in China several centuries before Europe discovered a method of making it. The paper produced in Europe was more suitable for printing, while that in China had a quality especially adaptable to the impression of engraved wood blocks. The Chinese and the Koreans developed a form of movable blocks for type; however, this method was somewhat difficult to use because of the numerous letter forms needed.

Johann Gutenberg is credited with having invented and built the first printing press in Europe in his native town of Mainz, Germany. Here the famous Gutenberg Bible was printed in Latin between the years 1450 and 1456. A beautiful, well-designed type was used and the pages were planned with margins carefully spaced. In fact, this is the finest example of printing ever produced, and in subsequent years it has never been surpassed in quality. Contrary to belief, the Bible was not the first book to be printed on this press, for there were earlier examples which made it possible for Gutenberg to experiment and bring his art to a high development before producing his masterpiece. The *World Judgment,* a book of seventy-four pages, was set in type and printed ten years before the date of the Gutenberg Bible. There were also an astronomical calendar and a Donatus (grammar) printed on vellum.

Bookbinding today has changed a great deal

from the historical examples noted. Hand-bound books are still made by professional binders who do binding as a form of expression or on private commission for patrons able to afford distinctively bound books for their own libraries or for special occasions. However, not many people today are committed to the profession of the hand binder, since the great commercial presses are able to produce such vast amounts at prices within the reach of everyone. The demands for knowledge have brought into existence the popular paperback editions, many of which have attractively designed covers. Although not permanent in binding, they serve a needed purpose in making more books available to more people.

The progress of man would have been greatly hindered without the book for the dissemination of knowledge. Through it the great cultures of the past are available for the needs of the present. The intellectual attainments now possible are due to the vast amount of literature, philosophy, history, and sacred writings that have come to us on the printed page. It is significant that the visual arts have played such a great part in this important aspect of our lives.

BINDING BOOKS

Bookbinding, although a less familiar craft than some, is within the range of all who wish to experience the pleasure of making and having books personally designed and created. The beginner should not let the lack of expensive equipment or of the years of training needed by the professional binder hinder him from doing a satisfying piece of work. The art of bookbinding has infinite possibilities for development. If the basic principles and techniques of book design are understood, the craftsman will find many opportunities for expressing his ideas through this medium.

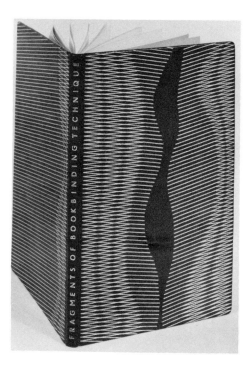

R. Wright: *Leather Binding.* London. Twentieth century.

Edgar Mansfield: *Leather Binding.* London. Twentieth century. Red-brown morocco inlaid in yellows, reds, brown, natural, and black. Tooled in gold and blind.

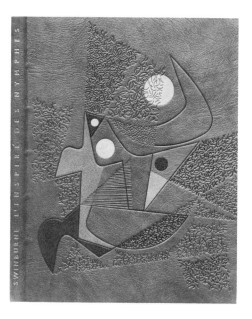

Georges Cretté: *Leather Binding*. French. Twentieth century. Grey-green box-calf mosaic decoration in dark olive and yellow-brown. Courtesy of *Graphis*.

G. B. Stevens: *Leather Binding*. London. Twentieth century. Letters on front onlaid in oranges and reds; those on back in blues, purple, and violet.

Ivor Robinson: *Leather Binding*. London. 1958. Inlaid with turquoise, terra cotta, black, yellow, and grey morocco leather, and tooled in black and gold. 16″ x 11″. Collection of Maurice Goldman, Esq.

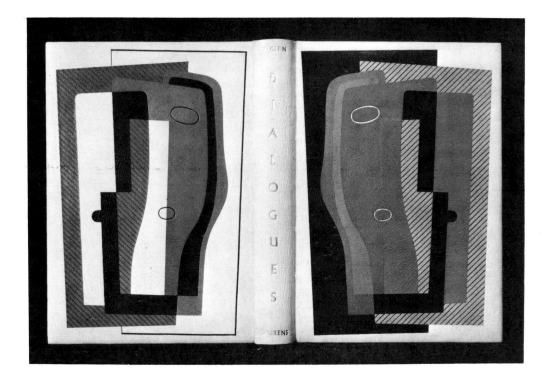

MATERIALS

Paper. All kinds of papers should be considered for use. A roll of butcher or kraft paper is excellent for general purposes and especially for making decorative papers for covers. Also available for covers are colored poster papers, Japanese colored origami and rice papers, silk span (used with airplane hobby kits), and newsprint. The intended use of the book, whether for sketching, writing, mounting, or other purposes, will help determine the type of paper most appropriate for the inside sheets. Cream manila paper, white drawing paper, sketch-pad papers, bond, newsprint, charcoal, and colored papers are suggested; however, other types should also be explored.

Cardboard. Backs of tablets may be used for cover boards. If they are too flimsy, two boards may be pasted together. Chipboard is available in various thicknesses in large-sized sheets. Rigid boards like tarboard and davey board used by bookbinders can be obtained from bookbinding supply firms and paper companies.

Cloth. Cloth is used as an outside cover material on books, either over the entire surface or as a partial binding around the spine, where it provides strength at the hinge where the book opens. In addition to its utilitarian function, the texture and color of the cloth provide design interest. Denim, sailcloth, hopsacking, Indian head, and linen are suggested useful binding materials. Plain material may be decorated with print or stencil patterns. Special book cloths such as vellum and buckram, the cover materials used on most machine-made books, are available by the yard or bolt from bookbinders and supply companies. They can be combined with decorative papers in making bindings for books, portfolios, scrapbooks, and other bound volumes. Special cloths, called super, are used in the binding process and are available commercially.

Leather. Leather is used on book covers either alone or in combination with other leathers or decorative papers. Most leathers, except skiver, reptilian, ostrich, and other thin pieces, need to be skived or pared around the edges so that they can be turned over the edge of the cardboard cover. There are many ways of adding decoration to the leather of a covered book either before or after it is bound. Calf or any leather that will hold an impressed line can be tooled and stamped. Design and pattern can be produced with *inlay* (inserting small pieces), *onlay* (gluing additional pieces on top), *mosaic* (gluing pieces next to one another), or *appliqué* (sewing). The leather cover may be left in its untreated state, with its natural color and texture contributing to the design; or color may be added by dyeing, staining, painting, or gilding the entire cover or parts of it.

We have seen in the history of bookbinding that many craft techniques and materials can be combined in the design of book covers. Enamel, ivory, metal, wood, and precious or semiprecious stone inserts are only a few of the many materials traditionally used in conjunction with leather bindings.

Thread. A natural-colored linen bookbinder's thread or heavy cotton or linen thread is necessary for some binding techniques.

Adhesives. Inexpensive pastes can be made of cooked flour and water mixtures, or powdered wheat paste combined with water. (See page 72 for directions.) Various rubber-based white glues, casein pastes, library pastes, vegetable glues, and rubber cements are commercially available. A flexible glue, preferably for the spine of the sewn book, may be obtained in liquid form or in gelatin loaf from local binders or bookbinding supply firms. Glue in gelatin form is cut into small pieces, placed in hot water, and melted in a glue pot or a double boiler. Water will need to be added occasionally to keep the glue in a thin and runny consistency. If bookbinder's glue is not available, a regular glue or musilage may be substituted. A stiff glue brush is preferable for use; however, a flat stiff varnish brush from the dime store is also satisfactory.

TOOLS

Needles
Scissors
Knife (with a sharp blade)
Steel square or ruler
Paper punch
Awl
Bone folder
Leather tools such as modelers, stamps, and
   skiving knives
Paper cutter

TECHNIQUES

Cutting. Cardboard for covers must be cut accurately. If the covers are not identical in size the book will be lopsided. The cutting of cardboard may be done on a paper cutter reserved for "rough" work, or with a steel square and a sharp knife or mat cutter. The steel square is used to get square corners and straight edges. Papers for the pages of books are most easily and accurately cut on a paper cutter, but if one is not available scissors or a sharp knife and a straight-edge may be used.

Pasting. In pasting it is essential to keep the work space and materials clean. Have a stack of newspapers cut in quarter-sheets available to put under the paper or cloth being pasted. Discard immediately after use. Thin paste should be used and applied rapidly before it has time

to dry. It can be put in the center of the paper to be pasted and spread outward toward the edges with a paste brush or fingers. Make certain that the edges are also well covered. After the pasted sheet is put on the cardboard it should be rubbed carefully with a bone folder or soft clean cloth, to make it adhere and to smooth out any wrinkles. Pasted cardboards will warp unless they are put under a weight or in a press until dry.

Pressing. Completed books are put to press as soon as they are finished, and left several hours until thoroughly dry. Various kinds of book presses are available; or one can be constructed simply, by clamping two boards together; or weights such as bricks or heavy books may be placed on top of the work to be pressed. Rough bricks should be wrapped with paper or covered with a soft flannel cloth, unless they are placed on top of smooth wood boards. A folded piece of waxed paper or a sheet of tin must be placed next to pasted areas when pressing, to prevent the dampness of the paste from going through to other parts of the book.

ACCORDION BOOK

One of the simplest types of bookbinding is the accordion book, so named because its pages are folded back and forth like pleats. When cardboard covers are attached to each of the two outside sheets, a book is formed. This type of book has an Oriental origin and traditional Chinese and Japanese books are made in this way.

MATERIALS

1. Cardboard
2. Paper—for inside sheets
3. Cover material—paper or cloth
4. Steel square or ruler
5. Knife
6. Paste
7. Bone folder or clean cloth

1 Take a long strip of paper and fold it back and forth into accordion pleats to form the pages of the book. If the book is meant to stand upright, stiff paper such as construction or tagboard will be needed. If a longer strip is desired, leave about ½ inch at one end for a tab to use as an overlap when adding the next strip or sheet. If a long strip of paper is not available for folding, hinge individual sheets together with strips of gummed tape, or 1-inch wide strips of white cambric attached with paste. If paste is used in hinging it should be kept very thin, and the sheets pressed under heavy weights until dry to keep them flat. This pressure will help prevent warping.

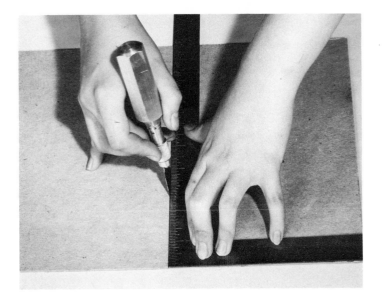

2 Cut two cardboards for the covers. If the book is to stand upright, as in illustration, the cardboards should be the exact size of the sheets. Otherwise they are cut ⅛ inch wider on each of the four sides. Measure boards carefully or use a right-angle steel square, and cut with a sharp knife.

3 Cut the outside cover material at least ¾ inch wider on each side than the cardboard. Put paste on the board and lay it on the cover material, or lay the material on the board. To smooth, rub well on both sides with a bone folder or a clean cloth.

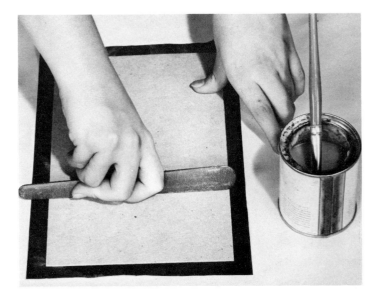

4 Cut off the corners of the cover material a distance from the board equal to the thickness of the board. This is called mitering the corners.

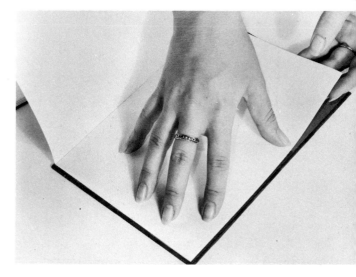

5 Apply paste with a brush to each of the projecting flaps. Fold over and press them down on the cardboard cover.

6 To attach the cover to the accordion-folded pages, paste each of the end sheets of the folded strip of paper to the inside of a cover board. This becomes a lining sheet.

7 If a different kind of lining is desired, paste it over the end sheet that has been attached to the cover board; or attach the accordion-folded strip to the cover boards by means of a 1-inch tab at each end, and then cover with a lining. Here a decorative lining is being made with strips of colored paper. Place wax paper inside of each cover and put the book in a press or under a weight for several hours or until it is dry.

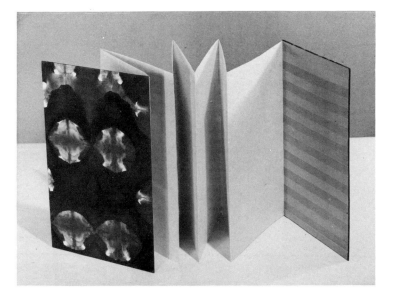

8 *Finished book covered with a decorative paper made with the fold-and-dye process, the inside sheets made of the accordion-folded paper, and a striped lining sheet.*

9 *Two finished accordion-fold books with printed decorative papers used on the covers. The one above is made with an eraser stamp and inside sheets of black paper. The one on the left has a wax-resist design and a lining formed with strips of colored paper.*

Portfolio. Vellum and decorated paper. Adult student.

Box-type Portfolio. Vellum and decorated paper. Adult student.

PORTFOLIO

A portfolio can serve a variety of purposes. The size and proportion depend upon its use. It may be designed to hold large sheets, charts, and drawings, or small items such as stationery. It may be kept simple in structure or have additional flaps around the edge that fold inward.

MATERIALS
1. Cardboard
2. Paper—for lining
3. Cover material—paper or cloth
4. Hinge material—book cloth or vellum
5. Knife
6. Bone folder or clean cloth
7. Paste
8. Ties

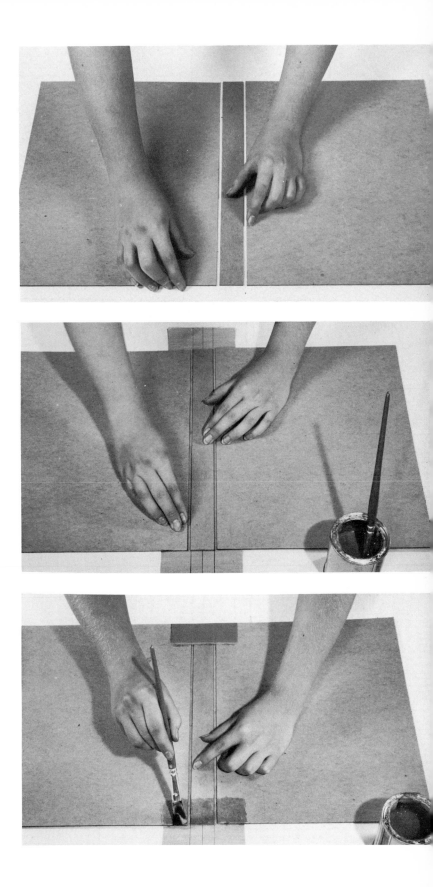

1 Cut two pieces of cardboard the same size for the covers. For a rigid back cut a third piece the same length and any desired width. Lay these pieces together to see if they line up evenly.

2 Cut a strip of cloth, book vellum, or tough paper 2 inches longer than the cover boards and sufficiently wide to overlap at least 1 inch on each board to make a hinge. A strip 3 or 4 inches wide will probably be sufficient. Draw a line down the center of the strip and measure on either side to indicate where to place the boards. Lines may be drawn across the top and bottom as additional guides in positioning the boards. Apply paste with a brush to the strip. Lay the boards down and press lightly into place. Turn them over and rub the strip well with a bone folder or clean cloth to smooth out any wrinkles.

3 Apply paste at the top and bottom, and fold over the extending flaps. If book vellum is used do not pull while damp or it will stretch. If wrinkles persist press with a warm iron. For large portfolios it is advisable to paste each cover board separately.

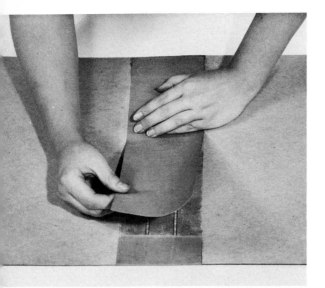

4 Paste a lining strip of the same material or of tough brown wrapping paper over the inside of the hinge area, about 1/8 inch from the top and bottom edges.

5 Cut the cover material for each side so that it overlaps the hinge material slightly and extends at least 3/4 inch beyond the boards on the other three edges. Paste the cover material to the boards and miter the corners as explained in illustration 4 on page 100. If ties are to be used, make slits through the cover board from the inside with a sharp knife about 1/2 inch from the edge.

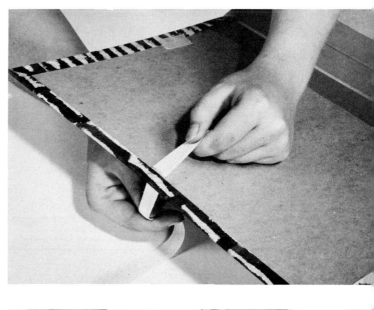

6 Insert the tie through the slit from the outside. A white booktape is used here; however, other materials that relate to the design may also be used.

7 Glue 1 or 2 inches of the tapes to the inside of each cover board. Select lining sheets of any desired paper that relates to the cover in color, texture, or pattern. Cut the lining sheets 1/8 inch smaller than the outside edges of the cover but slightly overlapping the inside hinge. Apply glue to cover boards, lay lining paper in place, and smooth with cloth or bone folder. Put protective wax paper over pasted areas and press until dry.

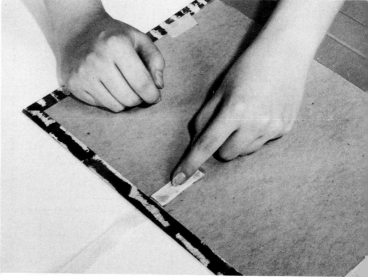

8 *The finished portfolio with a decorative paper cover and a book-vellum hinge.*

SCRAPBOOK

The scrapbook which may be vertical, horizontal, or square in shape, consists of single sheets held together between two covers. Precut scrap fillers may be purchased in packaged sets from stationery supply sources, or suitable paper may be purchased and cut to size.

MATERIALS

1. Cardboard
2. Paper—for lining and filler
3. Cover material—paper or cloth
4. Hinge material—book cloth or vellum
5. Knife
6. Bone folder or clean cloth
7. Paste
8. Fasteners at hinge

1 *Cut the sheets for the book to desired size. Fold a 1-inch tab on one end of each sheet. This tab will allow for expansion of the book as items are mounted on the pages. For neater folding, score the lines first with the slight pressure of a knife.*

2 *To make a cover that will be ⅛ inch wider at the top, bottom, and outer edge of the book when it is completed, cut a piece of cardboard the same width as the paper and ¼ inch more in length.*

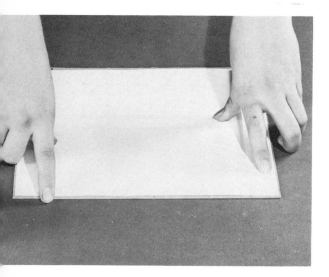

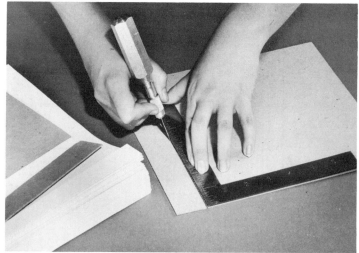

3 For the hinge cut a strip 1 inch wide from the side of the cover board.

4 Cut a strip of cloth, book vellum, or tough paper twice the width of the small cardboard strip plus 2 or more extra inches, and 1 inch longer at the top and bottom.

5 Crease the hinge strip in half vertically, open it up, and paste the narrow cardboard strip next to the center line. Rub well. Paste the large cover board next to it, leaving a space of $\frac{1}{8}$ inch or more if the cardboard is unusually thick.

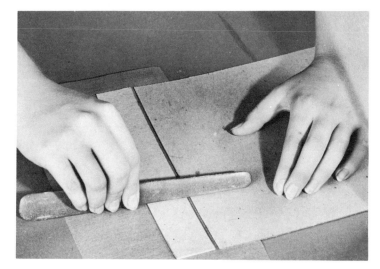

6 Cut off the corner sections on the unpasted half of the hinge material.

7 Paste the top and bottom flaps down on the cardboard.

8 Paste the remaining half of the hinge material; lay it over the cover board, pushing it down in the groove between the boards with the dull edge of a bone folder. This completes the front cover. The back cover may be hinged or not as desired.

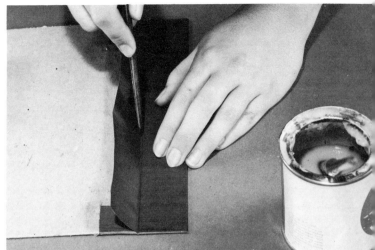

9 Paste the cover paper on the out-side of each cardboard, slightly overlapping the edge of the hinge material.

10 Miter the two outer corners on each board and paste down the flaps. Cut lining sheets ⅛ inch smaller than the outside edges of the cover but overlapping the inside hinge. Apply paste to cover boards. Lay lining paper in place and smooth with a bone folder or cloth. Put protective wax paper over the pasted areas and press both covers until dry.

11 Place the cover boards with the stacked sheets of papers between them so that the hinge edge is even with the folded tab edge of the papers. Make holes for fasteners or lacing through the narrow cardboard hinge of the covers and the papers between them. If a drill is used this can be done all at one time as in illustration 1 on page 109 for the side-sewn book. If a hand punch is used the holes in the covers can be made first and those on the papers marked through the cover holes so they will line up evenly. The book may be held together with ties, screw posts, rings, or side sewing, described on pages 108-111.

SIDE-SEWN BOOK

This method is used for binding single sheets. The sewing may or may not be visible on the finished book. If the sewing is to be concealed, the pages are first sewn and then covered with a hard-cover casing. When the sewing is visible and is used as a decorative feature of the book, it is referred to as a Japanese binding.

MATERIALS

1. Paper—for inside sheets and cover
2. Material for sewing—thread, yarn, cord
3. Needle
4. Drill or awl
5. Clamp or spring clothespin
6. Sewing clamp

Side-sewn Books. Vellum and decorated paper covers. Students at Jane Addams Junior High School, Seattle. Mary Kutila, Instructor.

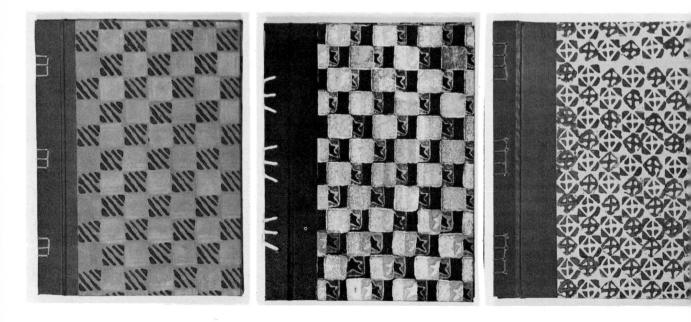

1 To make the pages for the book, stack single sheets of paper that have been cut to the desired size. For double pages use sheets folded in half. Later the fold will be on the outside edge and the open end will be bound. Soft covers for this method can be made by using single sheets of decorative paper of the same size as the pages. For greater strength, the cover may be cut double size and folded in half. Place the sheets between the cover papers with the fold edges kept together.

2 Draw a line ½ inch or more from the edge along the side to be bound. Make a series of holes through the covers and pages. The spaces between the holes may be equal or grouped in a pattern. If a hand drill is used, the book may be held in a sewing clamp, book press, or vise, with a cardboard placed underneath to provide a firm base against which to drill.

3 Holes can also be pierced with an awl, ice pick, or needle, or made with a hand punch, while papers are held in position with a clamp or spring clothespins.

4 Material for sewing may include cord, yarn, embroidery floss, coarse string, heavy thread, raffia, shoe lacing, or whatever seems appropriate. The sewing serves as decoration in addition to its function. To begin the sewing, bring the threaded needle up through the first hole at top end of the book, leaving a tail of thread 2 or 3 inches long.

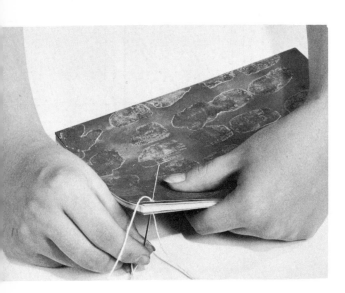
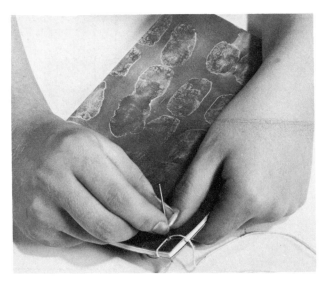

5 Bring the thread around the top end of the book and push the needle up through the hole again.

6 Then bring the thread over the back edge and again push the needle up through the same hole.

7 Pull the needle down through the second hole.

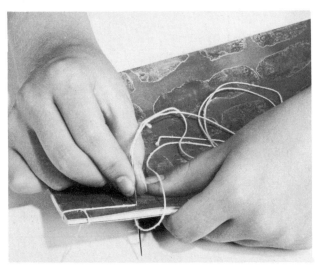

8 Bring the thread up around the back edge and push the needle again down through the second hole. Bring the needle up through the third hole. The thread goes around over the back edge and up through the hole again. Put it down through the fourth hole, come up around the edge and down through the hole again.

9 Continue until the last hole is reached, then bring the thread around both the top and side edges as explained in steps 4, 5, and 6.

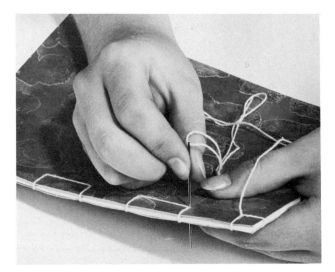

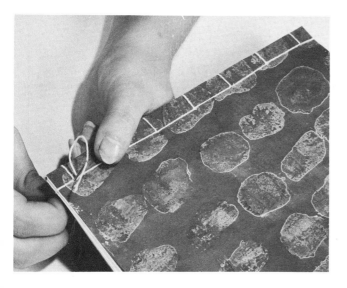

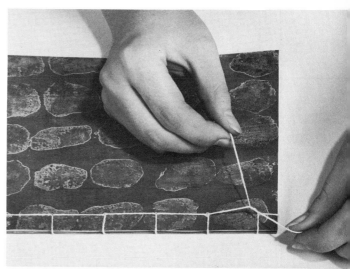

10 Retrace steps so that the space between holes is all filled by putting the needle down through one hole and up through the next until the opposite or beginning end is reached.

11 Tie the thread with tail that was left projecting at the beginning of the sewing. Unless the knot is too thick it can be poked into the end hole.

12 The book with the sewing completed. Other examples of side sewing may be seen in the illustrations following. Side-sewn books with hinged hard covers can also be made. Directions for making these covers will be found in the section on the scrapbook. A piece of book vellum or cloth is placed on the top and bottom of the pile of sheets and sewn in with them to form a hinge. The sewing is not brought over the top and bottom edges of the sheets as previously described. The cardboard cover can be pasted to the hinge and a narrower strip put over the sewing.

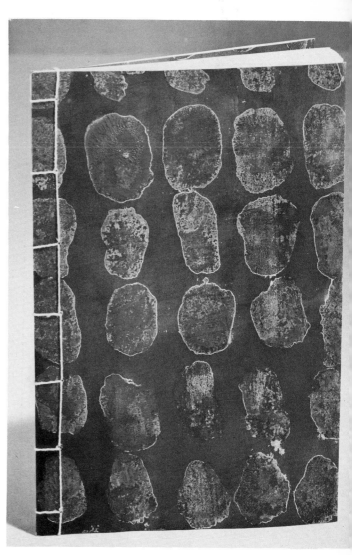

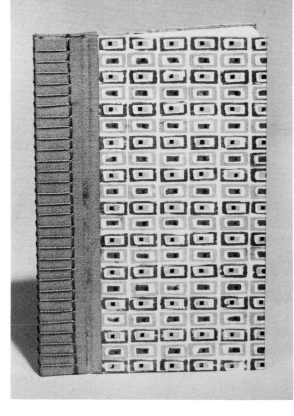

13 *Examples.*

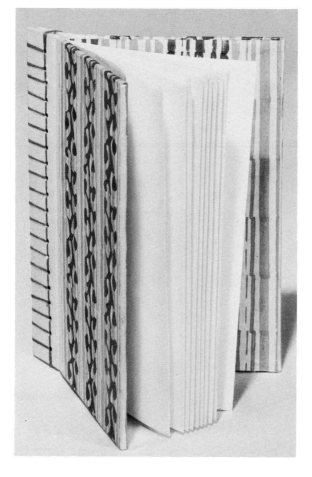

BOOK ON TAPES

Unlike the side-sewn book, the book on tapes is made by sewing folded sheets, grouped together into signatures, to tapes or cords, to form a sturdy binding. This method permits the book to be opened flat.

MATERIALS

1. Cardboard
2. Paper—for pages and lining sheets
3. Cover material—paper or cloth
4. Knife
5. Bone folder or cloth
6. Paste
7. Flexible glue or mucilage
8. Needle
9. Thread
10. Super
11. Tape
12. Sewing frame
13. Glue pot
14. Press

1 *Cut sheets of paper to size and fold in half, using a bone folder or the edge of the thumbnail to get a firm crease.*

2 *Arrange the folded sheets in groups of signatures or sections by inserting two or more together. The number inserted depends upon the thickness of the paper; however, four is the number generally used.*

3 *Stack the grouped signatures.*

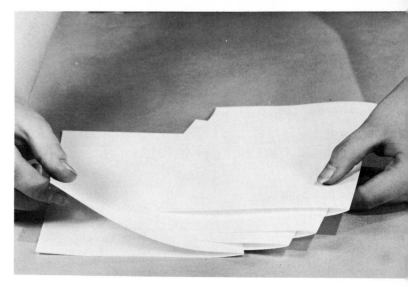

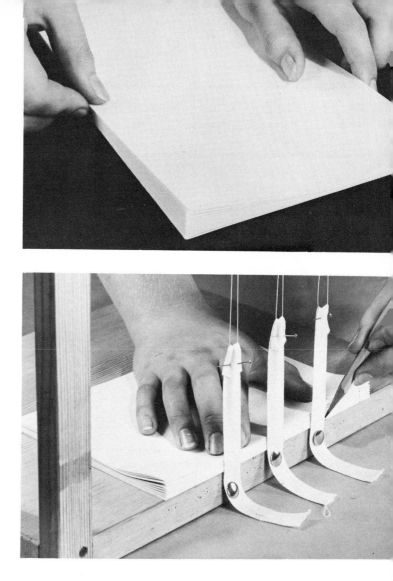

4   Place the stack of signatures on a sewing frame. A sewing frame can be simply made by attaching two uprights, with a crossbar at the top, to a flat wood base. Cut strips of white tape—three if the book is small or thin, four or five if it is larger. Allow 2 or 3 inches of tape to project on either side of the grouped signatures. To conserve tape, pin it to heavy thread tied to the frame. (If a frame is not available, place the stacked signatures near the edge of a work table and lay the cut tapes over the backs.) Mark two lines on the back of the signatures, $\frac{1}{2}$ inch from each end. Put one tape in the center. Space the others on either side between the end marks and the center. With the point of a sharp pencil mark a line on both sides of each of the tapes.

5   One signature is sewed at a time; therefore, all but the bottom one are removed from the sewing frame. Pick up the stack of signatures and turn them face down behind the sewing frame. Puncture each signature through the marked places with a large needle before sewing. (The marks at each end can also be cut with a coping saw to a depth of about $\frac{1}{16}$ inch. All the signatures are cut at one time before the sewing begins.) Use linen or any strong thread for sewing. Hold the signature open with one hand while inserting the needle through the first hole at the right end. Leave a tail of 2 or 3 inches of thread.

6   Bring the needle out through the next hole on the right side of the tape.

7   Place the needle into the hole on the left side of the tape. Be careful when crossing the tape not to catch it with the needle. Continue across the signature in the same manner until the end hole is reached.

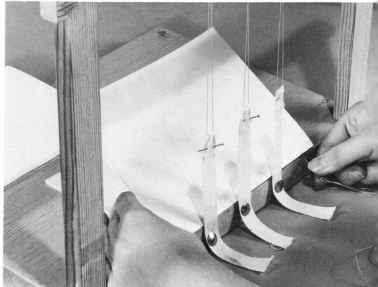

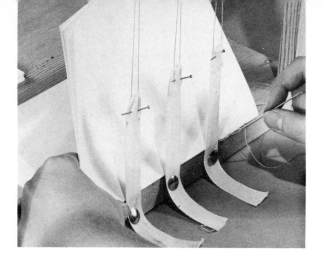
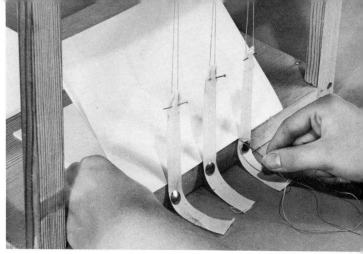

8 Take the next signature from the stack, turn it over, and lay it in position on top of the one just sewed. Place the needle in the hole at the left end. This process unites the two signatures. Continue to sew through the holes and across the tapes, as already explained, until the opposite end is reached. Tie the thread to the tail of thread left protruding at the beginning of the first signature.

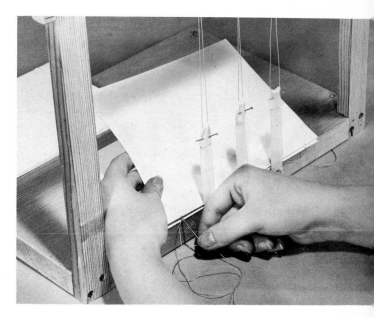

9 Flip the third signature over into place on top of the other two and sew from right to left. When the left end is reached, make what is called the kettle stitch by pulling the needle up through the stitch that links the first and second signatures. From now on, complete the kettle stitch at either end of each signature until finished. If it is necessary to add more thread, tie near the end so that the knot may be pulled through the end hole to the inside.

10 Cut the tapes from the sewing frame, leaving 1 or 2 inches extending on either side of the sewn signatures. Put the book in a press or vise with the spine projecting slightly beyond the edge. Or lay it near the edge of a worktable with a smooth board held firmly on top and a protective paper underneath. Apply sparingly a thin dilution of glue, preferably a flexible glue, and let it seep slightly between the signatures to hold them together.

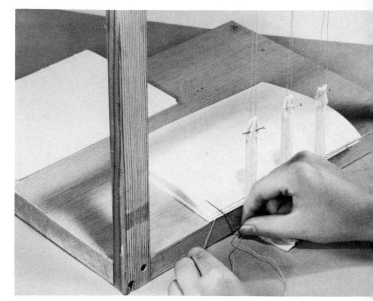

11 *After a book has been sewn the pages are sometimes uneven around the edges. They may be trimmed if considered necessary, but this should be done before the cover boards are measured. No more than absolutely necessary should be cut. Draw lines on the book at the top, bottom, and outer edges where the trimming is to take place. Large commercial cutters, such as those used in newspaper offices, or a plow and press can be used for this purpose. If no cutter is available, the pages may be trimmed by hand. To do this, place a heavy cardboard underneath the book for support and clamp it between two boards so that the part to be trimmed projects. Or lay a straight block of wood or a ruler on top of the book along the line to be cut; and, while supporting it firmly with one hand, hold a sharp knife or chisel upright and slowly cut across the book on the line marked for trimming. One page is cut at a time until eventually the entire book is cut through. It is recommended that an old magazine be used first to practice on until the skill of cutting is learned.*

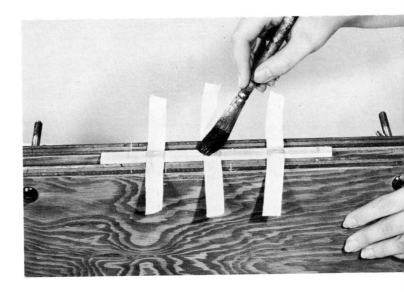

12 *Put the book back in an upright press. Cut a piece of book super, cotton cambric, or similar material so that when it is glued to the spine it will extend 1 inch on both sides and ½ inch from both ends.*

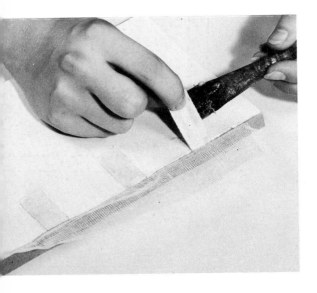

13 Cut a strip of heavy brown wrapping paper, lightweight cardboard, or tagboard the exact size of the spine, and glue to the back.

14 Paste the trimmed tapes to the top sheet of the book, using thinned paste.

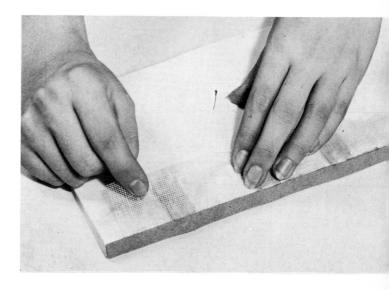

15 Paste the super to the top sheet, over the tapes. Apply the paste to the top sheet in the area to be covered by the super. Press the super down into place.

16 Trim the top page along the edge of the tapes and super to form a hinge. This will be used to fasten the book in its cover. The small portion on either end of the super may also be cut off.

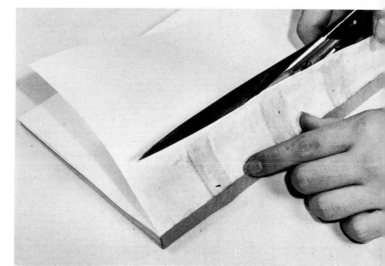

17 Two methods are shown for putting on a cover. In the first, put a piece of wax paper or paste paper under the hinge to protect the book. Paste the hinge, and place the cover board over it about 1/8 inch from the spine edge. If the cardboard is cut the exact width of the book and 1/4 inch more in length, it will extend 1/8 inch beyond the edges of the book when completed.

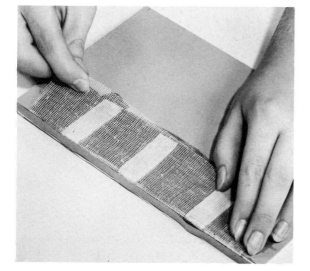

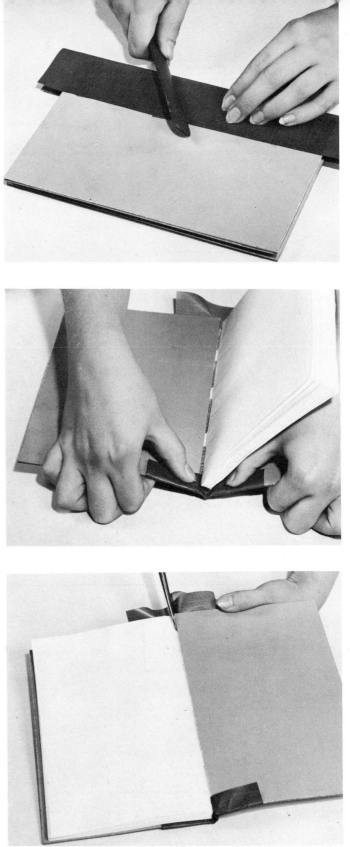

18   For the other method, two cardboards are used for each cover. They may be light in weight like tablet backs, or of different weights. If their weights are different, put the thinner board underneath. Place it under the hinge and paste the hinge to it.

19   Then apply paste all over the board and hinge, and lay the other cover board on top. When both covers are completed, put the book in a press or under heavy weights to dry so that it will remain flat.

20   The cover material may be cut in one piece, or two different materials may be combined. For the latter method, cut a strip of cloth, book vellum, or tough paper 2 or 3 inches wide and about $3/4$ inch longer at each end than the book. If desired, a piece of lightweight card or heavy paper the width of the spine may be pasted down the center of the strip, before the strip is attached to the boards. Lay the strip around the spine and paste it to the covers on both sides. Do not paste it to the spine. Rub well to smooth out any wrinkles.

21   Open the cover and turn in the flaps projecting at the top and bottom so they fit snugly under the signatures and against the cover board.

22   If the hinge was not trimmed away at the outer edges (step 16) before the cover was attached, snip it along the fold with scissors in order to allow room for the covering over the spine to be turned inward.

23 Paste the flaps to the inside of the cover boards.

24 Cut the cover material large enough to overlap the hinge slightly and to project about $3/4$ inch beyond the edges of the boards. Apply paste to the board, lay the paper on and rub it gently to smooth out wrinkles. Open the book and miter the corners as explained earlier.

25 To put in a lining sheet fold a piece of paper the same size as the book pages and tip it in. To do this put a small amount of paste on the top sheet of the book for a width of about $1/16$ inch along the inside edge and lay the folded sheet on. Apply paste all over the inside cover board. Press the lining sheet against it to form a liner. Do the same to the back of the book.

26 Put the finished book to press while it is still damp and leave it at least a day or overnight. To keep the moisture from penetrating through all the pages, put a folded piece of wax paper or a sheet of tin inside each cover.

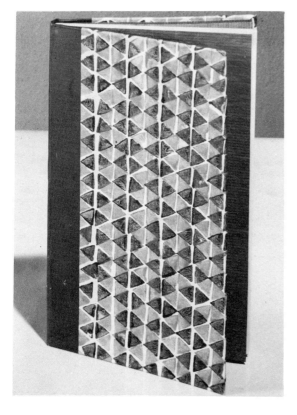

27 Finished book on tapes.

28 To rebind old books on tapes first remove the cover. Open the book and cut with a knife or razor blade along the spine separating the cover from the body of the book. Separate the signatures, and remove old stitching and dried glue from the spine. Repair any torn or weak spots with mending tissue or tape. If the old sewing holes are weak, make new ones. Rebind with the process already explained.

ADDITIONAL SUGGESTIONS FOR BOOKBINDING

The subject of bookbinding may be approached through the making of decorative papers in which the best results of exploration are kept for further use. Then when the student is introduced to simple book-construction problems he has design material to draw upon for covers and lining sheets.

In even the most simple book problems the student must be encouraged to become aware of the complete product and to observe the design effect from front to back, inside to outside, when the book is closed and when it is open. By experimenting with combinations of his decorative papers and additional colored papers, he can learn much about the final design integration of color, texture, and pattern.

Very young children can start by folding two or three sheets of paper together and stapling or sewing them through the fold (diagram). The outside sheet can then be decorated with a formal repeat pattern made with a potato or eraser or with torn or cut pieces of paper. Or a previously decorated sheet of colored paper can be used for the outside cover and stapled or sewed with the other sheets. Children can also make attractive little note pads by cutting narrow strips of paper, which may be 3-4 inches wide and about 8-9 inches in length, and fastening a decorated paper on top for a cover (diagram). Young children should not be forced to use measurements or mechanical means that result in stilted products; rather, the experience should be made simple and pleasurable and within their grasp and understanding.

Teachers may wish to have their students construct folders in which to keep class work. These

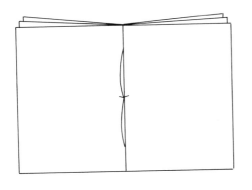
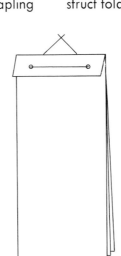
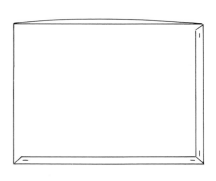

Cloth Bindings.

can be made from heavy wrapping or butcher paper by cutting a strip of paper twice the desired size, folding it in half, and stapling or pasting it across the side and bottom (diagram). Later they may be decorated with a printed repeat pattern.

A class may collaborate and produce a book as a group project by assembling individual chapters into signatures and sewing them on tapes. Or a large accordion-fold book can be made, using stiff paper such as heavy wrapping paper or tagboard for the inside sheets. The work of each student may then be mounted on the folded sheets and displayed by standing the book upright and spread open, on a table. The book can also be left lying flat and kept in the room library for reference.

WEAVING

Norwegian: *Bedspread, The Five Wise and Five Foolish Virgins*. c. 1800.
Tapestry, warp and weft of wool. 64″ x 48½″. Norwegian Folk Museum,
Oslo. Photograph courtesy of the Smithsonian Institution.

TEXTILE WEAVING AND DECORATION

The arts of weaving and textile decoration have been important parts of human culture from the very earliest times. Prehistoric man learned to stitch animal hides together to make clothing for his naked body. Later he invented simple plaiting techniques with reeds and grasses, and finally hit upon ways to spin plant and animal fibers into yarns for making cloth. Examples of prehistoric weaving have been found in many areas of Europe and Asia, although the materials used in weaving do not often survive the accidents of nature. Fragments of plain cloth from the prehistoric lake-dweller cultures of Switzerland indicate that this art had already reached a high degree of complexity. The art became so highly developed that, throughout later history, cloth played a role that rivals any other topic for romance and adventure. Early traders of cloth, yarn, and fabric dyes often changed the course of history and intermingled the products, customs, and knowledge of peoples from far-off corners of the world. Exploration, conquest, and cultural exchange followed the trade routes of the cloth merchants. Fine fabrics, rare dyes, and spun yarns were important economic items even in ancient Egypt and Babylon. The economic value of cloth has always been great because of its indispensable place in everyday life. In addition to these more common uses, the textile arts have added prestige and elegance to the lives of the wealthy and princely classes, and dignity and splendor to religious ritual and courtly panoply.

FIBERS FOR YARN

The earliest weavers used plant and animal fibers such as cotton, linen, and wool. The transformation of these fibers to cloth is remarkable, to say the least. Cotton has been used in India for over 3,000 years. When the Spanish explorers arrived in the New World, they found indigenous cotton growing. The fiber is obtained from the boll or seed pod of the plant. Linen, known since Neolithic times, is obtained from flax, a blue flowering plant; the fiber is found between the bark and the core of the stem. Wool and other animal fibers have also been used since ancient times. Wool has always been popular because of its warmth and texture, and its ability to take dye. Silk was introduced as a weaving material by the Chinese about 3000 B.C. Obtained from the cocoon of silkworm larvae, it must be patiently and carefully unwound from the cocoon, and several strands must be twisted together to make silk thread. At first the secret of making silk was jealously guarded by the Chinese weavers and merchants, for its unique qualities were highly in demand and provided them with a lively world market. Tradesmen carried silk yarns and woven stuffs by caravans over the brigand-infested trade routes through desolate countries and dangerous roads to the market places of the Near East. From there, the stuffs and yarns were exported to Europe as early as Roman times. But like all technological secrets, the process of raising silkworms and spinning the silken threads from the

Guatemalan: *Belt*. Twentieth century. Cotton. Woven on back-strap loom. The Seattle Weaver's Guild Collection of Guatemalan Textiles, School of Home Economics, University of Washington.

Mexican: *Woven Textile*. Twentieth century. Design made by brocading. Cotton. The Seattle Weaver's Guild Collection of Guatemalan Textiles, School of Home Economics, University of Washington.

Peruvian, Pre-Columbian Tiahuanaco Culture: *Textile with Overall Pattern of Faces*. C. 500 A.D. Cotton warps, wool wefts, 39" wide. In the Brooklyn Museum Collection.

cocoons soon leaked out and other areas developed this industry also. Weavers in southern Europe and in Japan began to domesticate the silkworm and spin their own silk yarns. Other natural fibers—hemp, bark, and the hair from various animals such as rabbits, llamas, and mountain goats—have also been used since ancient times, but these have never rivaled cotton, linen, wool, and silk as important economic and design materials except in limited areas.

Today, synthetic fibers have become common weaving materials. Their great variety and quality have made them successful substitutes for more traditional yarns. For the most part synthetic fibers have been used to imitate natural materials, but some innovations have been attempted, and perhaps one day synthetics will provide entirely new materials for the weaver.

COLOR

At first, the color of the yarn was provided by the natural color of the material; but although such materials as cotton and wool have a variety of colors, they are low in intensity and limited in color range. Therefore, early man invented processes for dyeing and pigmenting his yarns and woven material. Dyes made from vegetable sources provided considerable variety.

The yarns were prepared by being dipped in a colorless solution composed of lime or alum, which served as a mordant, causing the fiber to absorb the dye more fully and permanently. Then the yarn or fabric was immersed in the dye bath, prepared by boiling plants and other materials in water. The woad plant, a source of rich blue, was a popular dye during the Middle Ages. Onion skins yield a bright yellow or orange, dandelion roots a magenta, and elderberries a violet hue. Some colors were so rare and costly in ancient times that they were reserved for the rich or noble classes. The intense violet obtained from the murex sea snail was restricted in use to dye the robes of kings and emperors. Modern dyes have greatly augmented the weaver's palette. The range and selection of color available today would astound earlier weavers. Intense hues, golds and silvers, every tint, tone, and shade imaginable are easily made, permanent, and washable.

WEAVING TECHNIQUES

The basic principles of weaving plain cloth are very simple, although, as for the wheel, considerable ingenuity and experimentation were necessary for their invention. Essentially, plain weave consists of a group of yarns called the *warp* interlaced with a second group of yarns called the *weft*. The warps are bound together by a simple over-and-under threading of weft yarns to produce a continuous fabric or *fell*. To hold the warp yarns in place and keep them from tangling during the weaving process, the weaver threads them on a loom. Early looms, called *free warp looms*, consisted simply of a beam to which the warp threads were tied. Sometimes the loose ends of the warps hung free; sometimes they were held down with weights. Some American Indian weaving was done by tying the warp beam to the ridgepole of the long house (the communal dwelling), the warp ends hanging free. Indian grandmothers did the weaving—braiding or binding the warp with a weft by means of their fingers alone. The grandchildren sat on the floor and kept the warp ends from becoming tangled.

Weighted warps, from which the vertical loom originated, have been used since prehistoric times. The warp beam was suspended between two supports, and a weight of stone, metal, or clay was tied to the free end of each warp thread to keep the threads taut for weaving. The addition of a second beam to secure the free ends of the warp permitted the development of the horizontal loom. Probably the earliest application of this principle is found in the backstrap loom of ancient and primitive peoples. One beam was tied to some rigid support such as a tree or a wall; the other was tied to the belt of the weaver. The weaver kept the warps in tension simply by leaning backward and pulling on the warp. This loom can be used in almost any hand-operated weaving. It was employed by weavers all over the world, and is still in use by many Indian weavers in Central and South America, who weave with the traditional techniques and patterns of their pre-Columbian forebears.

The first weavers intertwined the weft into the warp one thread at a time, using their fingers as weaving tools. Early in weaving history two inventions were developed that greatly sped the process. These were the *shed stick* and the *heddle*. The opening between the warps through which the weft is passed is called the *shed*. In weaving plain cloth, the weaver forms the shed by pulling up every other warp thread, leaving an opening between the groups of warps. One shot of weft is passed through this shed; then the position of the warps is reversed, making a new shed. Making the sheds by hand is a time-consuming task. The shed stick, a long flat piece of wood woven into one of the sheds, can be used to open that shed. Pulling up on the shed stick, or turning it on its side in the warp, separates the warps and makes it easier to shoot a shot of weft. The shed stick can serve to open one shed only. To open the alternate shed, a system of heddles was devised. A heddle is a length of string looped around a warp thread. If the alternate warps are heddled and the heddles are tied to a stick called the *heddle rod,* when this stick is pulled up it brings with it those warps to which the heddles are attached, forming the second shed. Together, the shed stick and the heddle rod make it possible to form two alternate sheds on the primitive loom.

These mechanical aids, the shed stick and the heddle rod, were soon improved with rigid heddles, which led to the development of the hand loom as we know it today. Each addition facilitated the weaving process, and shortened the time needed to weave. Many of these innovations were added in medieval and pre-Industrial Revolution times only after great conflict, because the weavers' guilds and individual weavers saw them as positive threats to their livelihoods. Men, women, and children worked long hours at weaving, most often in extremely unpleasant and unhealthful working conditions. The weaver's trade, even in ancient Egypt, was difficult and offered only subsistence wages to its workers. The cloth merchants were often wealthy and influential in their communities, but the weaver generally existed in poverty. It was natural, then, that such inventions as the flying shuttle would be bitterly opposed by the weaver, for it was a threat to his already meager income. In spite of such obstacles, the improvements of the loom have made possible the industrialization of this craft. Today the hand weaver has a respected position and is thought of as an artist rather than a laborer.

THE BASIC WEAVING TECHNIQUES

There are five basic weaves: *plain weave, twill, compound, gauze,* and *knotting.*

PLAIN WEAVE

In *plain weave* the weft simply crosses over and under alternate warp threads. Considerable variations in color and texture are possible, and the weaver can make patterns by varying the colors of the warp and weft, producing stripes and plaids. When the warp and weft show equally in the finished cloth, it is called a *balanced* weave. Other treatments can conceal either the warp or the weft so that it is not visible in the finished cloth, producing *warp-faced* or *weft-faced* weaves.

Tapestry is a variant of plain weave. In a tapestry, the areas of color are used to build pictorial or patterned designs. The weft is not thrown across the entire warp, as it is in simple plain

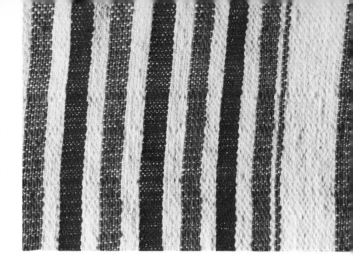

India: *Stripe Patterns and Plaid Patterns*. Twentieth century. Cotton. Courtesy of Elizabeth Bayley Willis.

Northwest Coast Indian: *Chilkat Blanket*. Tapestry weave, mountain goat wool twisted over strands of cedar bark. Courtesy of The Washington State Museum, University of Washington.

French: *Millefleurs Tapestry with Pelican in Her Piety*. Early sixteenth century. Wool with some silk. 40" x 86". Seattle Art Museum. Gift of the late Mrs. Donald E. Frederick.

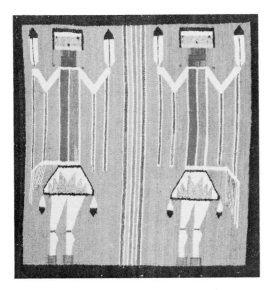

Navajo Indian: *Rug with Ceremonial Figures.*
Twentieth century. Wool, 36″ x 34½″.

India: *Woven Textile.* Twentieth century. Ikat
weave. Courtesy of Elizabeth Bayley Willis.

weave, but each separate color is woven back
and forth in its own area to complete the design.
By closely beating the weft, which is a heavier
yarn than the warp, the weaver can cover the
warp completely, producing a weft-faced fabric.
Pile weaves are also variants of plain weave. In
a velvet pile weave, extra warp or weft yarns
are introduced and held above the surface of
the cloth by means of small rods. After the
weaving is finished these rods are removed, leaving small loops of yarn. These may be left cut or
uncut, producing cut or uncut velvet. An interesting variation of plain weave is *ikat,* a process
in which the warp or weft or both are dyed in
patterns before the cloth is woven. It takes considerable skill and careful preplanning to dye
the skeins of yarn so that the design will occur
properly in the finished cloth.

The Chilkat blanket, Navajo rug, and Norwegian tapestry are examples of tapestry weaving. Chilkat blankets were prized treasures and
prestige articles of the complex Northwest Coast
Indian cultures, each blanket being worth many
valuable trade items. The yarn was made of
mountain-goat wool twisted over strands of cedar bark. Tribal symbols and totems were woven
into the fabric, so that the blankets served as
heraldic decorations; they were worn over the
shoulders during tribal rituals and religious
dances. Notice the handsome balance of darks
and lights, the sensitive use of negative space,
the great variety of sizes and shapes, and the
way the long fringe adds textural interest.

The Norwegian tapestry was designed as a
wall hanging. Its rich color areas were designed
to create a well-balanced dark and light pattern.
Made of wool dyed with natural materials, such
tapestries brightened the interiors of homes and
churches. Notice the way the figures and designs
have been adapted to the limitations of weaving
techniques and artfully arranged to fill the space.
Notice that the figures are carefully related to
pattern areas with repetitions of line and shape.

TWILL

In the twill weave the under-one, over-one pattern of plain weave is changed. Either the warps or wefts or both may go over and under the same number of yarns: over two, under two. In each row of weaving the skip is progressively moved one or more yarns to the left or the right, creating a diagonal pattern in the texture of the weave. In an irregular twill the pattern over and under is uneven—for example, over one, under two. Satin is an irregular twill in which the weft threads are concealed under the floats of warp. Sateen is also an irregular twill, but the floats that cover the surface are made with the weft instead of the warp. Although twills can be made on most hand looms, a loom equipped with heddles and harnesses in which the twill pattern can be threaded simplifies the selection of the pattern threads. Many variations are possible with the twill. Steep and reclining diagonals, herringbones, and bird's-eye designs can be made by threading different patterns of skips or by altering the sequence of the sheds.

COMPOUND WEAVES

Compound weaves are the result of using additional warps or wefts or both for design and pattern. Plain and twill weaves can be embellished by introducing extra shots of pattern weft or warp. In this case, the regular-weave weft, called a *tabby*, is augmented with extra weft shots, called *pattern weft*, introduced into the weave at intervals determined by the design. These pattern wefts do not interrupt the structure of the cloth, which is maintained by the tabby. *Brocades* are made in a similar way, but the pattern shots do not cross the entire width of the cloth. Many bobbins or shuttles may be used for the pattern weft, and these weft shots are introduced into the fabric where they are necessary for the design. Brocade offers a convenient method for elaborate ornamentation with rich variation in color and pattern.

American: *Bedspread, Boston Meeting House.* Nineteenth century. Double weave, wool weft on cotton warp. 84" x 76". Seattle Art Museum. Gift of Mrs. Agnes MacDonald.

Norwegian: *The Feast of Herod, The Beheading of St. John, and the First Judgment of Solomon.* Seventeenth century. Tapestry, wool, 76½" x 55". Oslo Museum of Applied Arts, Oslo, Norway. Photograph courtesy of The Smithsonian Institution.

Trude Guermonprez: Tapestry, *Bird Cage.* 1950. Copper and multicolored silk. Metal inlay in double weave. 21" x 21". Photograph by Charles Wong.

Ed Rossbach: *Double Cloth Floor Mat* (Detail). 1960. Linen warp, wool weft. Approx. 3' x 7'.

Left: India: *Quilt.* Twentieth century. Cotton, double weave. Pockets formed by double weave were stuffed as fabric was woven to form padding. Courtesy, Elizabeth Bayley Willis.

Double weave, sometimes called *double cloth,* is a compound weave in which two complete warps and wefts are woven simultaneously. Usually the upper and lower pairs of warps are strongly contrasted in value and color. The weaver makes pattern areas by reversing the position of the upper and lower warps and wefts, exchanging sections of the lower and upper cloths to make pattern areas. The exchange interlocks the two fabrics, making them one. The pattern is reversed in value and color on opposite sides of the finished weave. The design must be planned well so that the reversal of values does not destroy the quality of the design. Many early American quilts and coverlets were made with this weave.

GAUZE

In the *gauze weaves,* the warps are twisted around the weft as it is woven. The twists strengthen the weave and leave slight openings in the fabric. The weaver usually makes the twists in the same direction for each shed, alternating the directions on alternate sheds. *Leno* is a more elaborate gauze weave in which several warp threads are twisted together to form a pattern similar to lace; or rows of pattern twists are combined with rows of plain weave to produce stripes of open and tight weaving, which create a contrast of positive and negative spaces.

KNOTTING

The weaver makes *knotted weaves* by knotting the weft around the warp, usually leaving the ends of the knots protruding from the fabric. When the knots are closely packed, a pile results. This is the method used in many rug techniques. Usually short lengths of weft are knotted around pairs of warp threads. By using short lengths of different colors and values, the weaver can easily work a pattern into the weave. The famous rug weavers of Persia and Morocco use this tech-

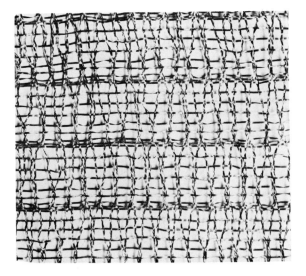

Top: Ed Rossbach: *Gauze.* 1951. Gauze weave. Courtesy, Henry Art Gallery. University of Washington.

Bottom: Lea Van P. Miller: *Casement Cloth.* Twentieth century. Gauze weave, black and yellow warp and weft.

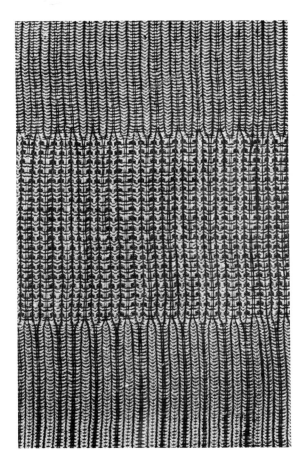

Moroccan: *Rug (Style introduced into Morocco from the Orient).* Courtesy of the Government of Morocco.

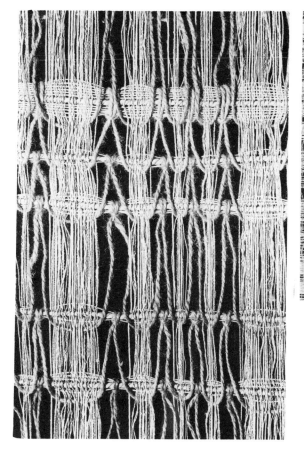

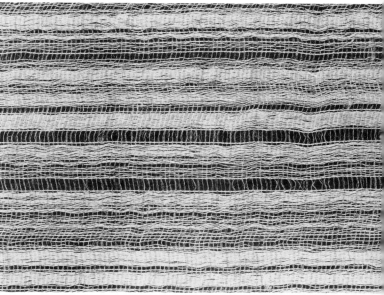

Jack Lenor Larsen: *Jason (Golden Fleece),* Casement. Egyptian cotton, goat hair, French gold lamé, leno weave. Jack Lenor Larsen, Inc.

Left: Mary Balzer Buskirk: *Space Divider.* 1959. Linen, silk, jute, 36″ x 36″. Courtesy of the American Craftsmen's Council.

nique to make the richly patterned, thick-piled rugs we esteem so highly.

WEAVING MATERIALS

Many materials can be used for weaving: paper, string, yarn, grasses, plastics, and even metal. Yarns are classified according to their fiber content, natural or synthetic. Cottons, wools, linens, silks, rayons, and nylons are available in a wide selection of color, weight, and texture. Rich hues and value contrasts are to be found in natural cottons, wools, linens, and silks. Undyed wools may vary in color from light off-white to deep browns and blacks. Vegetable dyes have long been used to color fiber for yarn. Elderberries, walnut shells, roots, and other plant materials boiled with the yarn provide a limited but handsome range of colors. In recent years chemical dyes have added an almost endless variety of hues, pure, intense, and brilliant, to the weaver's palette.

The fibers are spun and twisted into strands for single-ply yarns. Three- or four-ply yarns are made by twisting together three or four strands of single-ply yarn, and are therefore heavier in weight. Some weaving demands very fine yarn, lightweight but strong; other weaving techniques may use heavy, coarse yarn with a light twist. Many special yarns such as bouclé, slub, or rug roving have delightful textures that can add interest and variety to the woven material.

For the projects demonstrated in the sections that follow, cotton, wool, or synthetic yarns are suggested, but the weaver should experiment with many materials: grasses and reeds for screens, wall hangings, and place mats offer variety in color and texture; linens, silks, and metallic yarns are also useful additions to the yarn basket, for the textures they provide cannot be duplicated by other materials; even paper can be used for some weaving projects.

Stuart Davis: *The Magic Carpet*. Knotted rug. Collection of the Museum of Modern Art.

Jeannette Lund: *Bag*. Woven of fine wool and yellow wool and mohair on natural ramie and white cotton warp. 10½″ high. Courtesy of the Henry Art Gallery, University of Washington.

Ted Hallman: *Screen* (Detail). Acrylic plastics, cotton, and linen. Courtesy of the American Craftsmen's Council.

Mildred Fischer: *Mural No. 1, 1960*. Linen, cotton, rayon, wool, mohair, 53½″ x 32″. Photograph by Jack Foster Photos.

Hans Arp: *Rug*. 1938. Wool, 78″ x 59½″. Collection of the Museum of Modern Art. Mrs. John D. Rockefeller, Jr., Purchase Fund.

WEAVING   135

PAPER WEAVING

A valuable introduction to the weaving process is through weaving with paper, which provides a knowledge of simple weaving techniques as well as an opportunity for learning design. The study of color, value, and surface texture is a very important part of even the simplest kind of weaving. The strips used in weaving with paper may be varied in width to create different design effects. Narrow pieces may be overlaid, or decorative pieces may be added with paste, or subject matter may be woven into paper strip constructions.

MATERIALS

1. Paper
2. Scissors
3. Ruler
4. Pencil
5. Paste or staples

1 There are three ways to make the warp for a simple woven paper mat: the strips may be attached at one end, or at both ends; or they may be cut apart, placed parallel to each other, and secured to another surface. For the first method, mark a margin at one end of the paper with a pencil and ruler. Mark parallel strips. Cut up to the margin.

For the second method, fold the paper in half. Mark the margin opposite the fold end. Mark parallel strips and cut to the margin.

For the third method, assemble precut strips. For convenience in weaving, hold these strips in place by clipping or gluing them at one end to another sheet of paper or piece of cardboard. When separate strips are used, the warp colors may be varied.

2 To weave, take a weft strip and place it under the warp strip on the edge and over the next warp strip, continuing under and over across the warp. Weave the second weft strip in the opposite order, next to the first one, over and under and continuing across. As each strip is woven push it into place. In weaving, this is called beating. Repeat the process until the warp is filled in with strips.

136   CRAFTS DESIGN

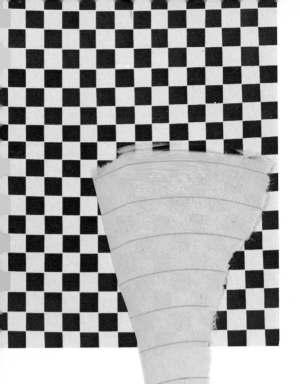

3 Finished v... This basic pattern is called a plain weave.

4 To weave a twill pattern, proceed as above but weave the weft strip under one and over two warp strips. The diagonal is made by shifting the under shot one space to the right each time.

5 The herringbone pattern is woven in the same manner as the twill, but the diagonal is interrupted and the steps repeated in reverse order. Note in the illustration that in some rows the weft passes over three warp strips.

6 The goose-eye pattern, which the weaver makes by inverting the herringbone to form intersecting diagonals.

7 Further variations can be obtained by weaving additional weft strips of contrasting color and value into place after the basic weave is finished. A pattern of pasted dots or other shapes may also be added.

8 A pattern invention based on dark-light alternation. The basic patterns illustrated in the steps above may be combined into many countless designs by changing the spacing, color, and value.

9 *Another way to vary the pattern is to shape the warp. Shaped-warp designs can be made by cutting the warp stripes on the diagonal or in curved lines.*

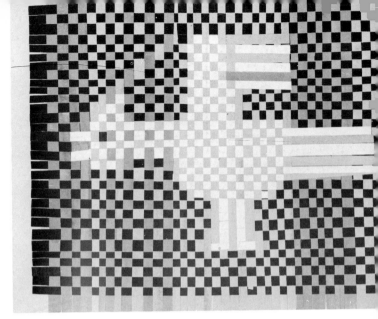

10 *Subject matter can also be woven in. In the illustration, the design strips were woven in where needed after the tabby weave was completed. Ends may be left unwoven to make fringe.*

FINGER WEAVING

Finger weaving is free warp weaving closely related to braiding and twining techniques. It is a traditional method employed by many primitive peoples all over the world. In this simple weaving process no loom is used. Changing the shed and shooting the weft is done entirely with the hands. Beginners will find it easier to learn the process if they use heavyweight yarn or rug roving and limit the warp threads to two colors, with a third color for the weft.

MATERIALS

1. Yarn, rolled into balls (three contrasting colors)
2. Scissors
3. Ruler or tape measure
4. String

SETTING UP THE WARP

1 *To prepare the warp cut the yarn into nine 1½-yard lengths—five lengths of one color, four of a contrasting color. For the weft cut one 3-yard length of a third color.*

2 *Lay out the nine warp yarns side by side on a flat surface. Alternate the colors. The two outside threads will be the same color.*

3 Lay the weft thread at one side of the warp, one end even with the ends of the warp.

4 Tie a knot in the warp threads. Keep the knot close to the end.

5 Instead of tying the warp yarns together in a knot, the individual threads may be tied separately with a square knot to a pencil in the order they were laid out.

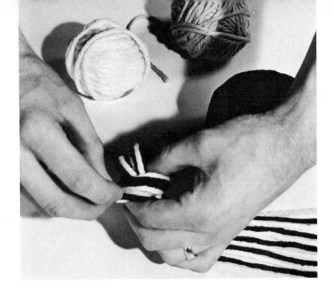

6 Secure the knot or the pencil to some stationary object such as a chair, table, doorknob, or drawer pull by tying it in place with string.

7 Separate the weft thread from the warp threads. Roll the weft into a ball and wrap it on a shuttle or around a small length of cardboard. Put this weft to one side.

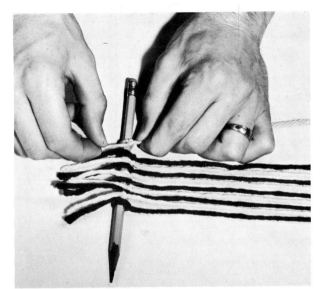

MAKING THE SHED

8 Pull the warp taut. Organize the warp threads in order in the right hand. Hold all the threads of one color between the thumb and index finger, the threads of the other color between the index finger and middle finger. This forms a space called the shed between the upper and lower warps.

9 Shoot the weft yarn through the shed opening.

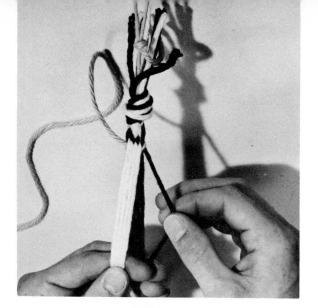

CHANGING THE SHED

10 Transfer the warp to the left hand without changing the relative positions of the threads. The left hand will hold the warp exactly as the right hand did.

11 Start on the right. Pick up the outside thread of the lower warp between the thumb and index finger.

12 Drop the outside thread of the upper warp and hold it between the index finger and the middle finger. Continue to pick up the lower warp threads and to drop the upper warp threads in order until the shed is changed and the warp is transferred to the right hand. Throughout this process hold the warp in tension.

13 The new shed has now been made.

14 *Shoot the next shot of weft.*

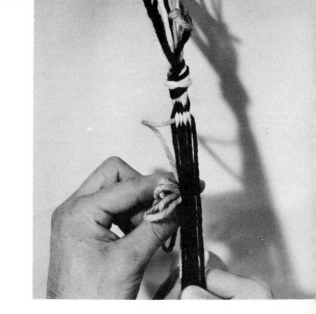

15 *Continue the process until the weaving is finished.*

16 *Finished finger-woven strip.*

SELF-WEFT FINGER WEAVING

SETTING UP THE WARP

1 *To prepare the warp cut ten 1½-yard lengths of yarn—five lengths of one color and five of a contrasting color. In this method no separate weft thread is used.*

2 *Separate the yarns on the fingers, making the shed as in step 8 above.*

WEAVING

3 *The outside thread in the upper shed becomes the weft. Separate this thread and pull it through the shed.*

4 Change the shed as in steps 10, 11, and 12 above.

5 The warp thread which has been used as the weft now takes its place on the left in the lower shed.

6 Pick up the next upper warp thread on the right, and use it as a weft as before. Continue weaving in this manner until the strip is complete.

7 Complete the strip of finger weaving with self-wefts. Note the diagonal pattern formed, in the example below, by using this method.

8 To vary the pattern use the upper warp thread on the left, instead of the right, for the weft. This will change the direction of the diagonals. The two diagonals may be combined in the same strip.

CHEVRON PATTERN

1 To prepare the warp use an equal number of two contrasting colors. The pattern is easier to weave if the number of warp threads is divisible by 2 and 3.

2 To begin, weave a few shots as in steps 3, 4, 5, and 6 above.

3 Divide the warp into two equal sections. Pick up the outside upper warp thread in each section and, using them as wefts, bring them through the sheds to the center. Cross them over each other so that the weft on the left joins the warp on the right and the weft on the right joins the warp on the left. Crossing the wefts fastens the two sections of warp together. Change the sheds and continue weaving.

4 *A variation of this method is to divide the warp into three separate parts. After a length of plain or chevron weave has been done, weave each section separately without crossing the weft threads. After three separate strips have been woven, they may be braided. At the end of the braid, rejoin the three strips by weaving them together.*

5 *The weft can be divided into as many sections as desired and woven in chevron and diamond patterns.*

RIGID HEDDLE LOOM

The rigid heddle loom is a simple structure made of wood, cardboard, string, or metal strips, through which warp yarns are threaded. It is used primarily for making belts and braids; however, if wider heddles are constructed, such articles as scarves or strips for purses can be woven.

The heddle consists of slots and holes which make possible the raising and lowering of the warp to form a shed. If the heddle is made of cardboard, a line is drawn horizontally through the center, along which are spaced holes with narrow slits cut between. If string is used, it is wrapped around a frame made of wood or cardboard. Knots are tied in the center for every other warp to pass through, and alternate warps are threaded through the slots. Heddles made of tongue depressors or ice cream sticks are usually adequate for beginners.

The heddle is moved up and down to change the shed of the warp and in effect operates like the harness in a more complex loom. The warp must be stretched tight when the weaver is working. It can be fastened between two stationary supports, or one end may be tied to a support and the other end tied around the weaver's waist or to his belt. The warps are either knotted together or spread out and tied to a stick or rod.

MAKING A RIGID HEDDLE LOOM

1 Ten slats are needed, six for uprights and four to complete the frame.

2 With a hand or electric drill, make small holes, large enough for yarn to pass through, in the middle of the six uprights. Lay the six uprights side by side with narrow spaces between them. Secure them between two slats at the top and two at the bottom. Fasten them with glue or staples, or tie them into place with string tied through holes drilled in the ends of the slats.

WEAVING ON A RIGID HEDDLE LOOM

1 To warp the loom, cut warp yarn in equal lengths (each about 2 yards long) for a belt. The number of warp threads needed is determined by the number of holes and spaces in the loom. Two more warps can be added by placing one on each side of the rigid heddle. In the example shown, this would make 13 warps. The warp threads may be all the same color, or two alternating colors may be used. Put one thread through each hole and through each space between the slats, as well as on the outside edges if two more warp threads are desired. Tie the ends together in a knot, or spread them out by tying each warp thread to a pencil or rod. Then secure each end of the tied warp to a solid object by fastening to a hook, doorknob, or clamp. One end may be tied to the weaver's belt or around his waist, by tying string to the end of the grouped warp.

2 Wrap a length of weft yarn around a shuttle. Shuttles can be purchased ready-made, or they can be constructed of wood or cardboard that is notched at each end to hold the yarn. Tongue depressors can also be notched at the ends, or a hole may be bored in one end, to which the weft is tied.

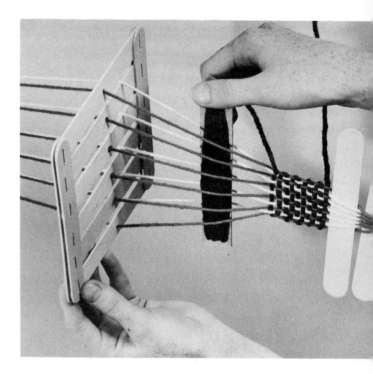

3 Raising and lowering the heddle changes the shed. Before starting to weave, make a shed and insert one tongue depressor or a narrow cardboard strip. Change the shed and insert another strip. These two strips spread the warp evenly.

4 To weave, open the shed by raising the heddle. Pass the shuttle through the shed, and beat the weft yarn into place. Either the shuttle or a coarse comb may be used for this purpose. Leave a 2-inch tail and tuck it around the end warp and back in the same shed.

5 Change the shed by lowering the heddle. Beat the weft yarn a second time, and return the shuttle through the shed, completing the second shot. Continue this process. As the weaving progresses the heddle must be kept a constant distance away to keep the strip an even width. Lean back to tighten the warp.

6 To add new weft threads, overlap the new thread with the end of the previous one an inch or so and beat into place.

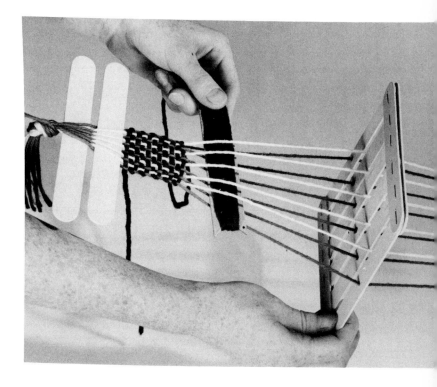

7 The design may be changed by introducing different weft colors and weaving them in strips or patterns created by threading two, three, or four heddles as shown on pages 189-193. Shuttles wrapped with different colors can be used alternately or together. Most weaving techniques—including inlay, knotting, and other types described elsewhere—can be introduced on the heddle loom. If the warp is very thin and the weft is heavy, the warp will be concealed.

8 When the weaving is completed, cut it free of the heddle and finish the ends by knotting or by stitching across. Each two warps may be tied together. The end of a belt may be folded and shaped into a point. Strips that are belt width may be joined at the sides to form wider strips to use for purses and bags.

9 A rigid heddle loom made of tongue depressors for weaving a wide strip. The warp ends are tied to a ruler.

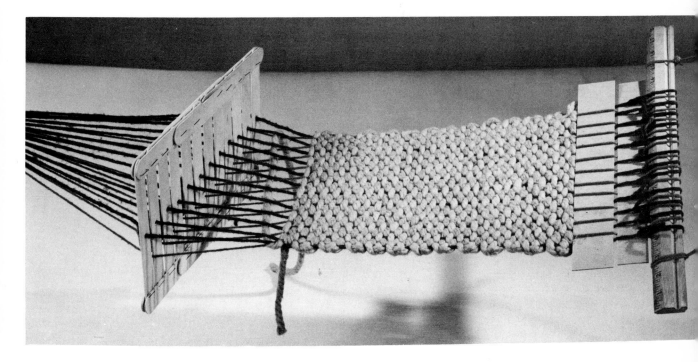

CARDBOARD LOOMS

The flat loom is a simple device for holding warp threads in a rigid position at fairly even tension. The warp may be put around the board, or stretched across it from one end to the other and held in place by nails, pins, notches in the ends, or holes cut into the board. Looms made of cardboard should be heavy enough to remain rigid when warped. Test the cardboard to discover in which direction it is less apt to bend. Shed sticks woven in to raise the shed in one direction, and string heddle rods for the other, can be used on all flat looms. In many parts of the world today, shed sticks and string heddles are the only tools used to change the shed, and very beautiful products come from these primitive looms. Mats, scarves, pot holders, bags, belts, and small rugs can be woven on the cardboard loom. Several woven pieces may be sewn together for larger articles.

MATERIALS

1. Rigid cardboard
2. Knife or shears
3. Yarn
4. Pins
5. Adhesive tape

1 To make the loom, cut a piece of cardboard the desired size. Draw a line 1/2 inch from the ends and mark off 1/4- or 1/2-inch intervals on each line, depending upon the size of the cardboard and weight of yarn to be used. These marks become the points of the notches and must be directly across from those on the opposite end. Cut the notches with heavy shears or a knife. If holes instead of notches are put in the cardboard, the warps can be placed closer together.

2 To warp the cardboard loom, fasten the end of the warp thread to the back of the loom with a piece of tape, leaving an end long enough to tie to the opposite end of the warp when the warping is completed.

3 Wind the warp back and forth across the face of the loom, looping it around the notches at each end. Keep the warp taut.

4 When the warping is finished, the warp thread should be at the opposite corner diagonally across from the beginning of the warp. Carry it around to the back of the board and tie to the beginning thread.

5 To weave, cut a length of coarse thread of cotton or four-ply knitting worsted yarn and fasten one end of it to a large blunt needle, or to a tongue depressor with a hole drilled in the end. If heavy cotton roving is used, tape it to the tongue depressor, because a knot would be too large to pass through the warp. The fingers may also be used for interweaving the weft as it is put over and under the warp threads.

6 Start weaving from either side. Weave one row across, leaving a 2-inch tail at the beginning to be tucked around the end warp and into the same shed.

7 Push the woven yarn to the top of the loom so that the weaving is firm.

8 Insert a ruler or stick under the opposite threads, turn it on edge to open the shed, and pass the shuttle through. This facilitates weaving with the left hand. Left-handed people can reverse the procedure and use the ruler for the right-hand side to open the shed, and the fingers or shuttle to pick out the threads in the opposite direction.

9 As the weaving continues, be careful to leave enough play in the weft so that the edges, or selvedges, remain even. If the weft is pulled too tight, the edges of the piece will become uneven.

10 A ruler, stick, coarse comb, or strip of cardboard may be used for a beater in pushing the weft into place.

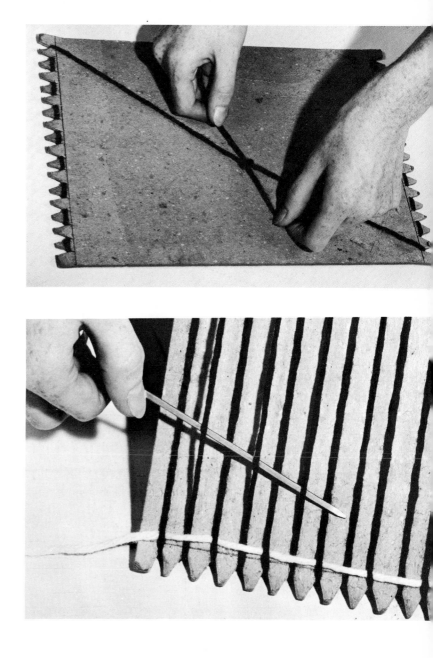

11 *The shed stick will have to be removed as the space becomes narrow when the weaving nears completion.*

12 *When the weaving is complete, weave the ends of the weft back into the body of the piece. Then remove the weaving from the loom by slipping the warp off the notches.*

13 *The ends of the warp may be finished in a variety of ways. If the weft has not been woven tightly against the ends of the loom, the warp ends may be chain stitched together with the fingers or a crochet hook; the edges may be sewn; a fringe may be left by knotting the warp ends and cutting the loops; or an additional fringe may be tied on.*

14 *Examples of weaving on the cardboard loom, showing variations of design produced by dark-light contrast, spacing, and alternation of warp.*

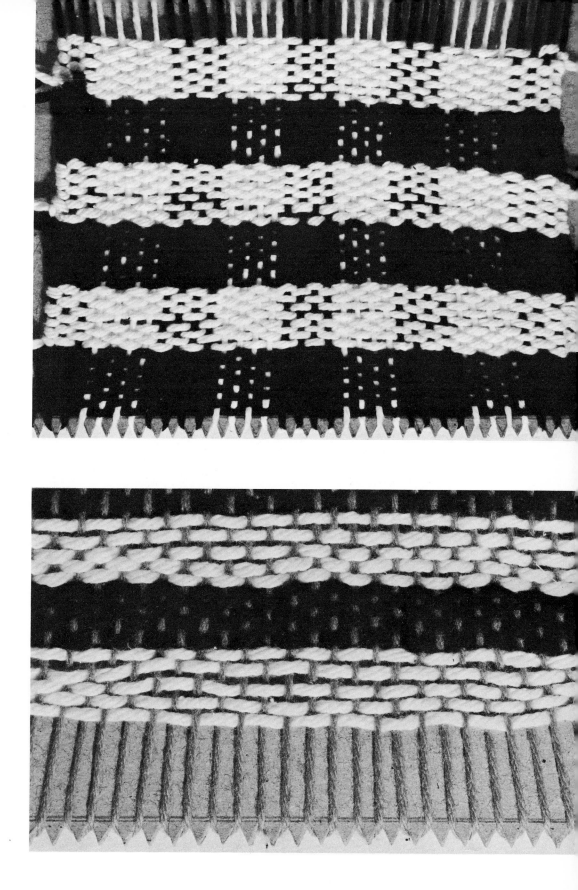

MAKING A BAG OR PURSE
ON A CARDBOARD LOOM

The weaver can make a bag or purse from a woven piece by folding it in half and sewing the edges together. He can line and finish it at the top with a zipper, a cord and button, or a drawstring. Or he can fold the mat in three parts, sewing the sides of two together and using the third part for a flap. A loop is crocheted, braided, or formed with a buttonhole stitch over strands of yarn and attached to the flap so that it can fasten over a button.

The weaver can also make a purse by weaving around a piece of cardboard so that it is closed on the sides and bottom and open at the top. The cardboard is removed when the weaving is completed. The loom may be made from a piece of cardboard or a cigar-box lid. Warp threads are held in position by an evenly spaced row of pins on one edge of the board, with the edges notched as explained in the directions for making a cardboard loom, or with holes poked across the ends of the cardboard. When holes are used, the warp thread is put through an end hole at the top, down through the opposite hole at the bottom, and up to the top again where it is tied. It is then put through the first hole again, and back through the next hole adjacent to it, and the process repeated so that there is always a warp on both sides of the cardboard. An extra warp is needed on one side so that there will be an uneven number of warps. In this way the shed will alternate as the weft is carried around the loom. The extra warp thread should be placed only on one side of the board, as near the outer edge as possible, to prevent a big gap as the weaving is carried around the board. Or an extra warp can be tied over the last warp on one side of the board.

1 *Put a strip of adhesive tape over the top edge of a piece of firm cardboard. The size of the cardboard will determine the size of the finished purse. Place pins along the taped edge of the cardboard at equal intervals of $\frac{1}{8}$ inch or more, depending upon the thickness of the yarns used for the warp and the weft. Press the pins firmly into place, allowing them to project about $\frac{1}{2}$ inch above the edge of the cardboard.*

2 *Tie the end of the warp thread to the first pin on the left.*

3 *Carry it around the bottom of the loom and back up on the other side to the top again encircling the same pin.*

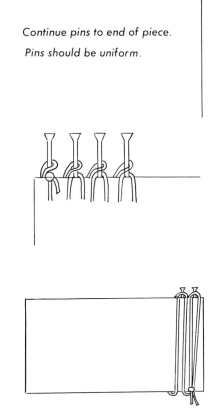

Continue pins to end of piece.

Pins should be uniform.

4   *Bring the thread back around the bottom of the loom, to the front, and hook it over the second pin. Continue until all the pins except the first have two loops over them (four warp threads to a pin, two to each side). The warp will then be on both sides of the loom.*

5   *When the last pin is reached, bring the warp thread down to the base on one side of the loom and tie to the end warp. This puts an uneven number of threads on one side of the loom, so that the weaving will alternate as the weft is carried around the loom.*

6   *To weave, start at the top and proceed as in steps 5 and 6 on page 149; however, instead of returning across the loom, continue around it. This will produce an article that is enclosed on the sides and bottom, like a sack.*

7   *When finished, weave the end of the weft back into the body of the piece, leaving the last end inside.*

8   *Pull out the pins to release the weaving and remove the cardboard loom.*

9   *Finish the bag with a cloth lining and put a button or zipper at the top.*

BOARD LOOMS

The board loom is made with a piece of plywood or any wood board, of whatever size and proportion desired. When the weaving is to be done on one side of the board only, headless nails ⅝ or ¾ inch in size are spaced at equal distance across each end about ¼ inch or more apart. A pencil line is drawn ¼ inch from the edge as a guide, and the place for each nail is marked with a point. It is easier to weave if the nails can be put in wood strips nailed on top of the board across each end. Or narrow slots can be sawed in the wood strip and the warp placed through them rather than around the nails.

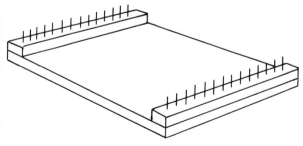

The warp thread is tied to the first nail at one end, pulled taut across the length of the loom where it is brought around the first two nails at the opposite end, and wound back and forth across the loom around each two adjacent nails until finished. The end of the warp is then tied to the last nail. When the warp is wound around two nails instead of one it lies parallel; otherwise, it would be at an angle.

If a longer warp is desired it may be obtained by continuing the threads around the board. A wood strip, 1½ inches wide and 1 inch longer than the width of the board, can be attached to each end of the loom. These strips hold the warp away from the surface of the board and permit the warp to be pulled around the loom easily. The warp may be cut in individual strips and each strip tied around the loom, or it may be wrapped around continuously in one piece.

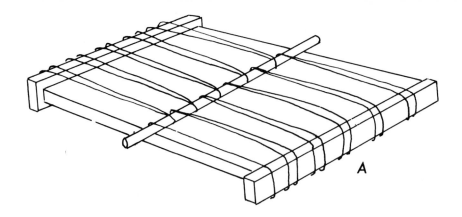

A

A method for putting on a continuous warp which can be pulled easily around the board is shown in the illustration. The dowel rod around which the warp is looped can be removed when the weaving is completed, releasing the ends. The rod is laid across the middle of the board, and the end of the warp thread is tied to one end of the rod. As the rod is held in place, the warp is brought around over one end of the board, under, and back up over the opposite end until it reaches the rod again. It is looped over the rod, brought back around the loom, and again looped over the rod. This is continued back and forth around the loom until the amount of warp needed is on the loom. The end of the warp is then tied to the rod. To weave, the rod and warp are moved up to end A. The loom is turned over so that the stick is underneath. The weaving is started at end A and pulled around the board as it proceeds.

A row of nails may be put across one end to keep the warps separate and spread. If they were put across both ends the weaving could not be drawn around the loom.

The weaving may be done by passing the weft thread over and under the warp with a shuttle, large needle, or the fingers; or a shed stick and a heddle rod made with string may be used to change the shed. A stick or ruler is inserted at the rear of the loom and slipped over and under every other warp thread. When this stick is turned up on its edge, the threads are raised, producing an opening or shed for the weft to pass through. Looped string tied to a dowel rod encircles the alternate warps and attaches them to the rod. When the rod is lifted upright, the warp threads are raised. The warp should not be tightly wrapped around the loom when the shed stick and heddle rod are used, or the warps will be difficult to raise.

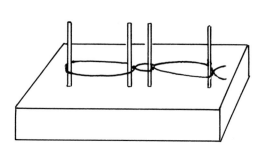

(a) *How to make the string heddles*

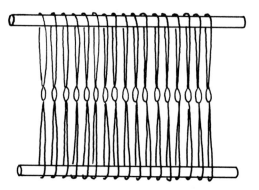

(b) *A heddle made of string*

The weaver may have difficulty keeping a straight selvedge on the sides while weaving, because there is a tendency to pull the outer warps and cause them to sag or curve inward. The weaver must make allowance for this by permitting a slack of the weft thread and not pulling it too tight as it goes around the warp at the edges. Beginners can use a rigid support by attaching a thin wire to the outer nails at each end of the loom along with the outer warps. This wire is included with the warps as they are woven, and pulled out when the weaving is completed. If a wire is not used, one or two extra warp threads may be tied to the same nails as the outside warp, to form a selvedge. If the weaving begins to pull in on the sides, the weft thread should be taken out and put in again more loosely.

Various types of weaving can be done on flat looms, ranging from the simple over-and-under tabby weave to the use of knots and more complicated patterns. The leno weave shown on page 200 was made on a flat loom, as were the pattern weaves of the tabby, herringbone, twill, and goose eye on pages 137 and 138. These weaves are explained earlier, in the section on Paper Weaving.

HUNGARIAN LOOM

The Hungarian loom, a simple loom for weaving strips or braids, consists of a piece of wood with rows of nails driven into it. The distance between the two rows of nails determines the width of the finished strip. If wider strips are desired a larger loom may be made, or several strips can be sewed together.

MATERIALS FOR THE LOOM

1. Forty-eight headless nails ($^5/_8$ or $^3/_4$ inch)
2. One board (12 inches long, $2^1/_2$ inches wide)
3. One strip of wood ($5^1/_2$ inches long)
4. Hammer

MATERIALS FOR WEAVING

1. Yarn
2. Scissors

MAKING AND WARPING THE LOOM

1 Assemble the loom according to the diagram. The nails to hold the weaving are placed alternately across from each other. Adjust the nails so that they are all approximately the same height.

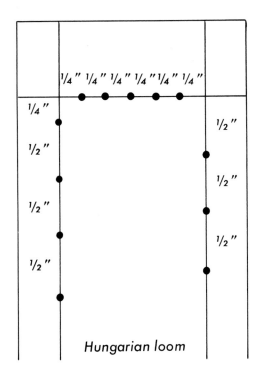

Hungarian loom

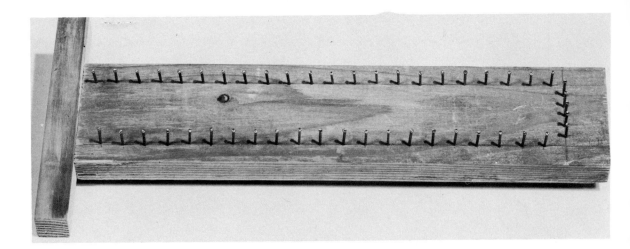

2 To prepare the warp, cut ten pieces of yarn equal in length, of which five are one color and five are another. The warp must be twice as long as the finished product. Three yards is usually adequate for the average belt or tie.

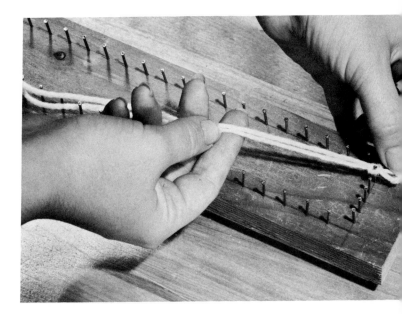

3 Fold each warp yarn in half, and make a knot about ½ inch to 1 inch from the loop end.

4 Fasten the knot of one of the warps over the first nail in the row across the top and tighten. Allow the loop to extend over the end of the loom. This loop will later be trimmed as a fringe on the finished piece. The length of the loop determines the length of the fringe.

5 Knot the opposite ends of the strip of yarn together.

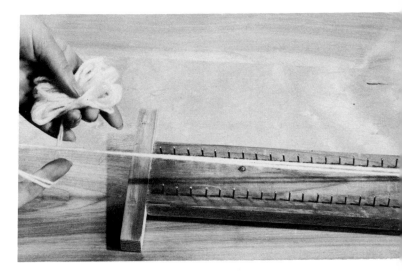

6 Shorten each warp thread to about a 15-inch length for weaving, by winding it around the fingers, putting it through a loop, and pulling it tight.

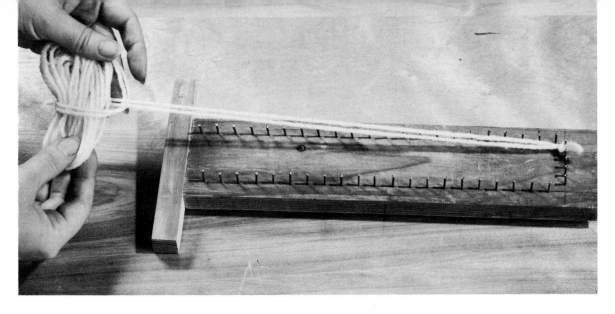

7 Or wind the yarn on a cardboard bobbin or a small plastic knitting bobbin such as is used for knitting argyle socks.

8 Continue by placing a warp yarn on each nail, using the five pieces of the first color.

9 To complete the warp, do the same for the second color, laying the yarns over the nails on top of the first row of warp threads.

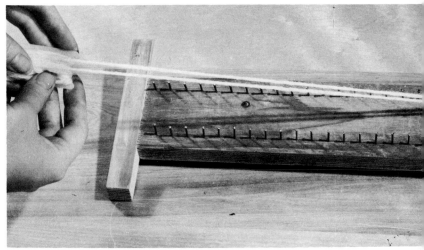

WEAVING ON THE LOOM

10 To weave, place the loom flat on the table with the nails on the right and the bar on the left.

11 Create a shed by carefully lifting all of the top layer of warp threads back over the top of the loom and resting them on the table without disturbing the attachment to the nails. To keep the knots from sliding off the nails, tie a piece of thread or stretch a rubber band around the end of the loom, over the loops.

12 Prepare the weft by winding a 10-yard length of yarn into a ball or on a bobbin, and fasten the loose end with a knot to the first nail in the row on the left, allowing the end to extend out with the other loops to become part of the fringe. Or the loose end can be woven back in with a darning needle after the weaving is finished.

13 Bring the weft straight across the shed, over the first nail in the right-hand row and then straight down to the bar at the end of the loom. Hold the weft in place with several twists around the bar where it remains while the shed is changed.

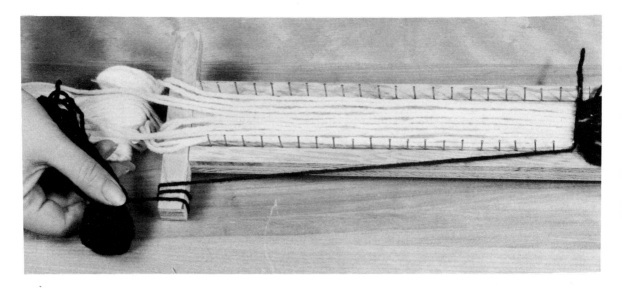

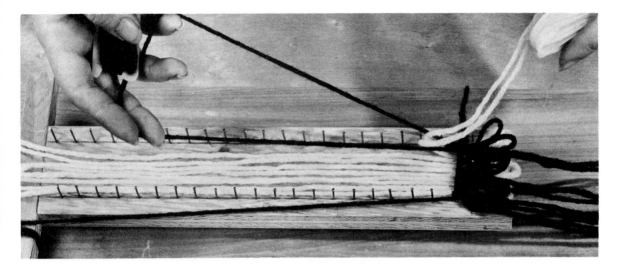

14 To change the shed, pick up the first double warp thread lying on the loom and pass it between the two parts of the first warp thread of the second color so that the two warp colors exchange places, one going through the other.

15 Repeat this all the way across the loom, until a new shed is created.

16 Unwind the weft from the bar. Carry it back directly across the loom over the nail in the opposite row, bring it down, and wrap it around the bar on the other side of the loom.

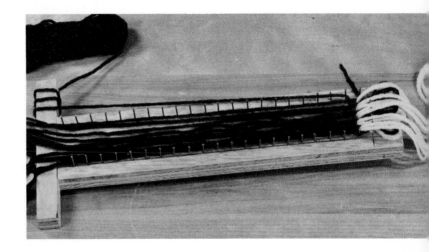

17 Change the shed by exchanging the colors again. The direction of the pattern depends upon the method in which the warp is exchanged—whether the left threads go through the right, or the right through the left.

18 To extend the weaving, carefully lift the strip from the nails.

19 Replace the strip where the weaving ended, over the group of five nails, and continue as before.

20 When the woven strip is finished, the ends may be stitched and cut, and left knotted with the loops attached, or the loops may be cut for a fringe.

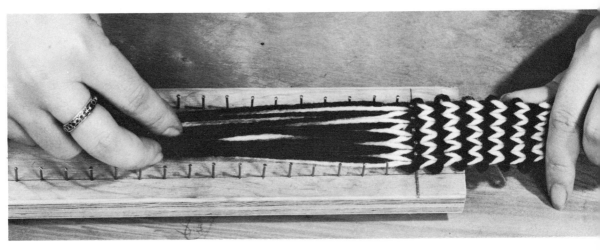

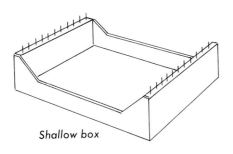

Shallow box

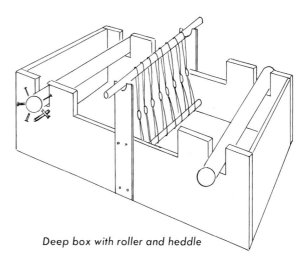

Deep box with roller and heddle

BOX LOOM

Boxes used for looms may be shallow, like tomato flats, or deep, like apple boxes. Cutting down or removing the sides will permit space for the hand or shuttle. Sanding the boxes will remove rough edges. Nails are driven in the ends as explained under the board loom. If a deep box is used, a rigid heddle placed inside it will facilitate the changing of the shed. Rollers around which extra warp is wound can be made with pieces of wood doweling that are inserted in slots or holes cut on the sides of the box. The warp is tied to the roller and secured with tape to keep it from slipping. Nails or pegs projecting from the roller on one side of the loom will hold it in place as the warp is held taut, if a large removable nail or peg is put near it in the loom.

Refer to the previous directions for making a rigid heddle. A heddle made of knotted string may be looped over two dowel rods and held in position by the top rod, which is placed across the box so that it rests in slots made in strips of wood nailed to the side of the box. The heddle is then lifted to raise the warp threads placed through the loops tied in the center. A shed stick is used to raise the alternate threads. To tie the strings for the heddle, drive four nails in a strip of wood and tie each string tautly around the nails using a square or weaver's knot so that the knots will not slip.

Mats woven on box or frame looms can be joined together to make rugs. They can combine tabby weaving with a pile made by knotted pieces as described on page 132. Small boxes such as cigar boxes, chalk boxes, shoe boxes, and hosiery boxes may be used for making small mats, purses, marble bags, pot holders, and similar articles. Pins may be put upright across the opposite ends, or notches or holes may be used for attaching the warp threads; the weaving will proceed as described for other flat looms.

FRAME LOOM

For the frame loom, four strips of wood are fastened together at the corners with nails, glue, bolts, or corrugated joint fasteners. Nails are driven in at each end, and the loom is warped in the following way: the end of the warp thread is tied to the first nail; the warp is brought to the opposite end around the first two nails, then back and forth around two nails each time, and finally tied to the end nail. Slots may be made with a saw and used in place of nails. Old picture frames are sometimes suitable for use as looms. If nails cannot be driven into the wood, the warp can be wrapped continuously around the frame. The weaving may then be done on the warp on one side only; it may be continued by pulling the warp around the frame as the weaving is completed, thus making a longer piece of weaving, as for a scarf; or the warp on both sides of the picture frame can be pulled together and used at one time. The weaving procedure here is similar to that described under cardboard and wood board looms.

Wood frame

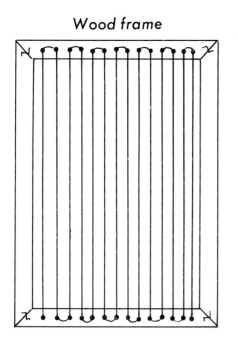

Picture frame

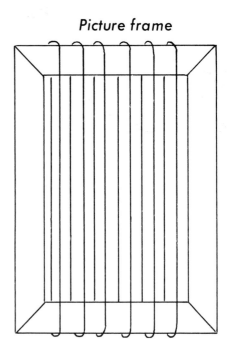

A sampler woven on a frame loom.

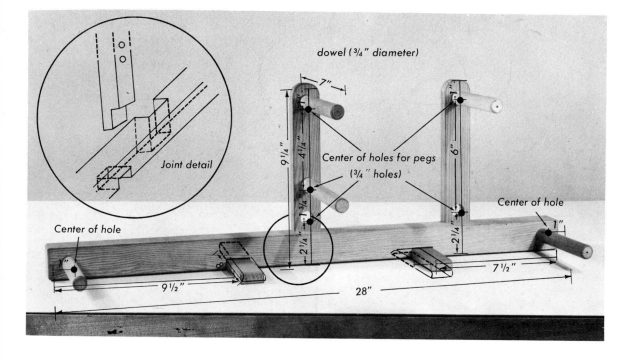

dowel (¾" diameter)

Joint detail

Center of hole

Center of holes for pegs
(¾" holes)

Center of hole

THE INKLE LOOM

The inkle loom, a very simple loom, derives its name from the Scottish word *inkle*, which means narrow band or strip. On this loom the shed is made with the assistance of string heddles attached to the loom. The warp is wrapped around the loom in a continuous band. The fabric produced by this loom is warp-faced; that is, the weft does not show in the body of the fabric. Therefore, the pattern building is done entirely with the warp. The warp may be made of cotton, linen, wool, or nylon. For beginners three- or four-ply wool is the simplest to weave. The woven strips can be used for neckties, belts, and strips of braid. The width of the strips can vary from very narrow to three and four inches wide. Strips may be sewn together to make wider strips of fabric for scarves, rugs, handbags, pillow covers, throws, skirts, jackets, and coats.

If an inkle loom is not available commercially, one can be easily made. Any kind of wood can be used, but hardwood is the sturdiest. The parts should be screwed together for stability. The dimensions (see above) are for a loom,

which, with standard warping, will produce strips up to 50 inches long. For longer strips the main beam of the loom could be lengthened.

MATERIALS

1. One board (2×2 inches—30 inches long)
2. Two boards (2×2 inches—9½ inches long)
3. Two boards (1×2 inches—8 inches long)
4. Five dowels (¾ inches—7 inches long)
5. Saw
6. Chisel
7. Drill
8. 1½ inch screws
9. One shuttle (½×2 inches—6 inches long)

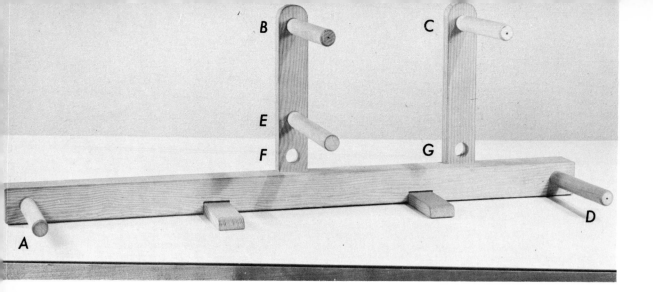

MATERIALS FOR WEAVING

1. Yarn—three- and four-ply wool, cotton, linen, or nylon
2. Scissors
3. Darning needle
4. Knitting needle
5. Two cardboard strips (1 $\times$ 4 inches)

MATERIALS FOR HEDDLES

1. Fine stout string, linen thread, twine, or nylon fish line
2. Scissors

MAKING THE HEDDLES

1 Move post E to hole F.

2 Loop the string around posts B and F, tie with a square knot.

3 Remove the loop from posts.

4 Repeat for each heddle needed. About 16 heddles are needed to weave a 1-inch width with four-ply wool yarn.

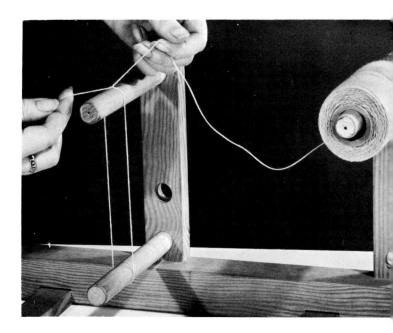

WARPING THE LOOM

Tying On

1 Select balls of yarn needed for the desired pattern. Move post E to hole E.

2 Tie the end of the first ball of yarn to post A.

3 Wrap the yarn around the post three times clockwise.

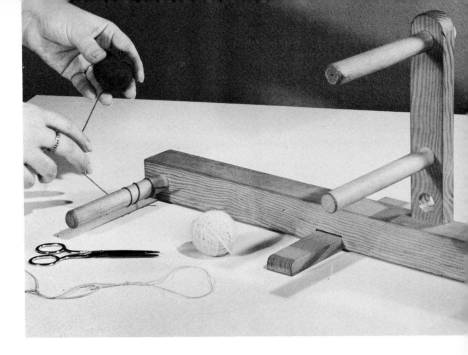

Making the Selvedge, Down Warp

4 Now take yarn between posts B and E and over post C.

5 Continue around post D back to post A. Keep the yarn fairly taut.

6 Repeat from A to C to D to A. Yarn warped in this way (not going over post B) is called down warp. These two down-warp threads form a selvedge for the material. Every warping is started and finished with two down-warp threads.

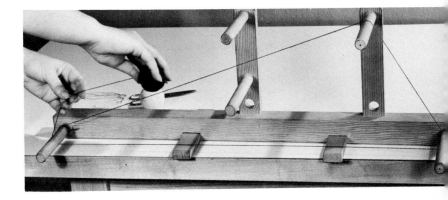

Up Warp, Attaching the Heddles

7 Now carry the yarn from post A over post B on to C to D and back to A. This is the first up-warp thread, going over post B.

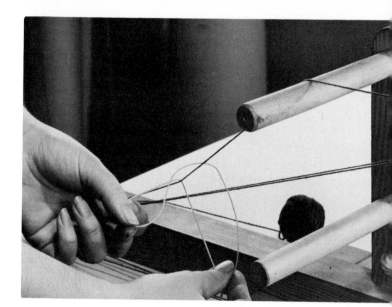

8 Lay the ball of yarn to one side of the loom and pick up a heddle.

9 Between posts A and B place the heddle over the up-warp yarn just warped.

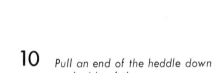

10 Pull an end of the heddle down over each side of the up-warp yarn. This forms a loop over the yarn.

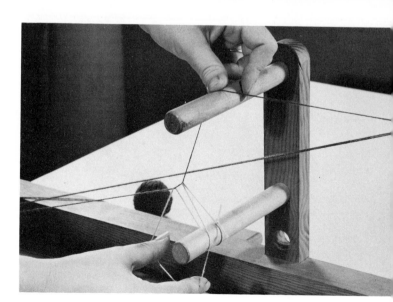

11 Loop the ends of the heddle over post E. Place the knot in the heddle under the post.

12 Continue to warp alternately up and down warp until the desired width is warped. Each down-warp thread is warped between posts B and E; each up-warp thread goes over post B and requires a heddle.

Changing Color of the Warp

13 When the color of the warp is to be changed, simply place the ball of yarn being used on the opposite side of the loom and tie on the new color, following instructions 2 and 3 above. The first color can be picked up and used again in the warp at any time. As many different colored balls of yarn as are needed for any pattern may be used. Place those not in immediate use to one side until the warping is complete. The warp yarns will cross over each other under post A as the colors are changed.

Tying Off the Warp

14 When the desired width has been warped, conclude the warping by laying two threads down warp, forming the selvedge on the outside.

15 Locate the first threads of each color where they have been tied at post A. Pull the threads gently to unwrap them from around the post. Cut the knots that tie them to the post, and hold the threads in the hand.

16 Cut the ends of the warping threads from the balls of yarn, leaving a little length of yarn on the end of each thread. Hold these ends in the other hand.

17 Pull both groups of threads gently to equalize the tension of the warp. Tie all the beginning threads to all the ending threads with a square knot. This knot should be made just under post A.

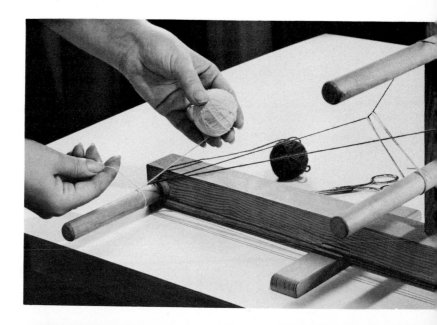

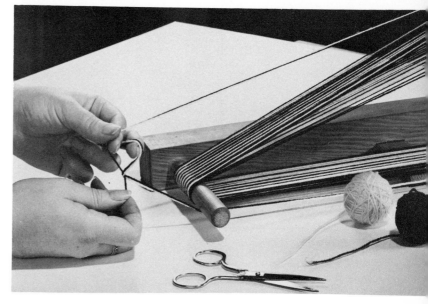

BASIC PATTERNS

There are three basic patterns in inkle weaving: vertical stripe, horizontal stripe, and checkerboard. Patterns are indicated on a graph to aid in setting up the loom. The upper squares indicate the *up warp,* the lower squares the *down warp.* An empty square indicates that no thread is used. The colors can be varied as the designer wishes, but for this diagram, X = one color and O = any contrasting hue.

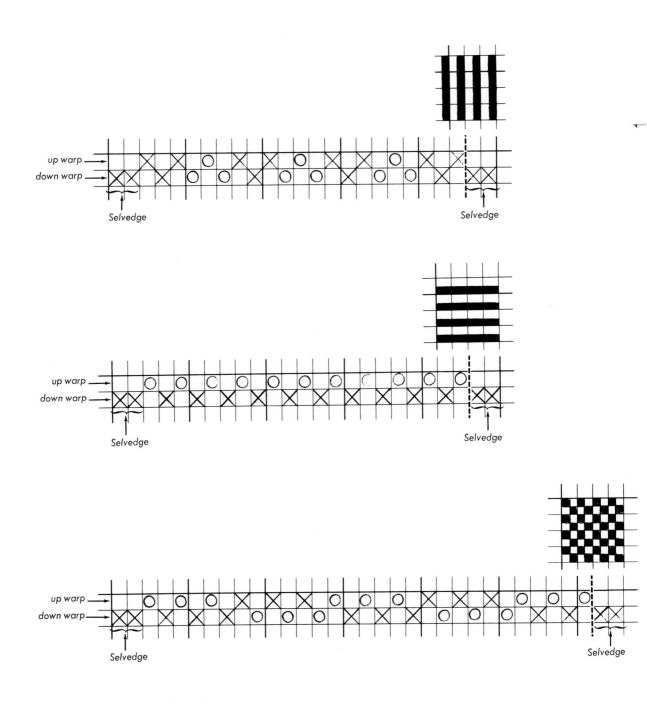

Changing the Shed

On the inkle loom, the shed is changed by lifting or lowering the down warp by hand. Place the hand under the down warp between the heddles and post C and raise the warp until the shed opening is large enough to pass the shuttle through. Depress the down warp to change the shed back again.

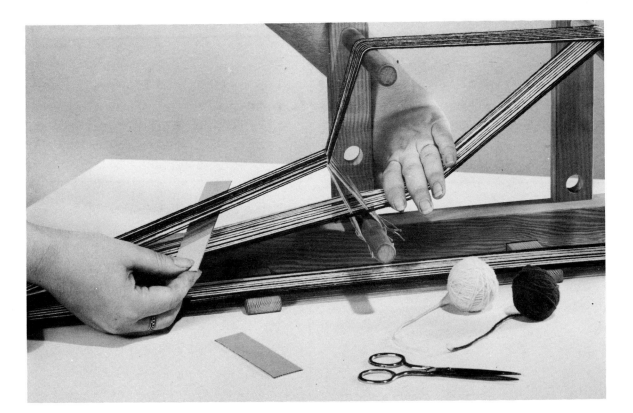

WEAVING

1 Before beginning to weave, lower post E to hole F. When lowering the post, grasp the heddles carefully so that they do not slip off the post.

2 Prepare two strips of cardboard about 1 x 4 inches. These strips are used to spread the warp.

3 Depress the down warp to the lower position, opening the shed. Lay in the first cardboard strip by inserting it through the shed opening.

4 Change the shed by raising the down warp as above and insert the second strip of cardboard. Arrange the warp threads so that they lay side by side, touching each other.

5 Change the shed by depressing the down warp. Beat the woven cardboard strips tightly into place by putting the hand in the open shed and pulling the hand toward post A.

6 Start to weave with the weft yarn. It is more convenient to wrap some of this yarn on a shuttle. If the weft on the shuttle is used up before the weaving is finished, more can easily be added. Shoot the shuttle or the ball of yarn through the shed.

7 Change the shed. Beat. If a shuttle is being used, beat the fell with the edge of the shuttle. This saves time, since the beating is done as the shuttle is being passed through the shed for the next shot. If the shuttle is not used, beat with the side of the hand, a piece of cardboard, or a ruler.

8 Shoot the next shot of weft through the shed. Continue this process until the fabric is complete.

Keeping the Selvedge Neat

9 Each time the shuttle is passed through the opening, care must be taken that the weft thread does not pull too tightly on the selvedge threads of the warp. To keep the edge straight, grasp the selvedge between the thumb and forefinger of the free hand at the place where the weft thread is to be pulled in. While the weft thread is being pulled through on the shuttle, keep the tension on the edge by pinching it between the thumb and forefinger. This will prevent the edge from becoming irregular.

Adding Weft to the Shuttle

10 If the weft on the shuttle is used up before the weaving is finished, push the end that is left down through the warp so it hangs free near the center of the width of the warp. Rewrap the shuttle and continue the shot, with the new starting weft slightly overlapping the old in the center of the warp, and also hanging down. After the weaving is complete and cut from the loom, these loose ends can be snipped off with scissors.

Moving the Warp Around the Loom

11 As the weaving progresses, the fell occupies more and more space between posts A and B, until the shed opening becomes too small to permit easy weaving. Since none of the warp is tied to the loom it may be freely pulled around the posts to give a better shed. Sometimes the beating itself will push the fell around post A toward post B. If this does not happen, move the warp. Grasp the warp between A and B, and gently but firmly pull toward post A. Certain warp yarns, such as bouclé, nylon, and fuzzy wool, have a tendency to stick in the heddles. To avoid this, loosen post E carefully and remove it while the warp is being pulled around; then reinsert it as before. As the weaving progresses, the warp is pulled around the posts until the fell has made an almost complete circuit, ending about halfway between posts C and D. At this point the two cardboard strips woven in at the beginning may be removed to make it easier to finish the weaving.

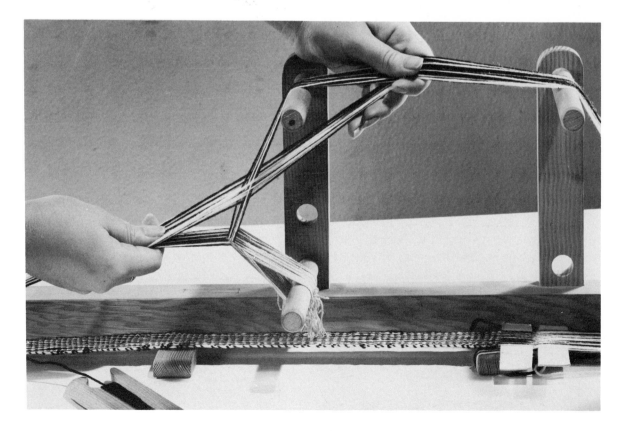

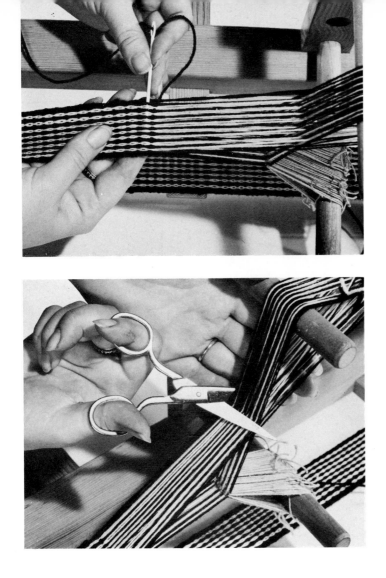

12 *When the fell has gone completely around the loom and is between posts C and D, the weaving is finished.*

Cutting the Fell from the Loom

13 *Before cutting the fell from the loom, thread the last shot of weft through a big-eyed needle and carefully weave it back into the fell. This will prevent the fell from unraveling. The fell is released from the loom by cutting through the warp above the shed between posts A and D. Do not cut the heddles; they can be used again. Pull the finished weaving from the posts, gently releasing the warp fringe from the heddles.*

THE FLOAT THREAD

In all the basic weaves that have been discussed, patterns are built by alternating the color or value of the yarn in the upper and lower warp. When the shed is changed, the upper warp goes under, and the lower warp comes up. To change this simple variation, hold up some of the threads that would otherwise be lowered, and retain them in the upper warp. These threads will not be woven into the fabric—that is, they will, for this shot of the weft, be *float threads*. Any thread or threads may be selected out of the warp and floated for as many as six shots of the weft. There is a danger of floating a thread for too many shots because,

since it is not woven in with the others, it is loose and easily snagged or pulled. But used well, the float thread is a basic pattern technique and can be used to create simple repeat motifs or complex designs.

THE LOOM STICK

The loom stick is a device used in making patterns on the loom. With it, some repetitive patterns are easier to make. It can also be used to pick up and hold threads needed for designs less clumsily than the fingers alone. Any smooth slender dowel or knitting needle will serve as a loom stick.

A SIMPLE PATTERN BASED ON THE FLOAT THREAD USING A LOOM STICK

1 Warp the loom. The single threads that are to be floated for the design are placed at appropriate intervals in the lower warp.

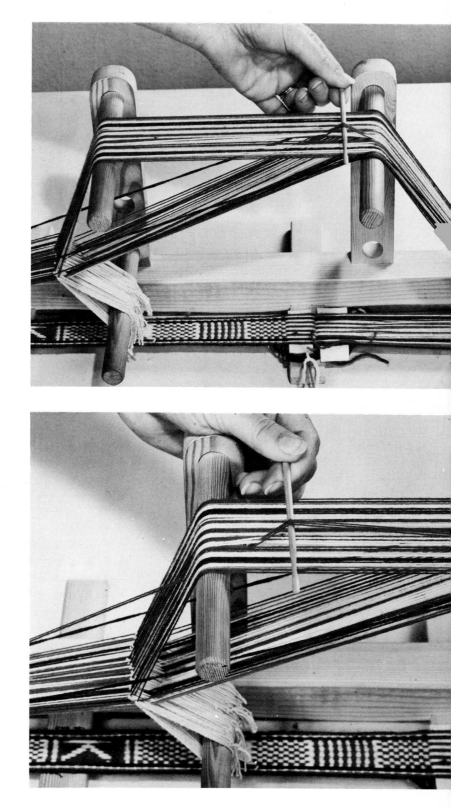

2 Pick up the loom stick. Between posts B and C near post C, locate the threads to be floated. Starting on the right, with the stick on top of the upper warp, separate the upper warp above the pattern thread, reach down through the upper warp, and pick up the pattern thread on the loom stick. Proceed to the left, locate the next thread, pick it up, and continue until all the pattern threads are on the loom stick.

3 Leave the loom stick, with the pattern threads over it, next to post C. Weave a few shots of plain weave.

4 When the lower warp is in down position, draw the loom stick toward post B. This will pull the pattern threads out of their proper place in the lower warp and place them in the upper warp, so that they become float threads for this shot. Weave the shot of weft.

5 Return the stick to its former position near post C, and continue weaving until another pattern shot is desired. Then repeat the above process.

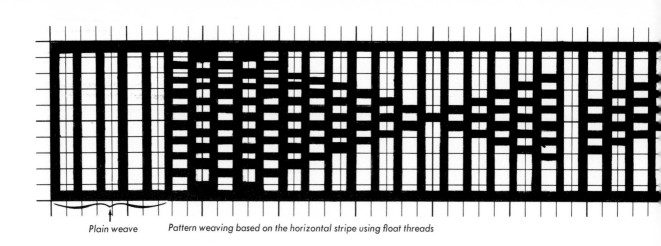

Plain weave *Pattern weaving based on the horizontal stripe using float threads*

PATTERN WEAVING USING FLOAT THREADS

Based on the Horizontal Stripe

In these patterns, which are more complex than those outlined above, the loom stick can be used between posts B and C or the pickups can be made directly on the shed. Complex designs can be made and carefully planned in advance. This technique is very like that used in traditional Navajo and Guatemalan belt weaving.

1 *Set up the loom for the horizontal stripe pattern. It is a good plan to include in the design a plain band on either edge. This will assist in keeping the selvedge even and regular. The contrast between dark and light in upper and lower warp should be strong enough to bring out the design clearly. The up warp should be light, the down warp dark.*

2 *Weave a few shots of plain weave to firm up the weaving.*

3 *Begin the pattern after changing the shed so that the lower warp is down. Hold the loom stick on top of the upper warp; separate the upper warp threads, and with the point of the stick bring up a lower warp thread on the stick. Make the pickups from right to left, proceeding to move the stick over the upper warp.*

4 *The pattern above was made by picking up every other dark thread from the lower warp on the pickup shot. On the next pattern shot the alternate threads were picked up, and so on. Each shot of weft, therefore, is held in place by the threads that were not picked up. If every thread from the lower warp were picked up with every shot, the weft thread would have nothing to hold it in place. In every pattern shot, therefore, pick up only alternate dark threads from the lower warp.*

5 *After the pickup shot, weave the next shot plain weave. Continue this process until the fabric is complete.*

6 *Designs can be worked out on graph paper and woven by counting the threads on each pickup shot, following the pattern.*

7 *When the finished weaving is turned over the pattern hardly shows on the back. Because the design is built by floating threads over the weft, only small breaks in the design appear on the reverse side.*

Based on the Basic Checkerboard Plan

This method will produce effects very similar to those on the Navajo belt loom. The pattern area may be combined with other basic weaves, such as vertical or horizontal stripes. For the first attempt at special patterns it is suggested that the pattern occupy a band down the center of the piece, bordered on either side by an edge of simple weave, which will help keep the edges of the weaving regular. The pattern is based on the basic weave of the checkerboard. By picking up or dropping out single checks in the basic pattern, the weaver can easily make many designs. The pattern shows equally well on both sides of the fabric in this weave. On the back the colors are reversed. It will help to plan the design on graph paper. Decide on the width for the design. Each square in the graph has the possibility of being either dark or light. Block in the design with a pencil, indicating square by square whether dark or light is to be used. No area of the design should be more than four or five squares long because, as will be seen, this requires a float thread, one that will not be woven into the fabric for this length.

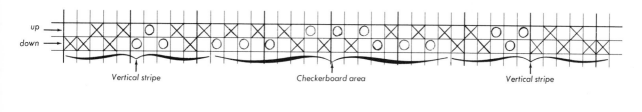

Vertical stripe   Checkerboard area   Vertical stripe

1 *After sketching out the pattern, warp the loom. Use the checkerboard basic pattern to warp the design area.*

2 *Begin the weaving. Weave a few shots of straight weave to stabilize the fell.*

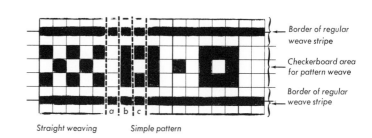

Straight weaving   Simple pattern

Border of regular weave stripe

Checkerboard area for pattern weave

Border of regular weave stripe

3 *Change the shed.*

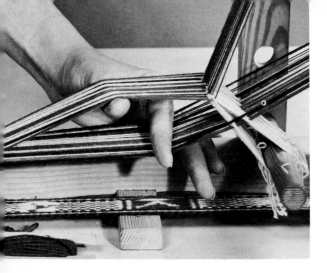

4 Instead of weaving a shot of the weft, insert the middle finger into the open shed. Keep it there, holding this shed open throughout the next steps.

5 Change the shed again. Do not remove the finger from the first shed (step 4). Introduce the index finger into the new shed to keep it open also.

6 With the other hand introduce a knitting needle into the lower shed opening to the point where the checkerboard pattern begins.

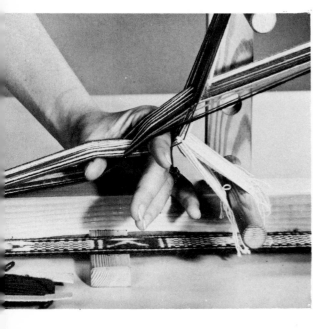

7 Pick up on the needle, from either the upper or lower shed, only those threads needed for the pattern. For example, in shot a in the pattern (step 1 above), the whole shot is light; therefore, the needle picks up the vertical stripe edge, then the first square, all in the lower shed. Push the needle up through the warp, then under the light threads that make up the middle light square in the upper shed, then back under the next light threads in the lower shed and on through the lower shed, completing the shot. This is the pattern shot through the pattern at a.

8 Remove the fingers, leaving the knitting needle in the shed.

9 Lift the knitting needle, separating the shed opening so that the weft yarn can be shot through.

10 Shoot the weft shot.

11 Change the shed again as in steps 3 through 5 above. Weave the next shot, determining whether from the upper or lower shed according to the design.

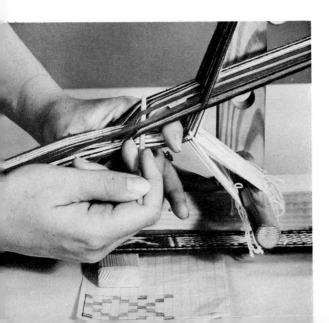

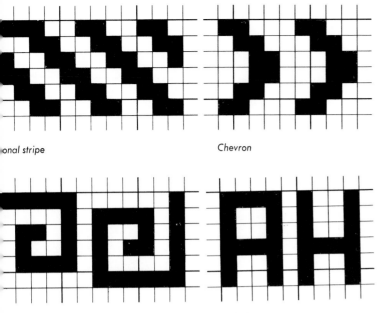

onal stripe

Chevron

k key

Alphabet

12 For the first attempt at this pattern technique it is good to make a sampler, trying many different designs, with an area of plain weave between each pattern area. This way many ideas can be tried to see which ones work well in weaving.

Once skill is attained with this pattern weave, a design may be made by sewing together two or three strips of weaving. Carefully plan the pattern on graph paper, then divide the design into widths convenient for weaving, and weave each width, following the plan. When all are woven, sew the strips together to complete the design.

13 Examples of weaving done on an inkle loom.

Front view.

THE TABLE LOOM

The table loom is very like the floor loom or foot-power loom in its construction, except that its harnesses are raised by means of levers. Looms are available in many sizes, depending upon the width of the fabric to be woven. The number of harnesses limit the variety of patterns that can be made. A two-harness loom is used for plain weaves and various pattern techniques such as leno, knotting, and tapestry. A four-, six-, or eight-harness loom greatly expands the pattern-building possibilities. The reed, which is used to keep the warp threads separate and to beat or batten down the woven fabric, is usually made of metal. It consists of a frame set with evenly spaced strips called *teeth*. The spaces between the teeth are called dents. The reed is purchased according to the number of dents to

the inch. A 15-dent reed is a practical and versatile size for most beginning projects. The heddles, made of string or metal, separate the warp threads into groups for making the sheds. Many weavers prefer metal heddles because they are more permanent and permit the warp threads to pass through them easily. A small table loom such as illustrated above is useful for many weaving projects. The necessity of changing the shed by hand levers, instead of foot treadles as in the foot-power loom, slows down the weaving process, and the narrower width limits the width of fabric that can be woven. However, it is an excellent loom for beginners to learn on, and many weavers use the small loom to plan patterns and make samples.

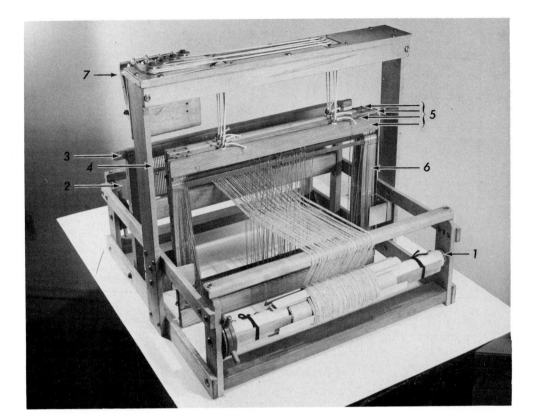

Back view.

1. Warp beam
2. Cloth beam
3. Beater
4. Reed
5. Harnesses
6. Heddles
7. Lever for raising harnesses

LOOM ACCESSORIES

Shuttles, leash sticks, and a raddle are necessary weaving equipment. They can be easily made if they are not available commercially. The shuttle is used for holding the weft while it is being woven. There are many kinds of shuttles for different purposes. A shuttle can be made by notching the ends of a short length of wood or cardboard. Often several shuttles are required. Leash sticks are used to separate the warp when it is being attached to the loom. They can be made of long sticks of wood with a hole drilled in each end so that they can be tied to one another and to the loom. The leash sticks should be about the same length as the reed so that they

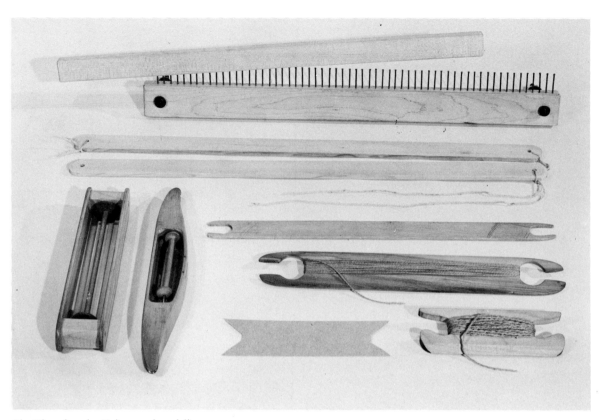

Shuttles, leash sticks, and raddle.

can hold the whole width of the warp. The raddle is used to separate individual warp threads when the warp is being wrapped on the warp beam. A raddle can be made of a strip of wood as long as the warp beam. Headless nails down its length in an even row, ½ inch apart, serve to separate the warp threads. A cap to cover the nail heads can be made by cutting a groove ¼ to ½ inch deep in another strip of wood the same length as the raddle. The raddle can be tied or clamped to the loom during the warping process. All wooden accessories should be carefully sanded so that they will not snag the yarn.

THE WARPING BOARD

The warping board is a device to measure out a number of warp threads all the same length, and to arrange them in order for easier threading on the loom. The warping board consists of pegs attached to a frame in an arrangement that will enable the weaver to wrap the yarn in desired lengths without a tangle, and provide a cross or a shed in the warp. The cross allows the warp to be separated easily for warping the loom. As the warp is being wrapped on the warping board, a count of warp threads is kept by tying groups of threads together by number. The first and last pegs on the board are usually removable to allow the warp to be easily taken off. Many kinds of warping boards are used, including some that are like reels and can be turned to make the winding easier. If no warping board is available, the upturned legs of chairs or tables will serve as pegs on which to wrap the yarn.

Before beginning to wrap the warp yarn on the warping board, allow at least one additional yard of yarn for tying to the loom. Then determine the number of warp lengths that will be required by counting the number needed for each inch of fabric width according to the dents in the reed. The warp may be of more than one color depending upon the pattern to be woven. The weaving techniques demonstrated on the following pages can be done with a one-color cotton warp.

THE WARPING FRAME

A warping board can be simply made by following the directions in the diagram. Any sort of wood will serve for the frame. The pegs should be 6 inches long. The corners of the frame can be held together with bolts and wing nuts; then it can be easily disassembled for storage.

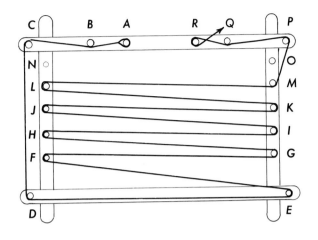

1 Determine the length the warp is to be.

2 Measure off a piece of yarn or string the same length as the warp.

3 Wrap it on the warping board to determine how many pegs will be used in wrapping the warp. Start at post A. Tie on the length of yarn, carry it under post B, around posts C, D, and E, then around posts F, G, H, and so on to posts P and Q, ending at post R, as in the diagram. The yarn must end at post R. Omit any number of posts in alphabetical order between E and P that are not needed. This preliminary wrapping is necessary to plan the wrapping pattern for the warp.

4 Select the warp yarn. Tie to post A. Follow the wrapping pattern determined in step 3, going under post B, around the board, under post Q to post R. When post R is reached, reverse the wrapping, this time going over post Q, around P and retracing the wrapping, going over post B to A, making the two crosses.

5 Continue wrapping, following the same procedure until the desired number of warps has been wrapped. Most weavers like to tie a short length of yarn around each group of 10 or 20 warps as soon as they have been wrapped to avoid losing count.

6 When the wrapping is done, secure the crosses and the end at A by tying a length of yarn through the sheds at A and B, and through the loop at A.

7   As an added precaution to keep the warps in order, the warp may be tied with short lengths of yarn between the other wrapping posts. This is necessary, especially if a long warp is being wrapped.

8   The warp may now be removed from the warping board. It may be rolled in newspaper as it is unwrapped from the board, or it may be chained.

9   To chain the warp, begin at post R. Put the hand through the loop at R, grasp the warp ahead of the loop, and pull it through the loop.

10   This creates a second loop. Put the hand through it, grasp the warp ahead of the loop, and pull it through as before. Continue until all the warp has been removed from the board. Chaining the warp is actually making a crochet chain of it.

11   Tie the chain at the end to prevent it from unraveling.

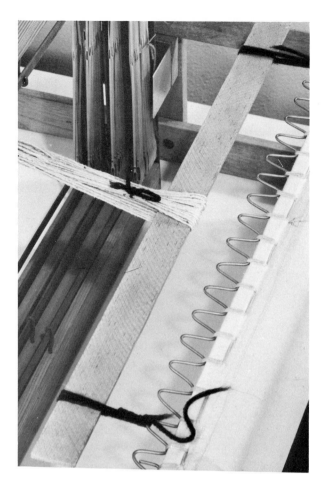

WARPING THE LOOM
MATERIALS

1. Loom
2. Chained warp
3. Raddle or warp separator
4. Threading hook
5. Leash sticks
6. Scissors
7. Cardboard strips or wooden sticks

1 *Push the heddles to one side to allow the warp to go through. Pass the chained warp through the loom from the front to the back and put the fly rod through the loop at the end of the warp. Tie the fly rod at each end to the warp beam at the back of the loom.*

2 *Insert the leash sticks into the warp shed made by the cross, and tie them to each other at the ends to prevent the warp from slipping out and losing the cross. Secure the leash sticks from slipping by tying them to the center post of the loom.*

3 *Untie the knots that held the cross.*

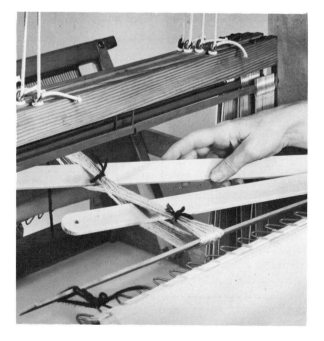

4 Roll the warp beam enough to permit the raddle to be attached to the back of the loom. Place a folded bit of paper or cardboard over the pegs on the raddle to hold the warp clear of the pegs. Space the warp into the dents of the raddle. The center of the raddle can be marked so that half of the warp lies on either side.

5 Put the cap on the raddle. This holds the warp threads in place.

6 Tie the center of the fly rod to the warp beam to keep it from bending during the tension of warping.

7 The warp is now ready to be rolled onto the warp beam. The leash sticks have been secured to one another and to the two center posts at the sides of the loom.

8 *During the winding of the warp onto the warp beam, it is best to have a helper hold the warp in tension from the front of the loom.*

9 *Wind the warp by turning the warp beam. As the warp is wound, keep it separated by winding in strips of flexible corrugated board or heavy paper. The corrugated board should be wider than the warp to keep the tension even.*

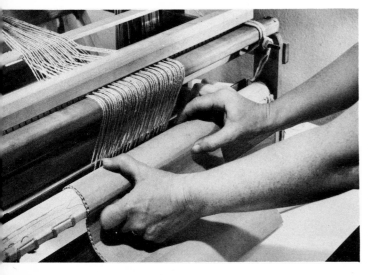

10 *Warp sticks may be used instead of cardboard or heavy paper. Space them evenly as the warp is wound.*

11 *Wind the warp until about 20 inches remains in front of the leash sticks. Cut the loop at the end of the warp.*

12 *Start from one end of the warp and thread each warp thread through a heddle following the heddle threading draft indicated for the design. Put the threading hook through the opening in the heddle from the front. Catch the warp on the hook and pull it through the heddle.*

13 *The warp threaded through the heddles. If the warping is wide, tie it loosely in groups as it is heddled.*

14 *Locate the center of the reed so that there are an equal number of dents on both sides. Count over the number of dents for half the warp and start threading, one dent at a time. Pull the threads through the dents with the threading hook. Push the threading hook through the dent from the front and pull the warp through the dent.*

15 *The warp threaded through the reed.*

16 *Starting from the center, tie the warp to the cloth beam, one section at a time. The cloth beam should be over the breast beam during tying. Divide the group of warps, pull half from under each side, and tie.*

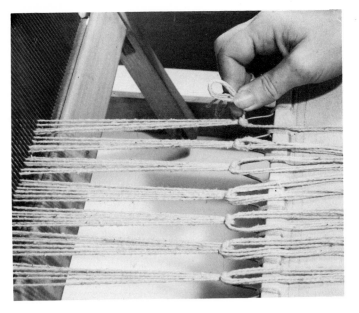

17 Pull the knot tight. Then tie a group on either side of the center. Work toward the sides, alternating groups.

18 The warp tied to the cloth beam.

19 Check the warps to be certain they have equal tension. Test the tension by pressing on top of the warps with the palm of the hand. Untie, pull taut, and retie any warp sections that seem slack. Complete the tying with bow knots.

PATTERN WEAVES

The weaver must have an understanding of three kinds of plans or *drafts* before he can plan designs and set them up on the loom. These are the *heddle threading draft*, which indicates the order in which the heddles are threaded as the loom is warped; the *pattern draft*, which is a diagram of the pattern; and the *treadle draft*, which indicates the sequence of raising or lowering the harnesses to bring the necessary warp threads into the proper shed during the weaving.

THE HEDDLE THREADING DRAFT

The heddle threading draft is laid out on graph paper. Each horizontal row of squares in the diagram refers to a heddle harness. A four-harness loom is indicated by four rows of squares. Each harness is indicated by the number beside the row at the right of the diagram, and each square in the row indicates a warp thread. The size of the diagram is determined by the number of warp threads needed for the pattern unit. The first row refers to the harness nearest the front of the loom; row 2 refers to the next-nearest harness, and so on in order. A square filled in on the diagram indicates that a warp thread passes through a heddle in that harness.

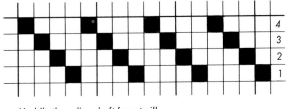

Heddle threading draft for a twill

The heddle threading draft is read from right to left. After the warp yarn is wound on the warp beam and is ready to be threaded through the heddles, push all the heddles on each harness to the left. The heddles are threaded from right to left; follow the draft for the pattern. For example, the heddle threading draft for the twill is read as follows: Starting on the right, the draft indicates the first warp thread on the right goes through the first heddle in harness one. Slide the first heddle on this harness to the right and pull the first warp on the right through this heddle. The second square marked on the draft, from the right, indicates the next warp must go through the first heddle in harness 2. Slide this heddle to the right and pass the next warp thread through the heddle. The third square marked on the draft indicates the next warp thread must pass through the first heddle in

harness 3. Continue warping, following the draft from right to left until the warp is all heddled. If a mistake is made, the threads must be pulled from the heddles and rethreaded to correct the error. Make a selvedge on both sides of the weaving by putting two warp threads through each heddle indicated in the draft. A selvedge of four heddle units will usually suffice.

If there are more heddles on each harness than are needed for the number of warp threads, the extra heddles should be divided before the heddling is started, so that half of the extra heddles will be on each side of the harness. This will keep the harnesses balanced and make the weaving easier.

THE TREADLE DRAFT

The name of this draft derives from the floor loom where each harness is raised by pressing on a foot pedal called a *treadle*. In the table loom used for the examples here, the harnesses are raised by a system of levers on one side of the loom. The harnesses may be raised singly or in groups. The treadle draft is determined by the sequence of harnesses that must be raised to provide the proper sheds for the pattern.

THE PATTERN DRAFT

Each row of the heddle threading draft indicates a separate group of warp threads that can be raised to form a shed for one shot of weft. The harnesses can be raised in any order the weaver wishes; this flexibility provides many possible combinations for pattern building. After the weaver has made a heddle threading draft, he can design pattern variations by trying different arrangements of sheds. He can plan these on graph paper to see how they will look when woven.

PLAIN WEAVE

The heddle threading draft for plain weave is very simple for a two-harness loom. The warps simply alternate—one through the front harness, one through the back, and so on across the warp. The four-harness loom requires a slightly more complex heddling. In the example above, the heddle threading draft is the same as for a twill, but in order to achieve the pattern indicated on the pattern draft, two harnesses must be raised for each shot of weft. The order in which they are raised is indicated in the treadle draft (opposite).

Variations on Plain Weave

The plain weave is basic to many weaving techniques. If the warp and weft are identical in color, texture, value, and weight, the result is solid unvaried weaving with no pattern change. Many pattern variations are possible, however, with simple color or value changes in either the warp or weft or both.

1. Vary the warp color. Two or more colors can be included in the warp. If these are grouped in units during the warping, a vertical stripe pattern will result.
2. Vary the weft color. Two or more colors may be used for the weft. Weave several shots of one color, then several shots of another. The number of shots of each color will determine the width of the stripes. This produces a horizontal stripe pattern.
3. Vary the colors of both the warp and the weft. This will produce a plaid pattern.
4. Use a lightweight warp and a heavyweight weft. If the warps are spaced to go through every other reed dent or even further apart, this will produce a weft-faced pattern.
5. Use a heavyweight warp and a lightweight weft. This will produce a warp-faced pattern.
6. Vary the spacing of the warps through the reeds. The spacing can be regular or random.
7. Use a combination of light and heavy warp with a combination of light and heavy weft.
8. Combine plain weave with laid-in or tapestry weaves.

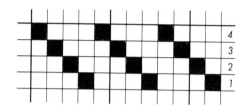

Heddle threading draft for a two-harness loom

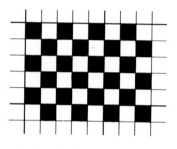

Heddle threading draft for a four-harness loom

Pattern draft

Treadle draft: 1 & 3, 2 & 4, 1 & 3, 2 & 4, etc.

TWILL

The twill pattern produces a diagonal pattern. The harnesses are raised in order. To reverse the direction of the diagonal, reverse the

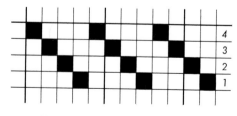

Heddle threading draft for a four-harness loom

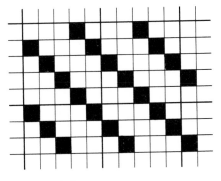

Pattern draft

Treadle draft: 1, 2, 3, 4; 1, 2, 3, 4; etc.

treadle pattern, 4, 3, 2, 1; 4, 3, 2, 1; etc. The heddle threading draft is the same as given above for plain weave, but only one harness is raised at a time.

Variations on the Twill

In addition to the variations listed above for plain weave, the twill may be varied by changing the treadling pattern. In the variations diagramed below, the heddle draft is not changed. By varying the treadle draft only, these and many other variations are possible.

Because this draft requires that two weft shots follow each other through the same shed, it is necessary to catch the weft on the selvedge before it is returned through the shed. To do

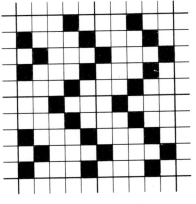

Herringbone twill Pattern draft

Treadle draft: 1, 2, 3, 4, 3, 2; 1, 2, 3, 4, 3, 2, etc.

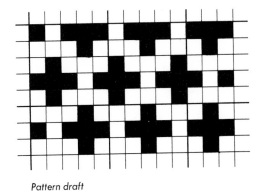

Pattern draft

Treadle draft: 2; 1 & 2 & 3; 2; 4; 1 & 3 & 4; 4; etc.

this, shoot the first shot, wrap the weft around the outside thread of the warp, then return the shuttle through the shed. Catching it on the selvedge prevents the weft from pulling back through the shed when the second shot is made.

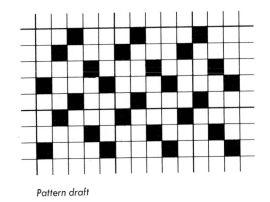

Pattern draft

Treadle draft: 1, 2, 4, 3; 1, 2, 4, 3; etc.

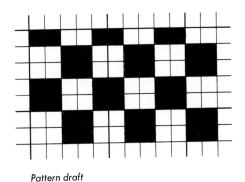

Pattern draft

Treadle draft: 1 & 2; 1 & 2; 3 & 4; 3 & 4; etc.

WEAVING   **191**

GOOSE EYE

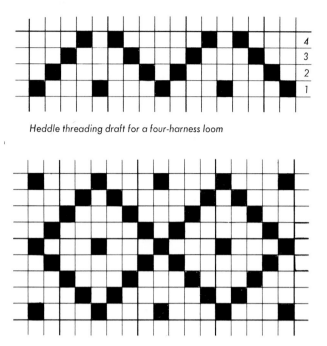

Heddle threading draft for a four-harness loom

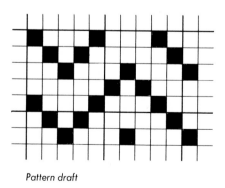

Pattern draft.

Treadle draft: 1, 2, 3, 4; 1, 4, 3, 2; etc.

Variations on the Goose Eye

Use the goose-eye heddle threading draft, but vary the treadling as in the twill above; or vary the color, value, texture, and weight of yarn as described under plain weave. The treadle draft below is only one of many possible variations.

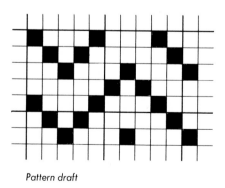

Pattern draft

Treadle draft: 1, 2, 3, 4; 1, 2, 3, 4; etc.

INVENTING NEW PATTERNS

The drafts diagramed above are included to demonstrate the simplest kinds of pattern building. For the beginner there are countless traditional drafts to be explored, and many other patterns will be found in the reference books listed at the end of this book. These drafts may be followed exactly as they are given, or variations can be made with treadling or color change or both. The greatest pleasure in design, however, comes with personal invention; and even the beginning weaver can design his own patterns as he is warping the loom, by carefully selecting the colors, values, and textures of yarn, considering the probable result of various combinations, and then experimenting with different weft patterns. Or, following the process of preparing drafts in advance, he can preplan a more controlled design and follow it just as in the simple pattern drafts given above.

1. Lay out a heddle threading draft on squared paper, one row for each harness of the loom.

2. Fill in the squares to indicate the arrangement of warps in each harness.

3. Try combining the rows in different orders, each requiring a different treadle draft. Make pattern drafts to see how the finished weaving will appear.

4. Try combining two or three rows in the same shed.

5. Avoid skips that are too long.

6. Remember that the color of groups of warp and weft may be changed if desired.

WEAVING ON THE TABLE LOOM

The loom used in these illustrations is a four-harness table loom. The basic processes of warping and weaving shown on this loom can be applied either to smaller two-harness table looms or to larger floor looms. The weaver made the design by alternating a shot of plain weave, called a tabby weft, with a shot of pattern weft. The tabby serves to strengthen the fabric, and is necessary because of the long floats in the pattern weft in this design. The basic procedures outlined below apply to every kind of pattern from simple plain weave to elaborate inventions.

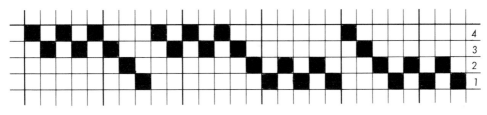

Heddle threading draft

Treadling draft. Tabby: 1 & 3, 2 & 4, etc.

Pattern: five shots 1 & 2, one shot 3 & 4, five shots 1 & 2; then five shots 3 & 4, one shot 1 & 2, five shots 3 & 4, etc.
Shoot one shot of tabby between each shot of pattern.

1 *Warp the loom according to the heddle threading draft required for the pattern. The heddle threading and treadling drafts for the pattern demonstrated in the following steps are given here as examples.*

2 *Weave in 3 or 4 strips of cardboard with plain weave before beginning the actual weaving. This separates the warps and gives a firm base for weaving.*

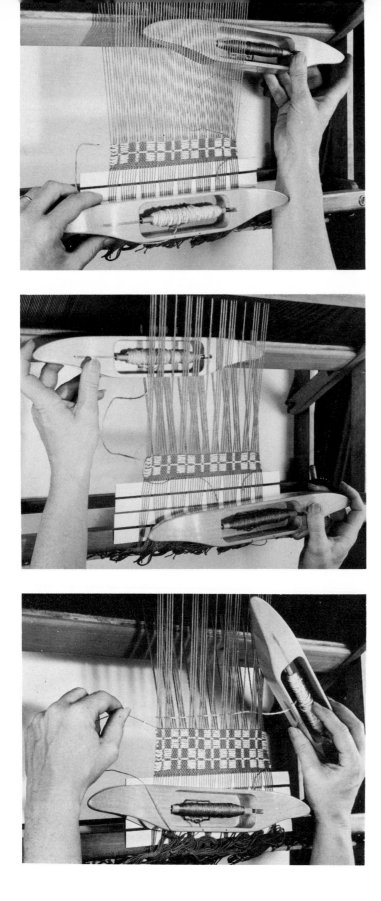

3 Begin to weave. In this example a few rows of tabby were woven in first to strengthen the edge; then the pattern was begun, each pattern shot alternating with a tabby shot. The tabby and the pattern weft each has its own shuttle. The tabby and pattern shots are always made in the same direction. In the illustration, the pattern shot has just been made, and the tabby shot is being thrown through its shed.

4 Beginning the pattern shot. Notice that the shuttle not being used is held at the front of the loom.

5 Ending the pattern shot. Notice that the pattern weft is crossed over the tabby weft at the selvedge. This serves to catch the pattern thread. If it were not held by the tabby, as in this example, it would have to be caught on the selvedge to prevent its being pulled out (in weaving where no tabby is used).

6 *Beating is done by pulling the reed firmly against the woven fabric both before and after each pattern shot.*

7 *Change the shed according to the treadling pattern. Notice that harnesses 2 and 4 are being raised together for a tabby shot.*

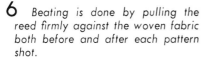

8 *As the weaving progresses, a rhythmic pattern develops. Shoot the weft, beat, change the shed, beat, shoot the weft, beat, and so forth.*

9 *Should either shuttle run out of yarn during the weaving, begin a new weft by starting on the edge, leaving a short tail.*

10 Change the shed for the next shot and pull the tail into the new shed. Pull a short length of it out of the warp, on top of the weaving. Continue to weave with the newly added weft.

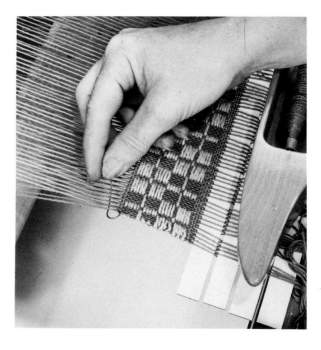

11 After a few rows have been woven, the end of the newly added weft that has been left on top of the weaving may be clipped off close to the cloth with scissors. A new weft can be started in the center as well as on the edge. Overlap the last of the old weft over a few warps. The tails of both old and new weft can be either pulled out the top of the weaving and clipped (as in the above example) or pushed out under the warp and clipped when the fabric is removed from the loom.

12 The space occupied by the fabric grows as the weaving progresses. In order to keep ample space for the weaving process, the fabric must be wound onto the cloth beam at regular intervals. Release the catches of both the warp and cloth beam, and roll the fabric onto the cloth beam. Shut the catch on the warp beam and roll the cloth beam until the warp is again in proper tension, then shut the catch on the cloth beam.

13 Continue weaving until the fabric is complete. If the warp has not been used up, the woven section can be left rolled on the cloth beam until all the warp is used. Or it may be cut from the loom in front of the reed, and the warp ends retied to the cloth beam.

14 If the weaving must be left on the loom between weaving periods, the warp and the woven fabric should be covered with a cloth to keep them clean from dust and dirt. Always release the tension on the warp between weaving periods, since warp kept in tension will loose its elasticity.

TAPESTRY WEAVING

Tapestry weaving is a variant of plain weave. Any kind of loom can be used. The warp is usually set up for plain weave or twill. The weft is woven loosely over the warp, so that when it is beaten into the fell the warp will be entirely covered. Any fine strong warp is suitable, but linen is preferred. The weft is usually of wool, but many other materials can be used. The design possibilities are greatly expanded over regular weaving techniques, for the woven areas are not bound to the vertical-horizontal pattern usually imposed by the warp-weft structure. Many colors, textures, and values can be combined in the same work with a surprising variety of shapes. Tapestry weave is used to make tapestries and rugs or to introduce pattern areas into any woven fabric.

1 Warp the loom for plain weave or twill.

2 Weave in three or four strips of cardboard to firm the edge of the weaving. Weave a few rows of plain weave.

3 In this illustration stripes have been woven with plain weave. The weft was loosely inserted into the warp or bubbled (see step 11), and then beaten firmly between each shot. If the weft yarn is too fine to cover the warp satisfactorily it may be doubled; that is, two strands of weft may be woven together. Use a separate shuttle for each color. Make color changes by introducing the new weft as in step 11, Weaving on the Table Loom (page 196). Weave back and forth with each color until the stripe reaches the desired width, then change wefts for the next stripe.

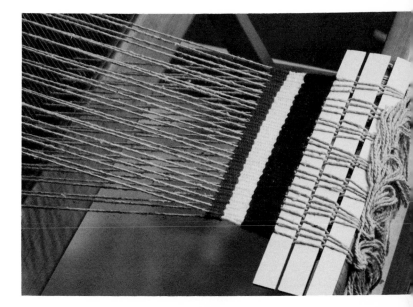

4 In this illustration, the weaver has made vertical stripes by weaving two colors of weft on alternate sheds. The first shed was made and shot with the first color of the weft. Then this shuttle was put aside, the next shed made, and a shot of the second color thrown. The second weft was then put aside; and the next shed was made and shot with the first color. This process was continued until the desired width was reached. Beat firmly between shots. To alternate the colors of the stripes, as was done in the last woven section on the loom, simply reverse the order of the weft colors.

5 In this section four pattern areas have been made. Four shuttles were used, one for each area. On each shed one row of weft was woven into the warp for each area. The two areas on the left have been joined by interlocking the wefts at the end of the shot. The weft threads come together from opposite directions, and before they are put through the next shed they are looped around one another. The weaver can also make a joint by passing the two wefts around the same warp thread before they are returned through the warp in opposite directions in the next shed.

6 The two areas on the right have not been interlocked. The two wefts are returned after each shot without looping around each other or around the same warp thread. This leaves a slit in the weave, which can be used to make obvious divisions in the pattern. If slits are used to define shapes they should not be made too long because they will weaken the structure of the material.

7 Weaving a diagonal with two wefts. One row of each pattern area has been woven in each shed. Simply move each weft yarn one or two warp threads to the right or left on each shot when they come together.

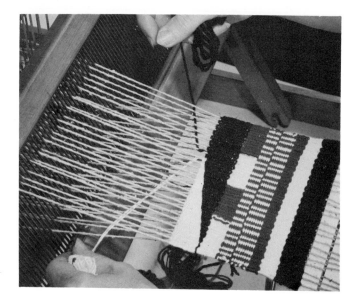

8 *In this illustration, a curved area is being started. Notice that two wefts are being used. Start the wefts by leaving a projecting tail, which will be clipped after a few rows have been woven. The wefts are not wound on shuttles, but have been looped and loosely tied, since only a small amount is to be used.*

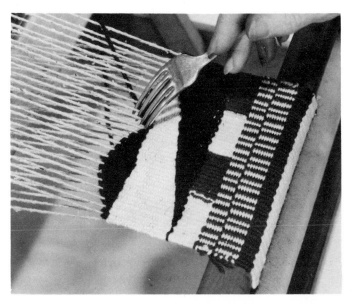

9 *The pattern areas are developed, following a curved outline. Since the irregular shape makes it difficult to build both the pattern and the background at the same time, the beating must be done on the woven areas as they are separately made. A fork serves as a beater.*

10 *The background areas are filled in. The shape behind the previously made pattern area required two separate wefts because of its irregularity. The wefts can be discontinued, and only one used to fill in the remaining space.*

11 *Bubbling the weft. The weft is shot loosely and then bubbled so that when it is beaten with the reed it will be loose enough to cover the warp completely.*

GAUZE OR LENO WEAVING

In gauze weaves the warp threads are twisted around the weft as it is woven into the fabric. In leno weaves, which are decorative variants of the gauze technique, several warp threads are twisted together to create pattern.

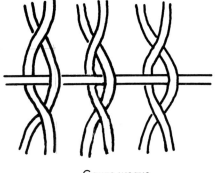

Gauze weave.

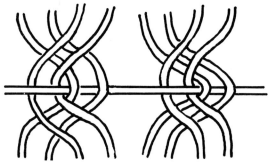

Leno weave.

1 Set up the loom for plain weave.

2 Weave a few rows of plain weave to firm up the edge.

3 Make a sampler of different gauze and leno patterns. Try combinations of plain weave, twisted weft, gauze, and leno for a variety of design effects. The open areas in weaving produced with these techniques can be combined with plain weave for decorative accent. Areas of plain weave can be alternated with open weaving for contrast of positive and negative space.

RUG KNOTTING

Rugs composed of knotted fringe can be made on any warped loom or on a special rug canvas obtained from commercial sources. Pieces of yarn are cut 2 to 4 inches or longer, depending upon the desired length of the finished pile. These strips of yarn are looped around the warp, or attached to the rug canvas with a special hook.

MATERIALS

1. Loom, warp or rug canvas, and hooker
2. Scissors
3. Yarns

KNOTTING A RUG ON A WARP

1 *Plan the design.*

2 *Warp the loom.*

3 *First weave a section with a tabby weave.*

4 *Cut pieces of yarn the desired length for the pile.*

5 *To make a knot, lay one of the pieces of yarn over two of the warps.*

6 *Pull the two ends of the yarn up between the warps.*

In the traditional rug-knotting techniques done on warps, several rows of tabby weave are put in first, after which several rows of knots are tied over the warp threads. The knots are tied to alternate warps, every other row.

The looms used may be the cardboard, wood board, frame, box, or any of the mechanical table or floor looms.

7 Tighten the knot by pulling the ends firmly so that the knot is formed and the two warps are pulled together. Pull the knot against the previously woven or knotted section.

8 To prevent slits in the weaving, alternate the warps in every other row, using one from each of the knots in the previous row.

9 Tie several rows of knots.

10 Weave a section of tabby weave between sections of knots. Five rows of knots and five rows of tabby make a good thick pile.

11 Starting another row of knots.

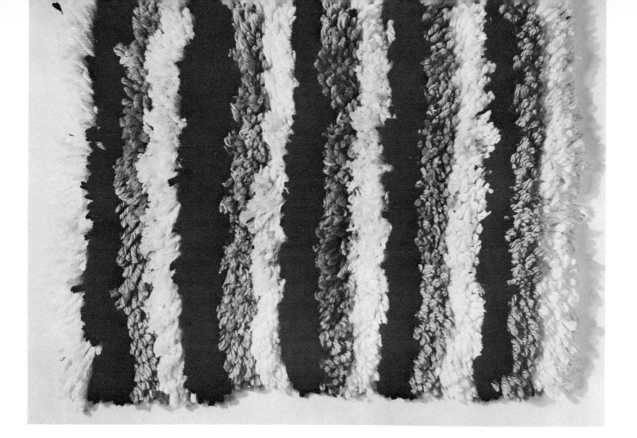

12 *The finished rug.*

MAKING RUGS ON RUG CANVAS

In rugs made on a rug canvas the pieces of yarn are secured to the material by means of a special hook available from commercial sources.

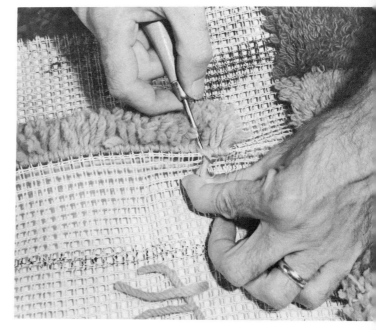

ADDITIONAL SUGGESTIONS FOR WEAVING

Essential to a weaving program is the search for and the procurement of the raw materials. These may be purchased, but often the immediate environment will yield many weaving materials. Children should be encouraged to look at home and elsewhere for scraps of colored yarns left over from knitting or unraveled from old sweaters, candlewick, fine and coarse string, cord, tape, narrow ribbon, raffia, cardboard and paper to be cut into strips, and cloth that can be torn in strips and dyed if necessary. Old gunny sacks can be washed and unraveled, and the threads dyed in beautiful colors for making bags and mats.

Natural sources should also be included in the gathering of materials. Children can look individually, or a class can make a trip as a group to search for materials. Various reeds, stems of flowers and plants, bamboo shoots, rushes, cattails, and other grasses might be found in the back yard, a vacant lot, woodsy areas, and by a river or marsh.

Both children and adults can profit greatly by starting to weave with paper strips, for the principle of weaving can readily be shown and explained. They can become involved almost immediately in the process, and experience the excitement of seeing the pattern of color and shape develop from the interplay of warp and weft. For young children, accurate measurement in weaving with paper is not necessary, and the standards for constructing the strips depend on the motor abilities of the age level. Free cutting without previous mechanical measuring is valuable training. A ruler may be placed on the paper along the edge where the warp or weft is to be cut, and marked with a pencil. Using the ruler as a measurement, the child can move it along and use its width for the space between lines. Never let anything become too tedious for children, however.

Older children will want to measure their strips with more precision and will find this good practice in using a ruler. Methods for cutting paper warps are explained on page 136. In order to study the effects of color and dark-light contrast, the weaver may weave several rows of one color, then several rows of another, continuing with additional colors until the end of the warp is reached. This is really a sampler, for it enables the weaver to try out various ideas from which to make a selection. He can also plan a pattern of stripes with the grouped colors. In fact, paper weaving can be used to plan design and subject matter to be woven with other materials.

Young children should work with materials that are large and coarse to avoid difficulty in handling. In addition to wide paper strips, these materials can include cotton roving, heavy rug yarns or four-ply wool, tape, ribbon, and large reeds. If felt strips are available children can work on a frame type of loom to weave colorful mats. The strips can be kept from pulling out of the finished mat if they are secured on the edge with stitching.

Child Weaving on Small Mechanical Loom. From *Our Expanding Vision*, by Fearing, Martin, and Beard. Courtesy, W. S. Benson and Co.

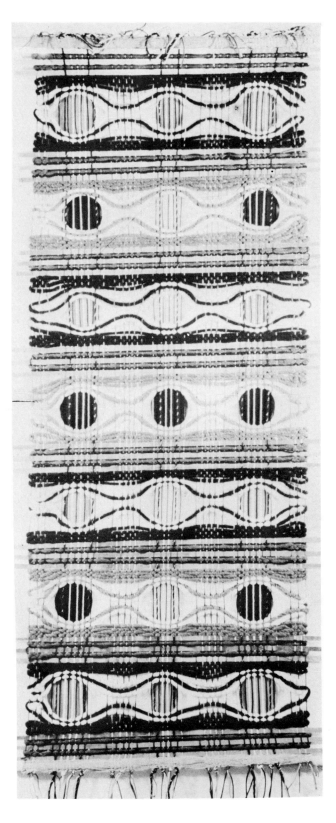

Wall Hanging. Plastic disks combined with heavy wrapping cord and yarn. Woven by 5th grade boy. From *Our Expanding Vision*, by Fearing, Martin, and Beard. Courtesy, W. S. Benson and Co.

It is advisable for students to make their own small looms whenever possible. Even young children can make and warp looms of cardboard and boxes. They may, of course, need assistance in measuring the space for slots, pins, or nails, and in using a hammer.

Very young children can start with simple over-under weaving, with which they can make little mats, bags, pot holders, and doll blankets. These can be planned with patterns of stripes. Older children will be interested in the rigid heddle loom made of tongue depressors, on which they can weave strips for belts, ties, purses, and scarves. Rug weaving, either plain weave or knotted, can be done on box or frame looms. The shed stick and string heddle rod can be introduced to facilitate the weaving process.

Although all weaving processes can be experienced at any age, some have special educational value at particular times. Children of adolescent age are intrigued by the inkle and Hungarian looms. They also find more complex finger weaving challenging. These students should have an opportunity to weave on table or floor looms also and to try various patterns. After first having the experience of creating on the loom, they can assist in the process of preparing and threading the warp.

The teacher needs to learn how to warp a loom and have it ready for use. When younger children are taught to weave on mechanical looms they can be shown how the warping is done even though they do not take part in the actual process. In all weaving, the teacher should first try out the process in order to discover any difficulties and pitfalls involved.

Mat Woven on Cardboard. Child age 6.

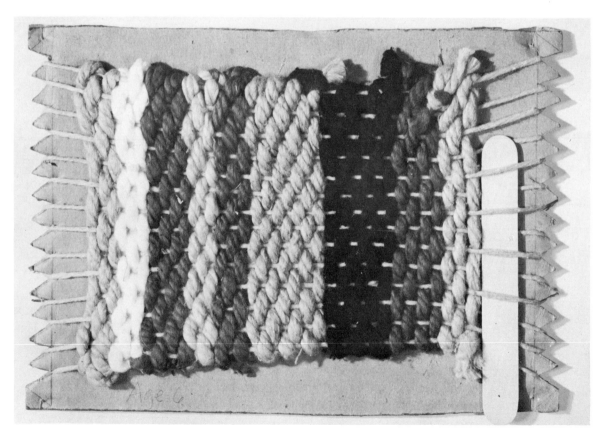

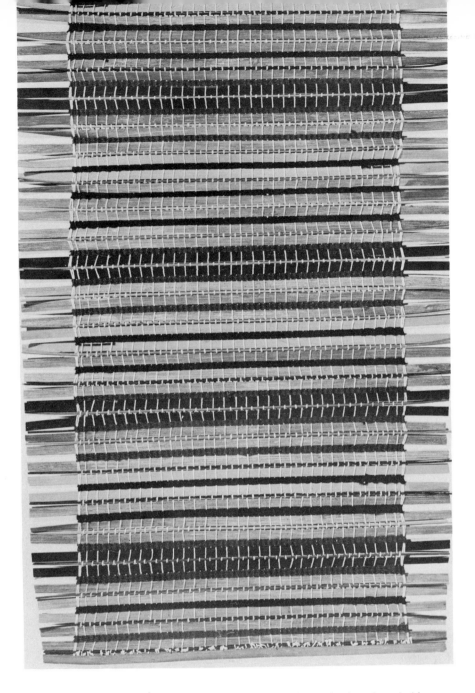

Table Runner. 1957. Woven strips of painted or stained reeds and pith combined with heavy crochet-type colored yarns on simple lap loom. High school student, Nancy Belfer, Instructor. Courtesy, *School Arts* Magazine.

DECORATED TEXTILES

Early American, Mrs. Caswell: *Caswell Carpet*. 1835. Homegrown dyed and spun wool worked with a chain stitch through coarse foundation fabric. 144" x 162". Present owner, Metropolitan Museum of Art, American Wing. Courtesy of the National Gallery of Art, Index of American Design.

DECORATED TEXTILES

Textile design accomplished in the weaving process is called *structural design* because the decorative design units are a fundamental part of the structure of the cloth. *Applied design,* another broad area of textile design, is perhaps as ancient in origin as weaving itself. Early designers discovered many methods of treating the surface of their woven fabrics to enhance their appearance with symbols and decorative motifs. These methods include embroidery, appliqué, printing, stenciling, painting, batik, and tie-dyeing.

STITCHERY OR EMBROIDERY

Stitchery has always played an important role in fabric design. Even before cloth was invented men probably used sewing to fasten hides together. Most weaving techniques produced widths of cloth that required several pieces to be stitched together for garment manufacture. This led quite naturally to decorative embellishment. Each culture and each period has produced individual stitchery techniques. Some motifs and pattern arrangements have become traditional for many parts of the world. There are hundreds of basic stitches and their variations, many of which are described in this book.

In addition to being used to decorate clothing and other useful items, stitchery has also been used to make monumental works of art. An example of this is the *Bayeux Tapestry,* sometimes called *Queen Mathilde's Tapestry* after the good queen, who, according to legend, designed and stitched it. It is known as a tapestry not because of its technique but because it was designed to hang on a wall. The tapestry depicts scenes of the Norman Conquest. Over its lively surface men, horses, and ships carry out an epic task. Equestrian soldiers do battle amid flying banners, men and horses cross the English Channel crowded into ships, councils are held, and even Halley's comet makes an appearance. These many details are lovingly portrayed and so well organized that, in spite of the many activities, a strong sense of order prevails. Repetition of line, shape, and color unifies the whole; negative shapes are beautifully planned and related to adjacent solids; groups of figures and animals are worked together to become pattern areas. This work is one of the art treasures of the world.

APPLIQUÉ

Appliqué is made by stitching cut-out shapes of cloth and other material to a cloth backing. Primitive artisans decorated their fabrics with appliqué design, sewing on pieces of leather, metal, feathers, stones, and many other materials. Craftsmen in India enjoyed creating patterns by stitching small mica discs, which reflect the light like mirrors, firmly around the edges to attach them to the cloth. American Indians appliquéd animal hooves and metal plates to their garments so that they would rattle or clang with the wearer's movements. In medieval times banners and flags and the caparisons for knights

French: *Bayeux Tapestry, Halley's Comet (They Look at the Star)*. Eleventh century. Embroidery. Cathedral Museum, Bayeux, France.

Bayeux Tapestry, The Norman Fleet Crossing the Channel.

Bayeux Tapestry, The Battle of Hastings.

India: *Costume* and *Detail of Costume*. Embroidery. Courtesy, Elizabeth Bayley Willis.

Peruvian, South Coastal, early Nazca near Pisco: *Detail of a Mantle*. Before 1000 A.D. Woolen yarns embroidered in stem stitch on woolen cloth. 98¾" x 35⅜". Courtesy of The Museum of Fine Arts, Boston.

Mexican, Yucatan: *Decorated Dress Yoke*. Twentieth century. Cotton with machine-stitched decoration. Decorated area, 4" x 9½" x 14".

India, Manipur State: *Manipur Naga Chaddar* (Cloak). Pattern of elephants, flowers, butterflies, plates, and spoons. Twentieth century. Embroidered cotton. 4' x 6'6". Courtesy of Mr. and Mrs. Elmer Kutila.

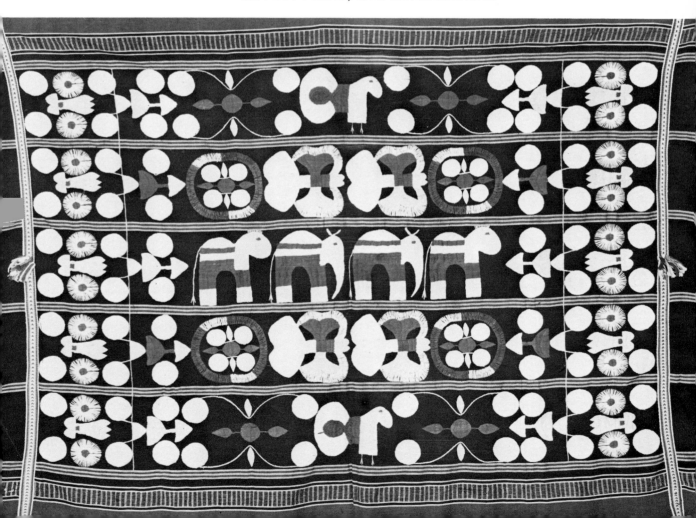

Pacific Islands, Polynesian: *Tapa Cloth.*
Design stamped on cloth made from
bark. Courtesy, School of Art, University of Washington.

Jean Laury: *Appliqué on Cloth.*

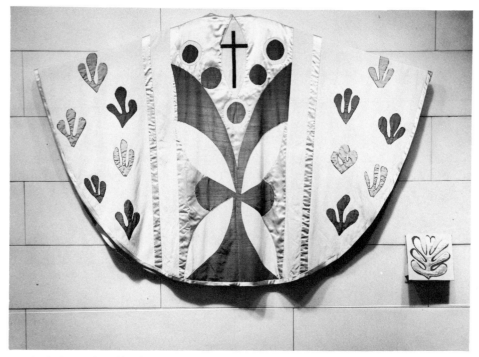

Henri Matisse: *Chasuble* (back). White silk with yellow and green satin
appliqué. 78½" x 49". Collection Museum of Modern Art.

India: *Textile Detail with Borders of Animals.* Twentieth century. Designs stamped on cloth. Courtesy, Elizabeth Bayley Willis.

India: *Textile Detail.* Twentieth century. Design stamped on cloth. Courtesy, Elizabeth Bayley Willis.

India: *Wooden Stamp for Printing Textiles.* Courtesy, Elizabeth Bayley Willis.

French (Probably Manufacture de Jouy): *Detail of Printed and Painted Fabric.* Late eighteenth century. Block-printed and painted cotton, detail of piece 31⅛" x 11⅝". Courtesy of The Museum of Fine Arts, Boston.

and horses were decorated with appliqué. Colonial America developed appliqué patterns—many of which have become traditional—for quilts, bedspreads, clothing, and household items. Some of these patterns were as random as the patchwork quilt; others were complex in design.

PRINTING

Printing is a method of applying design to the surface of fabric by means of a design cut from a block. The block is shaped or cut, inked, and pressed on the cloth. Once a block is made, it can be used over and over again on the same fabric to make a repeat pattern. This is the process used by the Polynesian peoples to decorate their *tapa cloths*. Traditionally, the men carve the pattern blocks from wooden planks, and the women print the cloth from these blocks; and Polynesian maidens print lengths of tapa just as Western brides-to-be work stitchery designs into materials for their hope chests. Usually the designs are geometric, and some deviation from a regular repeat is almost always present. The fabric for the tapa is not woven but pounded from fibers of mulberry bark.

Printing cloth is an ancient art, used in the Mediterranean area since early Christian times. India became famous for block-printed fabrics, and Europe imported great quantities of Indian hand-printed stuffs such as calicos and chintzes. Indian craftsmen employed cut-wood blocks to stamp the designs, using a variety of animal, plant, human, and geometric motifs. Many of these motifs have found their way into European folk art and contemporary commercial fabrics. Blocks for printing fabrics can be made of wood, linoleum, and rubber; even vegetables such as potatoes and carrots make excellent stamps for small quantities of material.

STENCIL

Stone Age artists used the stencil technique on the walls of their caves. A hand was pressed

Japanese: *Kimono Fragment*. c. 1750. Gold figured and silk embroidery on silk. 26″ high. Seattle Art Museum, Eugene Fuller Memorial Collection.

American: *Child's Coverlet.* Nineteenth century. Cotton with appliquéd cherry branches and fruit motifs of red, green, tan, and violet silk on white. 5'2" x 3'6". Courtesy, The Brooklyn Museum.

American: *Quilt, Star of Bethlehem,* or *Rising Sun.* Nineteenth century. Cotton, red, green, and brown pieced star with floral appliqués and border of glazed chintz. Courtesy, The Brooklyn Museum.

San Blas Indians: *Front Part of a Mola, or Shirt. Man and Fish, Probably a Reference to Jonah and the Whale.* Twentieth century. Combination of appliqué and cutout. Courtesy of the Delacorte Gallery, New York.

Katherine Westphal: *Textile Design*. 1956. Batik on cotton batiste, yellow, green, white, and black.

against the wall and powdered pigment blown against it. When the hand was removed, a negative impression resulted. Stenciling has long been used to ornament fabric with design and subject matter. The stencil can be made in one of two ways. Either the color is applied through an opening cut into the stencil, or the color is applied around it. Japanese designers have made very elaborate stencils by holding complicated designs together with a framework of human hairs. The hairs are fine enough not to affect the stenciled design but strong enough to support the intricate cut-out shapes, which would not remain intact without this delicate reinforcement. Contemporary designers prefer stencils supported on a silk screen. The silk-screen process, which has also become a popular medium for printmakers, permits a wide range of texture and shape, and a great freedom of design. In any stencil process, many stencils may be necessary to complete one design. Usually a separate stencil is used for each color.

BATIK AND TIE-DYEING

Just as yarn can be dyed before it is woven, so the finished fabric can be dyed to create pattern and design. In the *batik* method, long associated with the textile arts of India and Java, the design is painted or drawn on the fabric with wax, and then the fabric is dipped in dye; the waxed areas are protected from the dye and receive no color. For complex designs many applications of wax and dye are necessary. When the dyeing is complete, the wax is removed from the fabric by boiling it in water. The wax can also be applied with stamps cut from wood blocks. Other dyeing techniques include tie-dyeing and fold-dyeing. In tie-dyeing the fabric is knotted or small areas of fabric are pushed into tentlike shapes that are tightly bound with thread. When the fabric is dyed, the tied areas do not take the color; this process produces a pattern.

India: *Textile Design*. Twentieth century. Tie dye on cloth. Courtesy, Elizabeth Bayley Willis.

Above: Peruvian, Central Coast (Ancon Region): *Painted Cotton Textile*. Fifteenth–sixteenth century. Cotton. 23″. M. H. deYoung Memorial Museum, San Francisco. *Below:* Japanese: *Stencil of Broom Straw Grass and Flowers*. Eighteenth–nineteenth century. Mulberry paper, 14³/₄″ x 20″. Seattle Art Museum, Eugene Fuller Memorial Collection.

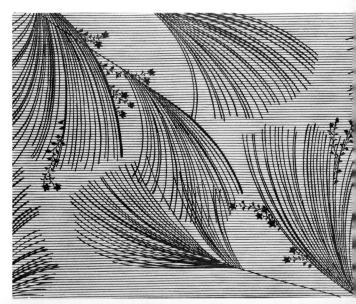

DECORATING TEXTILES

BLOCK PRINTING

The artist may transfer designs to cloth by printing from stamps made from inked blocks of wood or linoleum. Other materials may also be used for stamps. (See Decorated Papers.) Any linoleum may be used that does not chip when cut; however, plain brown "battleship" linoleum is the best. It may be left unmounted or it may be mounted on a piece of wood with glue or nails. Premounted linoleum blocks are also available.

The design is planned first and traced onto the block with carbon or traced around a cut-paper pattern. It may also be drawn directly on the block.

The cutting is done with a sharp knife, a razor blade, or gouges. Cut away the parts not to be printed. Before printing on the cloth, make trial plans for organizing the repeat by printing the block on paper. The design units can be printed close together so that the shapes touch or so that spaces are left between. Experiment by making a number of separate prints on individual sheets and grouping them in various arrangements; endless possibilities can be explored before the final organization is selected.

A work space for printing should be provided where the material to be printed can be spread out and kept clean. It is necessary to use a pad underneath the cloth; this pad can be prepared from blanket material or cloth such as flannel, folded several times. It can be protected with a piece of unbleached muslin on top. If cloth is not available a pad can be made with a stack of newspapers. The material to be printed should not have too slick a surface. Cottons and wools are excellent. The fabric is placed in position over the pad and held taut by means of thumbtacks or tape. The places where the block is to be stamped are marked lightly with a pencil line or dots.

The block should be evenly inked for printing, placed face down on the cloth, and pressed with the hands or tapped with a mallet. If printing is done on the floor, the artist may print the block by standing on it and rocking back and forth slightly so that all the edges are printed.

MATERIALS

1. Fabric on which to print
2. Padding under cloth—blanket material, flannel, or newspapers
3. Stamping material—linoleum, wood, or other suitable stamps
4. Cutting tools—knife, razor blade, or gouges
5. Printing media—oil-based printer's ink, textile-printing ink, oil paint, brayer; a hard, smooth surface for the ink such as glass, tin, marble, or a linoleum tile

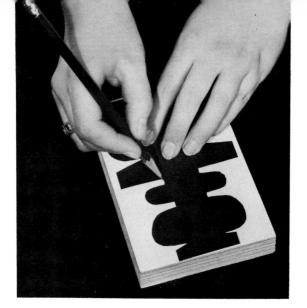

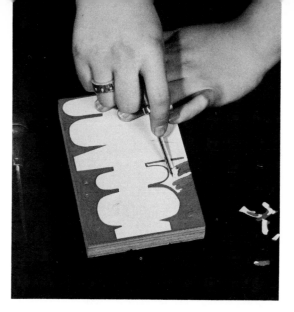

1 Plan a design with pencil, charcoal, paint, pen and ink, or cut paper.

2 Transfer the design to the linoleum block by drawing around a cut-paper pattern.

3 Outline the shape by cutting around it with a small gouge. Remove the areas not to be printed, by using a wider gouge or knife.

4 Squeeze a dab of ink from a tube on a hard, smooth surface. Roll the ink with a brayer until it is evenly spread and no longer sticky.

5 Roll the ink on the linoleum block with the brayer. Wipe off any excess ink where it touches the background, using a piece of cloth or crumpled paper towel, unless these accidental markings are desired as part of the design.

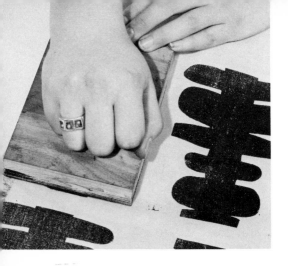

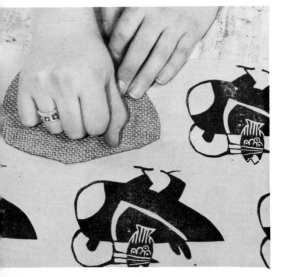

6 To print, place the cloth on the prepared padding and stretch tightly. Secure with thumbtacks or tape.

7 Plan the spacing on the fabric and lightly mark with lines or dots. Lay the inked block carefully in position, following the guide marks. Apply pressure with the hands on all parts including the edges, or tap with a mallet.

8 When unmounted linoleum is used for printing, the excess edges that might be accidentally inked can be trimmed off with heavy shears or tin snips.

9 Two variations of spacing. When grouped closely, the block prints form a pattern of vertical lines. The dark-light balance and the shapes of the spaces between are important considerations.

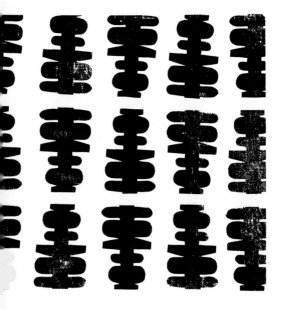

SILK-SCREEN PRINTING

Silk-screen printing is a technique for printing stencil designs. A stencil pattern is applied to and supported by the screen. Colored paint or ink is forced through the screen with a squeegee onto the surface to be decorated. The screen is moved as the process is repeated.

FRAMES

Silk-screen frames may vary in size and can be made of wood or cardboard. The screen coverings can be coarse or fine and are usually made of silk; however, nylon, nylon hosiery, organdy, or other net fabrics may be used. The screen fabric is stretched and fastened over a frame to create a taut surface through which the design is printed. 10XX silk is recommended for general printing. Finer screens tend to clog more easily.

SQUEEGEE

The squeegee is a length or strip of rubber attached to a wooden handle; it is used to force the ink through the silk. A squeegee length can be purchased by the inch and should be just long enough to fit inside the printing frame. Widths vary, and a narrow width, 2½ to 4 inches, is preferable for a small printing frame. Nails or dowels may be placed on each end of the squeegee to allow it to be supported by the frame when not in use. Window-washing squeegees and heavy cardboard may also be used to press the color through the stencil.

STENCILS

The stencil can be applied to the screen in a variety of ways, depending on the printing medium to be used and the number of times it is to be used. Oil-based colors require stencils that can withstand the ink or paint and the solvents required to clean them from the screen. Lacquer films can be used with oil-based inks and also with water-based colors. Lacquer film makes a more permanent stencil, which can be used and cleaned a number of times.

Stencils to be used for one run on one color may be of temporary material such as tracing paper, wax paper, newsprint, and typing paper; these materials are usually more successful with oil-based paint.

Water-based inks can also be used with paper stencils, crayon, gummed tape, or stickers. Crayon stencils, excellent for water-based colors, may be easily repaired as parts of the stencil wear away during printing.

A permanent stencil may be made with house paint or with spray-can paints or lacquers that can be sprayed over a paper or cardboard cut-out pattern, to create the stencil on the screen when the paper is removed.

INKS

Special serigraph inks and textile-printing colors are available with either oil or water bases. Oil-based colors require special solvents for dilution and cleaning. Water-based colors are easily diluted with water and can be cleaned from the screen with cool water, soap, and a brush if needed. Colors are opaque when used thick, and transparent when thinned. Follow the directions on the containers to obtain the desired color quality. Colors may be printed over one another when the first color is dry. It is usually advisable to print the light colors first.

FABRICS

Printing can be done on any fabric that will accept the textile color. Sized fabrics such as muslin should be washed and pressed before being used. If sized fabrics are not washed before they are printed, the filler washes out, taking the color with it.

THE WORKING AREA

The fabric ground must be secured to a padded working surface. Commercial printing surfaces have extended metal clamps that hold the fabric in place and provide straightedges against which to operate the screens. Additional adjustable straightedges provide further support. The beginner can pad a piece of building board or the top of a work table and secure the fabric over this with C-clamps, thumbtacks, or pins. Old cotton blankets, flannel, or a pad of newspapers may be used for padding.

It is important to organize the work area to avoid accidents of spilled ink. Printing supplies can be conveniently placed on a tray or in a pan so that they may be moved around.

Paint or ink can be dispensed with a spatula or tongue depressor. Care should be taken to provide a clean area to place the screen if it is necessary to remove it from the printing surface. Spots of excess ink on the bottom of the screen can damage the printing.

THE SCREEN

A small screen is useful for printing patterned fabrics. It is easily maneuvered for printing, and easily cleaned. Silk may be stretched on a heavy cardboard frame and shellacked, or a wooden frame can be used. An embroidery hoop provides a sturdy frame on which the screen may be quickly stretched into place. Small wooden frames can be purchased or simply constructed.

MATERIALS

1. Hammer
2. Corrugated joint fasteners
3. Two pieces of wood (1 × 1 inch—9 inches with mitered corners)
4. Two pieces of wood (1 × 1 inch—12 inches with mitered corners)
5. Silk-screen fabric: 10XX silk is recommended or nylon, nylon stocking, netting, organdy
6. Stapler
7. Staples
8. Brown paper tape (2-inch width)
9. Shellac
10. Brush
11. Squeegee (2½ to 4 inches—cut to 6 inches long) or window squeegee or very heavy chipboard

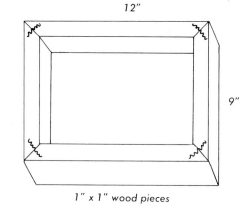

12"

9"

1" x 1" wood pieces

TO MAKE A WOODEN SILK-SCREEN FRAME

1 Assemble the frame according to the diagram.

2 Stretch the silk on the screen frame with staples. The silk must be stretched smooth and taut. To keep it even, begin at the center of one side, staple, pull the silk taut, and staple again at the center of the opposite side. Repeat the process on each end of the frame. Then gradually move from the centers to the corners of the frame, pulling and stapling the silk until the frame is covered.

3 Seal the inside edges of the screen frame with strips of gummed kraft paper tape. The tape should be folded so that half of it attaches to the frame and half to the screen fabric, forming a 1-inch mask around the edge. This prevents the color from getting between the under side of the frame and the screen, where it would spoil the printing. Reverse the frame and cover the back with strips of gummed tape, so that a 1-inch mask is formed to match the one on the top of the screen.

4 Shellac or lacquer the frame, covering the paper tape so that the shellac extends just slightly beyond the tape onto the silk. This prevents the ink from seeping under the tape.

5 Allow the shellac to dry thoroughly before printing.

CLEANING THE SCREEN

The screen is cleaned according to the type of color used for printing. Oil-based colors must be cleaned with solvents. After printing, remove the excess color from the screen with the squeegee and a rubber spatula. Press the solvent through the screen onto clean newspapers, and repeat the process until the screen is free of all color particles. The final cleaning may be done with soap and water if necessary. Hold the screen up to the light to see if any meshes are still filled. Remove any clogged areas that develop during printing, by rubbing the screen with a small cloth soaked in solvent. If the clogging cannot be removed while the screen is held vertically, it must be placed flat and rubbed against a newspaper-covered surface. Care must be taken to keep the bottom of the screen free of any excess paint, which will damage the design during printing.

Water-based colors can be removed from a screen with cool water. Stubborn spots may be treated with soap or detergent and scrubbed lightly with a small brush. Clogged areas that develop during the printing process can be rubbed with a damp cloth. A sustained sequence and order of printing, once a color run is begun, helps prevent clogged screens.

MATERIALS

1. Screen with stencil
2. Squeegee
3. Fabric
4. Padded work area
5. Newspapers
6. Tacks, pins, or clamps
7. Water-based textile color
8. Spatula or tongue depressor
9. Tray or pan
10. Water, soap, and brush if necessary

TO PREPARE TO PRINT

1 Stretch and fasten the fabric to be printed to the work surface with pins, tacks, or clamps.

2 Protect surrounding areas with newspaper.

3 Arrange the printing materials in a tray or pan so that they can be moved quickly and easily without soiling working area or fabric.

4 Put the stencil on the screen.

DESIGN WITH GUMMED STICKERS

Gummed stickers and pieces punched from gummed labels may be arranged in rows or patterns to make stencil designs.

MATERIALS

1. Screen
2. Masking tape
3. Gummed stickers, reinforcements, labels, and notary seals
4. Paper punch

1 Mask off the design area with masking tape. The area of the silk left uncovered will provide the area in which to plan the design.

2 Arrange a design of stickers on the bottom of the screen.

3 Print an allover pattern by placing the screen so that the design areas are adjacent. To prepare to print, put the screen in place on the fabric and spread about 1/3 cup of color along one end of the screen with a spatula. To print, pull the squeegee across the screen with even pressure. This forces the pigment through the stencil onto the fabric.

4 Clean the screen with cool water.

5 Heat set the fabric according to the directions given on the label of the color. The artist can set some colors by pressing them with a hot iron for four or five minutes, or by wrapping the printed fabric in foil and placing it in a warm oven.

DESIGN WITH CRAYON

Crayon may also be used to draw the stencil on the screen.

MATERIALS

1. Screen
2. Crayon

1 Plan the design on paper.

2 Lay the screen in place over paper; trace the design on the screen with crayon. With the crayon, fill the screen meshes solid in the areas not to be printed.

3 Print the design so that an allover pattern is formed.

4· To clean the screen and squeegee, wash them with cool water. The crayon design may be removed from the silk with soap and a brush, or dissolved with a solvent and rubbed with a cloth or brush.

5 Heat set the fabric as previously explained.

DESIGN WITH STENCIL PAPER

Designs may be cut from stencil paper and attached to the screen with tape.

MATERIALS

1. Silk-screen stencil paper
2. Stencil knife
3. Pencil
4. Tape

1 Plan the design.

2 To transfer the design to the stencil paper, cut a piece of stencil paper the size of the screen. Lay the paper over the plan, so that the design is centered, and draw and cut the design with a stencil knife.

3 Tape the stencil paper to the bottom of the screen.

4 Print in an allover pattern.

5 To clean the screen, remove the stencil and wash the silk.

6 Heat set the fabric according to directions accompanying the color.

LACQUER-FILM STENCIL

Stencils that withstand a number of printings and that may be used with either oil- or water-based colors can be cut from lacquer film. Lacquer film adheres to the screen with a special fluid, purchased with the film.

MATERIALS

1. Screen
2. Lacquer film
3. Adhering fluid
4. Block-out lacquer, brush
5. Stencil knife
6. Newspaper
7. Cloth
8. Lacquer thinner

1 Make an accurate drawing of the design on the film. The film should cover the bottom of the screen.

2 Cut the lacquer-film stencil. To cut, cut only the top film layer, and carefully peel the parts away.

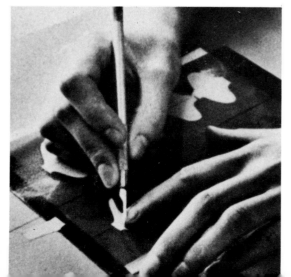

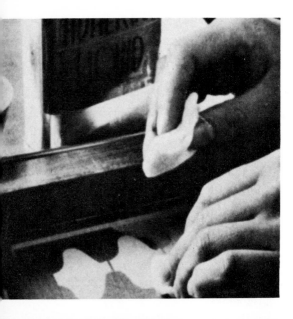

3 To make the stencil adhere to the bottom of the screen, place the stencil, paper side down, on a newspaper-covered working surface. Lay the screen, bottom down, in place over the stencil. Rub the silk with adhering fluid until the stencil sticks to the silk. Areas that wear during printing may be repaired with block-out lacquer and a brush.

4 Turn the screen over and carefully pull the paper backing from the lacquer film.

5 Measure and mark off registration for printing an allover repeat pattern on the stretched fabric.

6 Pour about 1/3 cup of water-based textile color onto one end of the screen.

7 Print the first color run.

8 Wash the screen and squeegee in cool water. Do not remove the stencil.

9 Print additional colors required for the design.

10 Clean the screen with water. The stencil may be removed with lacquer thinner.

11 Heat set the fabric according to the directions on the label of the color.

STITCHERY

Stitchery or embroidery is made with yarns and similar materials stitched on any cloth that will provide a base for holding stitches. Successful stitchery is accomplished when a relationship is established between the design and the stitching process.

The stitches presented herewith are simple traditional stitches. Their importance lies in their simplicity. They are easy to learn and easy to do; but through variation in placement and size of stitch, weight and color of thread or yarn, weave and texture of the base material, and thoughtful use of spacing, an infinite number of designs can be created. Scrap yarns and pieces of various lengths may be used in the design, as well as other materials: string, metallic cord, raffia, and narrow ribbon. These often add a variety not achieved through use of usual embroidery threads.

Beginners will find it helpful to make samplers using basic stitches singly and in combination. The combination of a good background knowledge of basic stitches and the attitude that new stitches are yet to be invented should help the student of stitchery to create constantly new and fresh designs. Sewing machines that can be adapted for a variety of stitches can be used in conjunction with hand stitches for stitchery and appliqué.

MATERIALS

1. Fabric on which to sew—any plain or textured fabric such as cotton, linen, or wool cloth, netting, burlap, felt, or canvas. The fabric may be heavy or light, depending on either desired visual effect, or ultimate use of the piece.
2. Material for stitches—cotton or wool yarns, string, mercerized embroidery cottons, thread, narrow ribbons, metallic cord.
3. Appliqué materials—buttons, beads, etc.
4. Needles
5. Scissors

FLAT STITCHES

1 *To make sample stitches preparatory to designing, use a coarse, loosely woven fabric such as burlap and a medium-weight yarn. Try a simple running stitch. Make variations by (a) making the stitches and spaces between them the same length; (b) making the stitches longer than the spaces between; (c) making the stitches shorter than the spaces between. When they are grouped, rows of stitches produce a compact effect. You can make patterns by grouping the stitches in evenly spaced rows, close together or far apart.*

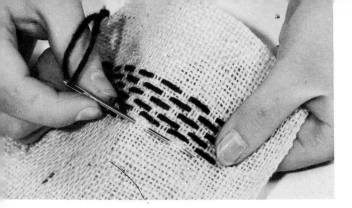

2 Stitches can be grouped in alternating rows.

3 Flat stitch. To begin the flat stitch, bring the needle and thread up through the fabric. Finish the first stitch and begin the next by bringing the needle up again adjacent to the beginning of the previous stitch. Repeat the process until a group of parallel stitches is made.

4 Satin stitch. The satin stitch is developed by use of flat stitches placed close together. This is a space-filling stitch. The tension of the thread should be kept as even as possible for a smooth, satiny texture. These stitches are known as flat stitches because they lie flat on the surface of the fabric. However, in the satin stitch, as in others, use of underpadding with back and forth running stitches, or even with additional heavy fabric sewn in the area to be covered by the satin stitch, can give three-dimensional quality to the traditional "flat" satin stitch.

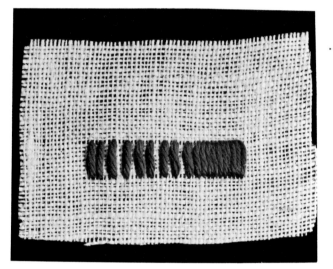

5 Bundle stitch. For the bundle stitch, three or more parallel stitches are caught and held in the middle by a fourth stitch to form a sheaf or bundle. To start the stitch, group three flat stitches as described in step 3. For the final or catch stitch, bring the needle up through the fabric at the center of the middle stitch. Pull the thread around the stitches and return the needle through the same place in the fabric. Tighten the thread to pull the centers into place. Repeat to produce a pattern.

6 Cross stitch. The cross stitch is a very useful space filler, widely used in folk embroideries. It has ranged in use from the comparatively coarse embroideries of Europe and Central and South America to the delicate petit point embroidery of the European courts.

When cross stitches are used as a space filler, the stitches must cross in a constant direction if precision is desired. To accomplish this, bring the needle up at the bottom left point of the cross. Put the needle down through the top right point of the cross and bring it up at the bottom left of the next cross. Continue working all the stitches in the same direction for this half of the cross. When these are complete, work all the top stitches in the opposite direction to complete the cross. This stitch may be made singly or in groups, and instead of all the stitches crossing in the same direction, the crosses may be formed at random for another kind of texture.

7 Herringbone stitch. The herringbone stitch is made very similarly to the single cross stitch. It is worked from left to right along a double line. Insert the needle from below the fabric at the lower left. Push it down at the upper right, bring it out again at the upper left, and stitch through again at the lower right. Bring up through the fabric to start the second stitch at a point to the left of the previous stitch. Continue across the fabric.

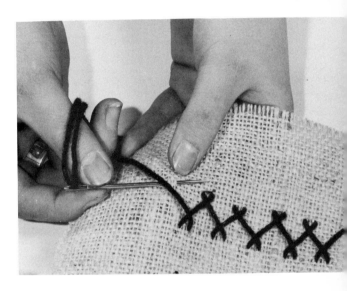

8 Back stitch. To make the back stitch, bring the thread up through the cloth, insert the needle down directly behind it and pull out again directly in front. For the next stitch, repeat the process with the needle inserted each time in the hole made directly behind. This is a good line stitch. The length of the first stitch determines the length of the second, and so on.

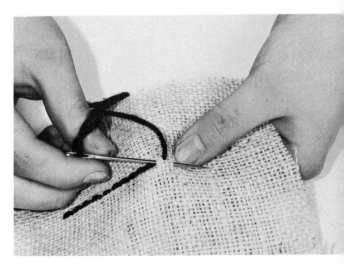

DECORATED TEXTILES 233

9 Outline stitch (also known as the overcast or whip stitch). *Visualize a line and make a stitch to overcast the line, moving from left to right.*

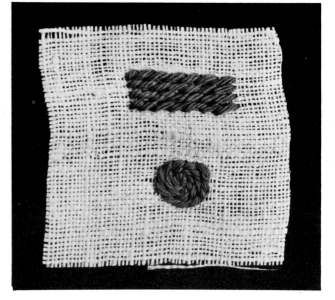

10 Padded outline stitch. *A padded outline stitch is just as described in the directions for the outline stitch, except that instead of visualizing a line to be overcast, a thread is actually laid out and overcast.*

11 Outline stitch variations. *Two very effective and different uses of the outline stitch are the spiral outline stitch and the row-on-row outline stitch. These are made just as they are named—the spiral starting from the center of an area of fabric and working out spirally, and the other worked row on row, with the rows touching each other. These stitches not only are good outline stitches, but, used as above, are excellent for filling in design areas.*

12 Three-sided stitch. *Bring the needle up through one hole, down through the next, over to the third hole, then back down through the second one again, up through the third, and down through the fourth, which is right next to the first one. When one triangle is formed, the next is continued, only reversed in position.*

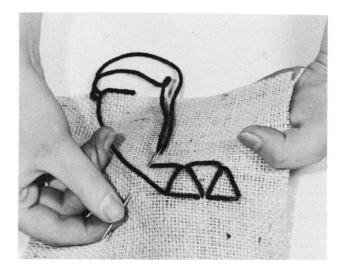

13 Trapunto. *Trapunto is accomplished through the use of two layers of cloth and gives a third dimension to the fabric without altering the surface texture of the material. Baste two fabrics together and stitch along both edges of the design to be raised with a simple running stitch from the back side of the fabric. When a design area is stitched, pad it with heavy yarn, quilting cotton, wool, or waste fabrics. Insert the padding material into the design areas between the two fabrics. A small opening must be cut in the back fabric to allow for insertion. Clip the ends as each section is completed.*

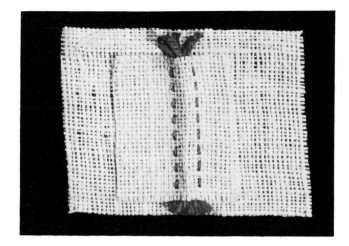

LOOPED STITCHES

Looped stitches are valuable both as binding for raw edges of fabric and as decorative fill for design areas. They are flat stitches formed by looping the thread around the needle before completing the stitch. The techniques for all looped stitches are basically the same and yet the difference visually is great.

1 Blanket stitch. *The blanket stitch is a simple loop stitch. With the thread coming through the fabric at the lower edge, insert the needle above and to the right, bringing the needle out above the thread at the lower edge.*

2 Buttonhole stitch. *The buttonhole stitch is an edging stitch made identically to the blanket stitch, except that the stitches are worked as closely together as possible to prevent the fabric edges from fraying. This stitch is utilized in cutwork and appliqué as well as in fill work.*

3 Feather stitch. *This is a simple loop stitch following parallel lines. The left side loops to the left, the right loops to the right. Stitches can be spaced far apart or close together for the desired effect.*

4 Feather stitch (slanted). *In this variation of the blanket or buttonhole stitch, two buttonhole stitches are made on a diagonal. The needle is then brought under and through the cloth to a spot below where the needle first came through the fabric. The process is continued.*

5 Scroll stitch. *This stitch is to be worked from left to right. The thread is brought out of the fabric, the needle inserted to the right and brought out at the left. The thread is then looped from left to right around the needle. The loop is tightened and secured with the left thumb, the needle is pulled carefully through the loop, and the stitch is formed.*

CHAIN STITCHES

The simple chain stitch is very similar in appearance to a crocheted chain. It is a stitch that fills the surface of the fabric quickly, with little thread appearing on the underside of the fabric.

1 Chain stitch. *Bring out the needle from behind the fabric. Insert the needle again in the same hole, looping the thread under the needle as it is brought through the fabric. Bring the needle out and repeat.*

2 Lazy daisy stitch. *This is an individual chain stitch that the stitcher ends by securing the loop and going on to the next stitch, rather than continuing the chain.*

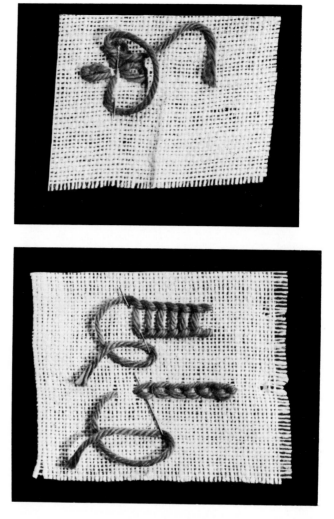

3 Open chain stitch. *This is the simple chain stitch that the stitcher can broaden by returning the needle through the fabric a length away instead of in the same hole.*

4 Double chain stitch. *In the double chain stitch, the loops are formed first to the right and then to the left. The first two stitches are feather stitches; the stitch is continued with the needle emerging twice in the same hole in the same loop.*

5 Wheat ear stitch. *Make two flat stitches diagonally to each other and work a chain through the base of them without catching the fabric with the needle.*

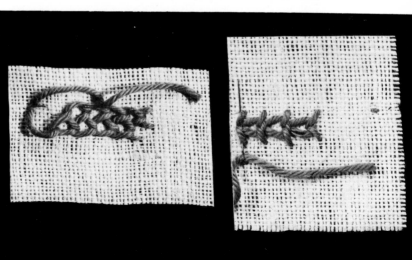

KNOTTED STITCHES

These stitches provide an interesting textural effect, different from all others. They are, simply, knots, and can be used imaginatively either singly, in areas, or in lines.

1 French knot. *The needle and thread are brought through the fabric from the back. The thread is wrapped around the needle two or more times, and the needle is returned through the fabric near the point of entry. The stitch works easily if the tension on the threads is not too great and if they are held by the thumb after the needle passes through.*

2 The bullion knot *(also called a long French knot). A short stitch is made; the thread is then twisted around the needle with as many twists as will cover the length of the stitch, or more if a looped effect is desired, and the needle is carefully pulled through the wrapping while the twist is held down with the thumb.*

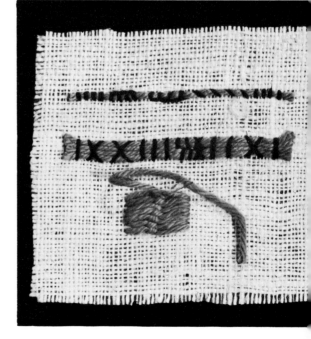

COUCHING

Couching serves to secure yarns or threads to the surface of the fabric. A great variety of stitches may be used to secure one or many yarns to the fabric. Cross stitches, whipping stitches, and chain stitches, among others, are very satisfactory for this purpose. Variety may be obtained also by the placement and angle of the various couching stitches used.

Yarns that are too thick to penetrate a dense or closely woven fabric can be applied to the surface of the cloth. The use of stiff or supple yarns, or yarns with varying thicknesses, adds to the texture of the design. Couching is actually the appliqué of yarns and threads rather than cloth, and can be used more delicately for linear effect as well as for fill areas. The yarn or thread is simply placed where it is desired. A second thread of contrasting color or value, or the same color or value, is brought through from the underside to secure the surface yarn in the chosen stitch.

DETACHED STITCHES

These are so named because they are attached to the fabric only at the edges of the section to be stitched, or to the base stitches, rather than to the fabric itself. They are quick fill stitches. All the thread remains on the surface of the fabric. Detached stitches can be used over appliqué or couching for further textural variety.

1 Stemstitch. *The base threads are simple flat stitches spaced as desired. The fill is simply whipped around each base stitch from right to left.*

2 Circular stemstitch. *The base threads are placed radially from a center spot. The fill stitches are worked as in the simple stemstitch from the center out to the edges.*

3 Ceylon stitch. *The Ceylon stitch resembles a knit stitch. It begins with a simple flat stitch. The second row loops through this flat stitch and returns to the other border. The third row is looped twice, and so on; the thread is kept at an even tension all the while.*

4 Honeycomb filling. *This is a weaving stitch. Threads are laid horizontally, then diagonally, and the second diagonal is woven in and out of the two previous layers of threads until the section is complete. The fabric is caught only at the edges of the section.*

DRAWN WORK OR HEMSTITCHING

This stitch involves drawing or pulling threads out of the base fabric itself. The threads remaining after the pulling are then secured in a pattern by the hemstitch. The name *hemstitch* is derived from its original and primary use in decorative hemming. However, sectional areas of hemstitching or drawn work may be used with success anywhere in a design.

The threads to be pulled in an area are clipped at their confining limit, so that they will not pull beyond that area. Before the hemstitching is begun, the two outer edges of the pulling must be secured by a buttonhole or satin stitch to avoid fraying.

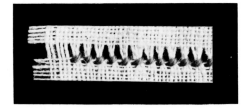

1 Simple hemstitch. *For a very simple hemstitch, a simple back stitch is used. Working from right to left, insert the needle behind the threads to be gathered up and draw the needle down into the fabric. Bring the needle in front to the right and put through the back, picking up the next section of threads to be gathered. Repeat until the section is complete.*

2 Hemstitching. *Bring the thread through the fabric near the edge of the pulling to be secured. Pick up as many threads as needed to make the design and pull the needle out. Bring the thread over the picked-up threads and stitch vertically from underneath the fabric. Continue the process until the area is complete.*

Depending on the design desired:
  a. *Leave the top as it is.*
  b. *Work the top row in the same way as the bottom.*
  c. *Divide the threads of one section in half at the top and secure with half of the threads of the next section.*

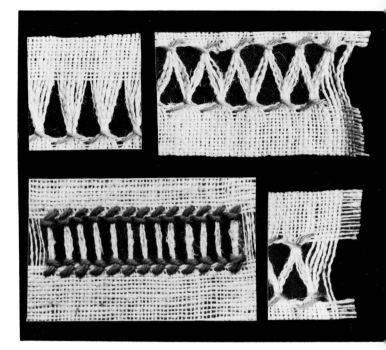

3 Drawn Work. *For a more open type of work than that shown in the basic hemstitching steps above, many threads are drawn, leaving the perpendicular base threads free for many varied types of treatment. Yarns can be woven into the base threads. Knots tied around various areas create differing effects. The edges are either treated with decorative edging or left plain, as desired for the design.*

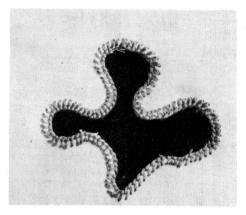

CUTWORK

By means of cutwork entire areas of fabric can be cut out according to the desired pattern. In the past, cutwork has been used primarily in tablecloths, and in altarcloths for churches. It is associated with fine embroidery, but can be used to advantage in any stitchery pattern where negative shapes would enhance the design.

The outline of the entire cut-out area is stitched with a fine buttonhole stitch, the loop part of the stitch facing the part to be cut out. After all the stitching is complete and securely fastened, the area to be cut out is cut with very sharp scissors as close to the stitch as possible without cutting the stitching thread.

TASSELS AND LOOPS

Tassels and yarn loops can add to the surface quality of a design in stitchery. These, like every other type of stitch used in stitchery, must be considered in the over-all design of the work.

1 To make a tassel wind the yarn around a cardboard cut as long as the length of the tassel. The amount of yarn wrapped around the cardboard determines whether the tassel will be thick or thin. Cut the yarn at one end of the cardboard. This makes several identical lengths of yarn. Tie a knot around these lengths at their center with another piece of yarn. Allow the yarn lengths to hang down from the center knot, and wrap yarn tightly and evenly around them just below the knot. The end of the wrapping may be tied or stitched back into the tassel or sewn into the fabric to which it is to be attached.

2 Make loops of any length by bringing the yarn through the fabric and looping it around a cardboard of the desired width. A pencil or stick will serve for small loops. After the loop is complete, make a simple knot at the base of the loop next to the fabric and return the needle through the fabric to begin the next loop. The loops may be cut or not, as wished. They may be made singly, in a line, or to fill an area.

APPLIQUÉ

Appliqué is applied ornamentation. Through use of appliqué, large areas of the design can be filled simply and relatively quickly. Fabrics of a texture or color very different from that of the base fabric, when applied, add a richness of texture to the over-all design.

The technique of appliqué varies, depending upon the effect desired and the fabric to be applied. If a tightly woven fabric or felt is used, almost any stitch can be made to secure it to the base fabric. Complex shapes are possible with felt and very tightly woven fabric, because such materials can be secured to the base at any place without regard to fraying edges. However, if a loosely woven fabric is to be applied, a tight stitch such as the buttonhole or satin stitch must be used to secure the edge. If a tight stitch is not desired in the design of the piece, the appliqué fabric may be cut larger to allow for a small hem, which is turned under and basted before application. The appliqué fabric may also be stitched down with a sewing machine or, in some cases, glued.

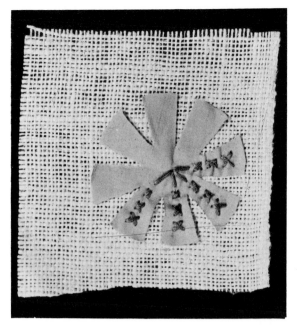

Any amount of decorative stitching may be used in conjunction with the necessary edging stitches. Buttons, beads, ribbons, tassels, when worked successfully into a design, extend the possibilities for creative applied stitchery.

ATTACHING FABRIC

Often in stitchery, extra, loose pieces of cloth may add to the texture. If these are to stand out measurably from the surface, a stiff cloth such as felt should be used. If the added piece is simply meant to hang loose, any cloth would be adequate, as long as it has been hemmed or otherwise treated to prevent fraying. Any stitch can be used to attach the extra cloth. Attach one end of the added fabric to the base fabric, allowing the other end to hang free.

RUG HOOKING

Hooked rugs are made on a base of heavy cloth in which the fibers are not tightly woven, so that the hooker can penetrate the cloth with the yarn or other material used to form the pile. Sized or unsized burlap, gunny sacks that have been opened and washed, or a special rug canvas is suitable for use.

There are two methods used in hooking rugs. When a rug hooker is used, the yarn is pushed through the back. When a large crochet hook is used, the yarn is pulled through from the front. The material must be stretched tight on a frame when the hooker is used. However, a frame is optional with the crochet hook. Adjustable frames can be purchased ready-made, or they can be constructed with strips of wood an inch or so wide and secured at the corners. The material is tacked to the frame on one side, usually at the center of the edge first, and then stretched and tacked at the center of the opposite side. Next it is tacked at the centers of each of the ends. After it has been stretched in this manner, it is tacked at intervals of every two inches or so from the center out, alternating back and forth from the opposite edges.

The design is planned first on paper and then transferred to the cloth with carbon, or cut out and traced on the cloth. If a pattern of stripes or simple blocked areas is used, it may be drawn directly on the material.

The frame may be supported and held in place with clamps between two stationary objects.

MATERIALS

1. Frame
2. Base on which to hook—burlap, gunny sack, rug canvas
3. Materials to use for hooking—yarns, wool, cotton, nylon, or cloth strips
4. Tools for hooking—hookers, large crochet hook
5. Nails, thumb tacks, corrugated joint fasteners, hammer
6. C-clamps

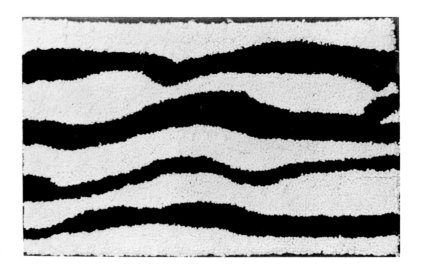

Hooked Rug. Yarn on burlap. Bryant Junior High School, Dearborn, Michigan. Patricia Cyr, Instructor. Courtesy, *Arts and Activities* Magazine.

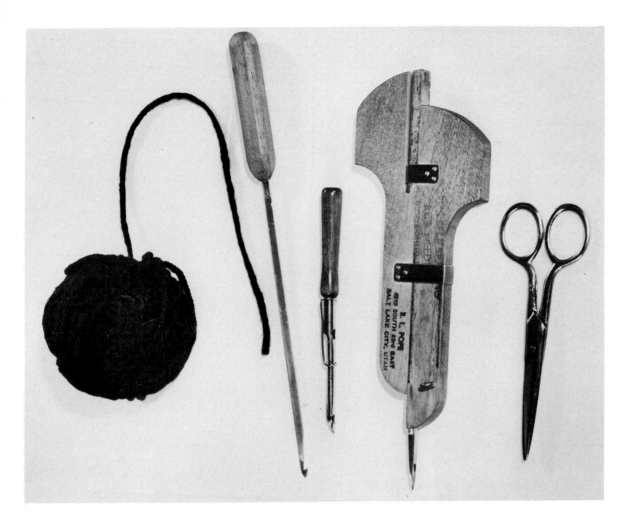

1 Make a frame of four wood strips held together at the corners with corrugated joint fasteners, nails, or glue. When a small frame is used, several pieces can be hooked and later sewn together to produce a larger size rug.

2 Nail the burlap to the frame.

3 Draw lines on the burlap for a simple pattern of squares or stripes.

4 Thread the hooker by pulling the yarn through the holes, leaving a tail of yarn 2 or 3 inches long projecting from the tip. Follow the directions enclosed with the particular hooker purchased.

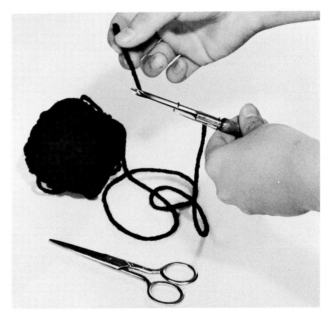

DECORATED TEXTILES 245

5 Hold the frame with one hand, or clamp it between two stationary objects. Working from the back, hold the needle upright and push it through the cloth to the right side where a loop is formed. Pull the needle back. The loop remains in place. Push the needle through again, leaving a short space between stitches.

6 Continue making stitches, placing them in rows by moving back and forth until the area is filled. Use contrasting colors in adjacent areas so that the design becomes defined.

7 Example of a pattern of stripes placed in an alternate arrangement. A different type of hooker is being used in the illustration.

8 If you use a large crochet hook, push the hook through the burlap from the front to the back and grasp the yarn with the hook.

9 Pull the yarn through the burlap to the front, to form a loop. Continue making loops until the spaces are filled.

10 To make a larger rug all in one piece, construct the size of frame needed.

11 Plan a design to form a repeat pattern. A dark-light alternation makes a strong design. The pattern in the illustration is of cut paper.

12 Divide the burlap for the rug into squares, using charcoal or pencil. Apply the design to the cloth by tracing around cut-out shapes, or trace the design with carbon paper.

13 Place identifying marks in areas to contain the same color. Hook all the areas of one color before proceeding to the next color.

14 When the hooking is finished, the back of the rug may be sized with rug size or backing to hold the yarn securely in place.

15 Remove the rug from the frame, turn the edges under, and make a hem.

ADDITIONAL SUGGESTIONS FOR DECORATED TEXTILES

The same techniques used in cutting and printing designs on paper can be used for decorated textiles. When permanence is desired, waterproof paints and inks must be used.

Young children can make prints with wood sticks, erasers, potatoes, cardboard, and shapes cut from inner tubes. Older children may use the same processes and in addition will find linoleum block printing just enough more difficult to challenge their abilities.

Although cardboard and inner-tube prints are especially adaptable to the use of young children because of their simplicity, they can also be used for the production of more serious mature prints and should be considered as good material for older students as well.

Wood for stick printing can be secured from scrap pieces, old spools, and meat skewers. Pieces ¼, ½, and ¾ inches square provide a good selection with which to work. Older children can file or cut designs in the ends of these shapes.

Since cutting linoleum requires strength and considerable control, this type of experience is more suitable for junior and senior high school students and for adults. The only essential tools needed are a V-shaped gouge for digging out lines, and a U-shaped gouge for scooping out larger areas. Large black masses should be retained to balance light areas. Lines and texture patterns created by groups of lines and dots may be tried out first on scrap pieces of linoleum.

Linoleum that is hard to cut becomes more pliable after it is warmed on a radiator. Teachers should give a careful demonstration of how to hold the block for cutting and emphasize special precautions—for instance, that students should take care not to jab the hand that steadies the block.

Students need to realize that the slight variations of tone resulting from hand printing are often desirable and should be accepted and appreciated. A poorly printed area can be reprinted.

If a great deal of material is to be printed, as for drapery, several students can work together and divide the responsibilities by having one person ink the block, one place it in the correct position on the cloth, and another hammer it to make the print.

At the end of each printing period, the slab, brayer, and linoleum block should be cleaned with paper towels, rags, and turpentine; for if the ink is allowed to dry, it is difficult to remove. This responsibility must be demonstrated and instilled in students, for they are often reluctant to give proper care to materials. Finished prints can be hung over or pinned to a line stretched across the room, pinned to a bulletin board, or left spread out on papers on a table or floor to dry.

Older students are capable of ambitious projects—for instance, the making of draperies for a student lounge. Or they can help children in an elementary school make draperies for their classrooms, using the children's designs but as-

Stitchery. Yarn on cloth; yarn on burlap. Jane Addams Junior High School, Seattle. Mary Kutila, Instructor.

sisting by carrying out the technical process of printing.

SUGGESTED PROJECTS

Articles for which fabric decoration may be produced include mats, handbags, shopping bags, belts, ties, lunch cloths, napkins, tray cloths, handkerchiefs, skirts, shirts, dresses, cushions, draperies, bedspreads, screens, wall hangings, bindings on books and portfolios, stage costumes, and doll clothes.

All age levels of beginners can work with stitchery by starting with a knowledge of a few basic stitches most commonly used. It is advisable to make a sampler of the stitches, preferably on a material that has some body to it like burlap, Osnaburg, monk's cloth, or a heavy cotton. The stitches can be repeated and grouped in such a way as to produce a pattern, and the sampler can be attractive as well as instructive.

Students can combine cotton or wool yarns with other types of materials such as those listed under weaving. They will discover which stitches they prefer for outlines and which for fill-ins, and will begin to create some stitches of their own as they become familiar with the purposes.

The teacher can guide the students when they are making decisions about color placement or dark-light emphasis. Sometimes just a question will challenge the student's thinking; or a suggestion that he turn his work upside down will enable him to study the total effect.

A class may collaborate on a large problem such as draperies, or each student can make an individual section to be sewed to the others to form a wall hanging. Unity can be achieved if each student uses the same colors and materials in his design.

Rug hooking is of interest to students of intermediate-grade age on up. They can usually make their frames quite easily; but sometimes, they may need a little assistance. Since rugs can be made with cloth strips or combinations of various materials, as well as with yarns, many items can be brought from home, including old gunny sacks to be used for the rug foundation.

Designs for rugs should avoid stereotyped patterns; they should be decorative rather than representational. Sometimes younger children can use their paintings for subject matter, for these are often quite rich in their patterns of shapes and colors.

Springing Birds. Glue serigraph. Child age 8. Bethune School, Charlotte, North Carolina. Courtesy, *Everyday Art* Magazine.

DECORATED TEXTILES 251

Wall Hanging: Stitchery combined with appliqué. Adult student. Courtesy
Beaudette Smith. *Right: Textile Design.* Stencil print on cloth. Adult student

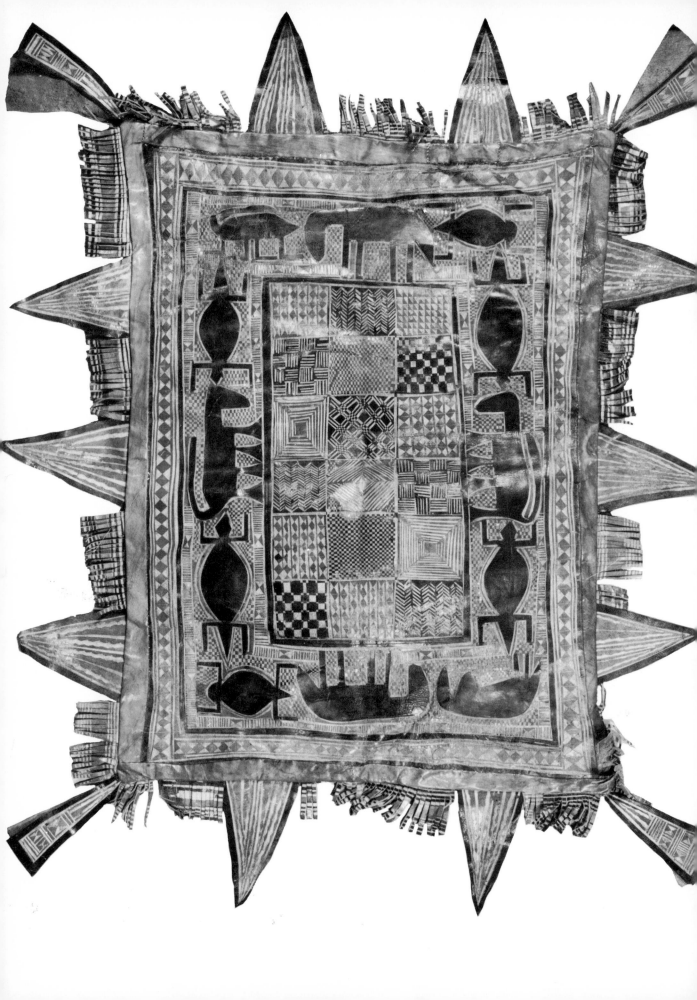

LEATHER

African, N. Nigeria; Provenance, Bida. Nupe Tribe: *Cushion Cover or Mat.*
Leather hide decorated with animals and birds. British Museum.

LEATHER

Leather has occupied an important place in many primitive societies, where it has practically been the basis of life. Early man used skins of animals for clothing and for many other articles, including drinking cups and vessels, examples of which have been found that date back to the Neolithic period. Tools used at this time for scraping leather have also been found, as well as handles of weapons wrapped in leather strips. Early man rubbed the skins with fat and smoked them over a wood fire to cure and preserve them.

Articles fashioned of leather have also been discovered in Egyptian tombs. The Egyptians developed a method of curing and preserving leather by soaking the skins in fermented oak or chestnut barks containing tannic acid. From this has come the process of tanning leather, which is now accomplished by chemical modification in processing plants called *tanneries*. Tanning arrests decomposition, increases the strength and pliability of the skin, and keeps it from becoming soluble in water.

The Eskimo is an example of a primitive culture that has been dependent upon the skins of animals for the necessities of life. The seal, walrus, deer, bear, and beaver have furnished the material for their beautiful fur-lined and hooded parkas, mucklucks, and mittens. Their tentlike dwellings are made of skins, and their hunting canoes, called *kayaks,* are formed of sealskins stretched over a pointed frame with an opening in the middle where the hunter sits. Eskimo women chew the leather to soften it for making articles of wearing apparel.

The American Indian, especially of the Plains tribes, lived a hunter's life centered around the buffalo, deer, antelope, elk, and beaver. From these he derived the rawhide needed for his clothing, moccasins, leggings, robes, packing cases, drums, trappings for horses, quivers for arrows, shields, and tents. He decorated his gear and clothing with fringe and feathers, which blew gracefully in the wind while he was riding rapidly on horseback; and he decorated his tents, robes, and teepees with painted designs—pictographs made on buffalo hides.

American Indians developed the art of embroidery on leather to a high degree, using colored glass beads imported from Europe (after 1800) and distributed by traders. Of greater antiquity, however, was quill embroidery, a typical American Indian art thought to be several thousands of years old. Porcupine quills were softened in water, flattened, dyed, and sewn to garments, pouches, moccasins, or other articles—producing a glossy appearance in arrangements of abstract patterns. The Indian also produced a leather known as buckskin, an unusually soft, pliant material quite resistant to water, which he used for clothing and other purposes.

Tribes in Africa have used hides of animals for clothing, quivers, bags, sheaths for knives, and wrappings to cover tool and weapon handles. Shields were made of heavy rhinoceros

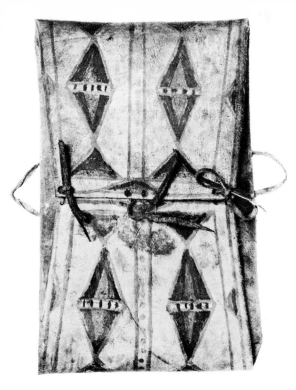

American Indian, Blackfoot: *Parfleche*. 1875-1900. Painted hide, 16" x 24". Chicago Natural History Museum.

American Indian, Sioux: *Dance Shield*. Painted buffalo hide. 22¼" diameter. Museum of the American Indian. Heye Foundation.

American Indian, Chippewa, Turtle Mt., N. Dakota: *Knife Sheath*. 1900. Beadwork on rawhide. 16½" long. Museum of the American Indian. Heye Foundation.

American Indian, Chiricahua Apache, Arizona: *Saddle Bag*. 1910. Cut leather, rawhide. 19½" x 44". Museum of the American Indian. Heye Foundation.

American Indian, Ottawa, Cross Village, Michigan: *Pouch*. 1825–1850. Quilled buckskin dyed black. 6½" x 6½". Cranbrook Institute of Science.

African: *Bottle Cover, Sierra Leone*. Dark red leather embroidered with fine strips of dried palm leaf. British Museum.

African: Yeruba Tribe, Nigeria: *Bag of the Shango Cult*. Appliqué on leather. British Museum.

hide; rugs and headdresses were made of long-haired monkey fur.

The Chinese made screens and chests of thick heavy leather, upon which they painted designs, and elaborate boxes covered with appliquéd cut-out patterns attached with heavy stitches. The Japanese also made screens of leather, which they decorated with paint.

Of unusual artistic quality are the ornate and highly original puppets made for shadow theaters in Java and Siam. The older puppets were cut from dried buffalo hide and beautifully decorated. The unnaturally long arms fastened to the body of the puppet are moved by means of little sticks attached to them. These puppets are held in front of a large cotton screen and manipulated to illustrate the action of the story being told by the storyteller. The shadows of the puppets are thown on a screen with a lamp.

Leather was also used as a writing material for books during medieval times. Vellum and parchment were prepared from the skins of

Moroccan: *Sweets-holder*. Leather pieces applied to terra cotta pottery jar. Courtesy, Elizabeth Bayley Willis.

Moroccan: *Carved Wood Stamp*. Used to stamp designs on leather. Courtesy, Elizabeth Bayley Willis.

Siamese: *Shadow Puppet, A God and His Vehicle*. c. 1820. Leather with perforated pattern. 28¾″ high. Seattle Art Museum, Eugene Fuller Memorial Collection.

calves and sheep and polished with pumice stone to provide a smooth surface on which to write.

Leather was used quite extensively during the early part of the Renaissance in Italy and Spain, and also in Morocco, where leather tooling was developed to a high state of perfection. Morocco became a center of leather production, and a leather known as *Moroccan goat* was produced for use in binding books. Many of the traditional leather techniques are still practiced in Morocco, handed down by hereditary craft guilds which have existed for centuries in the workshops of the ancient Fez Medina. The bowl, used for holding sweets, is formed of terra cotta and covered with leather inside and out. Smaller pieces are appliquéd on top, and the leather has been modeled over the knob on the lid. The traditional shape of this bowl is derived from containers made of brass in many sizes, used to hold sweets, cakes, and bread. The bag, carried by soldiers in the service of a *caid* or local ruler in what was formerly Spanish Morocco, is richly

Moroccan: *Shikara. Traditional Bag Carried by Men. Appliqué on leather.*
Courtesy, Elizabeth Bayley Willis.

R. Wright: *Leather Binding.* London. Twentieth century. Blue Niger morocco with gold tooling.

Moroccan: *Berber Shoes.* Embroidery and appliqué on leather. Courtesy, Elizabeth Bayley Willis.

decorated with an intricate pattern of tiny appliqué pieces, lacing, and cut strips to form a fringe. Looped leather tabs hold the cord and there is a fastener also made of leather. Each locality developed its own patterns and colors on bags like this, which are part of traditional Moroccan dress. Carved wood stamps are used by Moroccan craftsmen to stamp designs in gold, silver, or finely ground pigments on leather. Embossing is also used for decoration. This method of patterning was used to decorate the amulet case, made of red-dyed leather, laced with a whipstitch, and attached to a cord so that it could be worn around the neck. Such amulets, embossed with protective religious symbols, are worn by Berber tribesmen to ward off evil.

The Moorish tradition from Morocco was also implanted in Spain, where beautifully decorated objects stamped with gold and richly tooled were produced. Even wall panels, made of

Moroccan: *Amulet Worn by Men of the Berber Tribes.* Design pressed into red leather with lacing around edge. Courtesy, Elizabeth Bayley Willis.

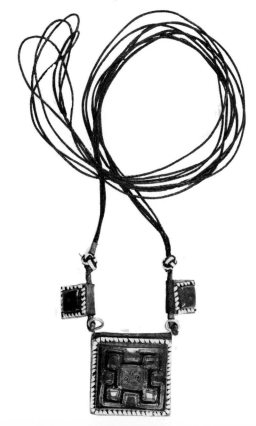

Spanish: *Chest.* Fourteenth century. Leather repoussé with animal forms and metal attachments. The Cluny Museum, Paris. Courtesy, Caisse Nationale des Monuments Historiques.

Persian: *Front, Book Cover.* 16th–17th Cent. Leather, 11⅛" x 6¾". Seattle Art Museum, Eugene Fuller Memorial Collection.

whole hides, were intricately tooled and colored. The hides were spliced to fit together to cover the walls of large rooms in palaces and villas.

In addition to tooling and stamping, the Spaniards did carving, inlaying, and embossing. They knew how to model the leather to form it into bottles and cases in various shapes. Objects made of leather included chair backs, boxes, chests, saddles, and harnesses and trappings for carriages. Royal personages were clad in elegantly decorated belts, jackets, caps, boots, and leggings of leather.

The early American colonists made chairs and screens of leather and sometimes covered their doors with it. Leather doorhinges were also used.

The leather-covered saddle has become identified with the American West. Trappings of fringe, as well as inlay, stitching, and large floral carvings, have characterized this particular craft. The leather is stretched over a form and shaped. Saddles coming from the saddleries and harness establishments of an earlier period were more original in design than those of today, which are primarily stereotyped repetitions of former styles.

Leather occupies a more significant place in our culture today than might be imagined. It is used for coats and jackets, hats, shoes, bags, gloves, luggage, and furniture. Hides and skins with the fur retained are made into coats and rugs. In contrast to the examples from the past, however, the utilitarian aspects assume the chief importance and less emphasis is placed upon creative ideas. Standardization has established forms from which there is slight variation.

Navajo: *Saddle.* c. 1880-1900. Skirt 24" long. The Museum of Northern Arizona. Christy G. Turner II, photograph.

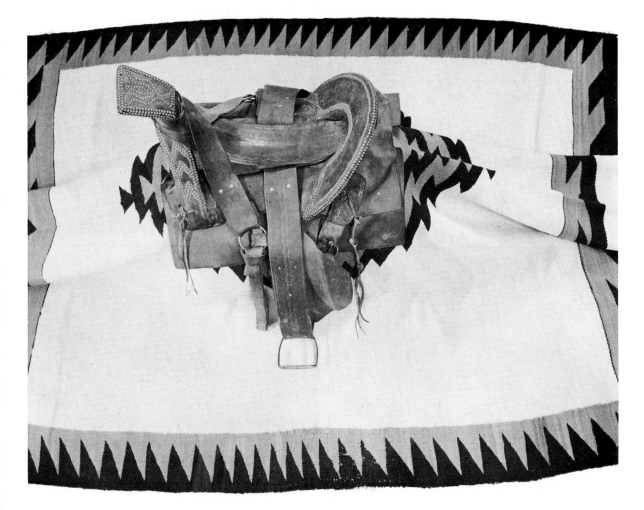

Mies van der Rohe: *Barcelona Chair*. Leather. The Museum of Modern Art.

Bill and Marty Holm: *Bag.* 1959. Leather combined with cloth woven with wool and nylon on linen warp. 12″ x 8″ x 6″.

LEATHER PROCESSES

Objects made of leather are durable as well as pleasing to see and handle. They may be constructed of well-known varieties like calfskin, sheepskin, goatskin, steerhide, cowhide, and pigskin, or of the less common and more exotic types, which include the hide of deer, antelope, seal, walrus, camel, elephant, ostrich, lizard, and alligator.

Leathers from large animals are referred to as hides; those from small ones are called skins. They are generally sold by the square foot in whole or half hides (or skins). Smaller amounts are sold by the square inch and are somewhat higher in price. Leather scraps, which are the odds and ends of assorted pieces, are available by the pound. If a whole hide is obtained the best parts may be selected for bigger projects and the weaker or disfigured sections, usually found near the edges, may be used for smaller objects or for patterns where small pieces to be fitted together are needed.

In some instances it is better to secure precut pieces for specific purposes. For instance, it is rather difficult to cut a long strip of thick leather for a belt and have it straight. Wallet inserts are also available with various kinds of pockets, and are less bulky and clumsy than those individually constructed.

The type of leather selected depends upon the purpose it is to serve. Cowhide is suitable for heavy belts, whereas calf and goat, being pliable, are good for wallets and key cases. Leathers that are firm will hold a tooled or stamped pattern better than those that are loose and stretchy. Some leathers, such as Morocco goat, pigskin, and ostrich, have interesting surface textures and do not need additional surface pattern enrichment.

Heavy leathers must be cut with a sharp knife; thin ones may be cut with scissors. If the leather is too thick to fold, as in making wallets, it is pared or skived on the edges until it is sufficiently thin to turn under.

Pattern can be applied to leather with modeling and carving tools, metal stamps, and wood or linoleum blocks. Other ways of achieving pattern are by inlay, onlay, appliqué, or mosaic. Leather may be dyed by the whole piece or by selected parts to make designs.

Leather parts are held together by lacing, by sewing by hand or sewing machine, or by an adhesive.

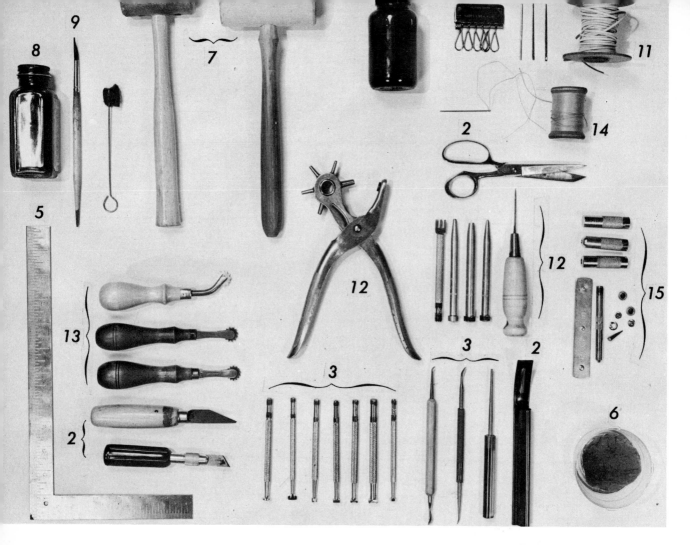

MATERIALS

1. Leather
2. Cutting tools—knife with sharp blade, skiving knife, scissors
3. Tools used in decoration—modeling, carving, and stamping tools
4. Work surface—masonite board, hardwood board, marble slab, lithograph stone
5. Steel square or metal-edge ruler
6. Sponge
7. Mallet
8. Color sources—dye, stain, shoe polish, paint, ink, food coloring
9. Brush
10. Atomizer or spray gun
11. Leather lace
12. Tools for lacing—awl, round drive punch, three- or four-prong thonging chisel, revolving punch, lacing needle
13. Tools for sewing—space marker, needle
14. Thread
15. Snap setter, snap sets, rivets, eyelets

CUTTING

1 To cut thick leathers, use a sharp knife and a steel square or metal-edge ruler.

2 To skive leather, so that it will be thin enough to fold over on the edges, pare it on the underside. Lay it face down on a hard surface with the flesh side up, and with a skiving knife remove a few pieces at a time. Be careful not to cut off too much at once, since there is the danger of cutting a hole clear through. Remove scraps as they gather to keep from marring the outer surface of the leather.

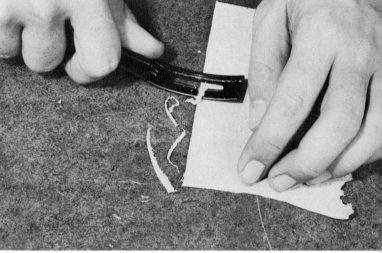

TOOLING

There are several different kinds of modeling tools, but the one in general use is pointed at one end and flat at the other. The pointed end is used for indenting lines and for stippling. The flat end is used to make depressed areas in lowering a surface.

1 Wet the leather on both sides with a damp sponge.

2 Place the leather piece on a hard surface with the right side up. Use the narrow end of the modeling tool, point turned upward, and press firmly while pulling the tool to make a line. To keep lines straight, use a steel square or metal-edge ruler.

3 *For simple curves, cut a template of stiff paper, using the edge as a guide for the modeling tool. More complex designs may be drawn lightly with pencil directly on the leather. Or a pattern may be drawn on paper, secured to the leather with tape or paper clips, and the design transferred by being pressed through the paper with the tool. The tape may be placed around under the leather to the flesh side to avoid marking the surface.*

4 *To depress larger areas, use the flat end of the modeling tool. Press firmly between tooled lines, using short or long moving strokes as needed.*

STAMPING

Stamps are used to transfer shapes to leather to produce a pattern. They may be plain, or cut or engraved on the end in various designs. Engraved metal saddle stamps are available from commercial sources. Original stamps can be made by filing designs on the ends of ⅛- or ¼-inch brass bars or the tops of large-headed nails. Designs may be cut in wood or linoleum and stamped on the leather by means of a press.

1 *Dampen the leather on both sides with a sponge, and place it grain side up on a hard surface. Wait until the top is almost dry, since leather that is too wet will not retain the impression.*

2 *Hold the metal stamp upright and tap it with a mallet or hammer. Arrange stamps in a pattern or in combination with other stamps.*

CARVING

Carving, sometimes called *incising,* is another method used for decorating leather. The design is traced on the leather and the lines are cut with a swivel knife. Background areas are depressed with a flat modeling tool or metal saddle stamps. The best leathers for carving are calf, sheep, goat, and cowhide.

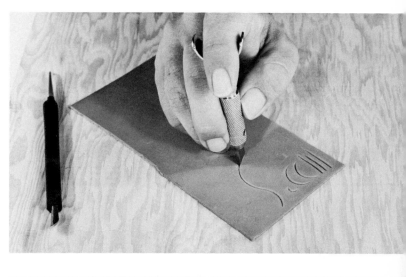

1   Dampen the leather on both sides with a wet sponge.

2   Transfer the pattern as explained in step 3 under Tooling.

3   Before cutting, moisten the grain or top side of the leather again so that it is slightly wet. Hold the swivel knife between the thumb and the middle and fourth fingers with the index finger resting on top. Let the little finger move on the leather to help steady the hand. Hold the knife in an upright position. Do not tip it sideways, either to the right or to the left.

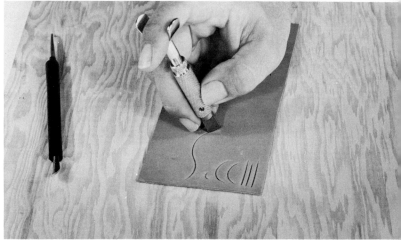

4   Cut with the corner of the blade. Begin and end each cut with light pressure. This makes the cut shallow at each end and deeper in the center. Cut to about one-half the thickness of the leather. No leather is cut away; it is merely incised. Rotate the knife to change directions. Use a straightedge for help in making straight lines. Do not go over lines or cross one line over another.

5   To complete the effects of the carving, model those background areas that are to be depressed to make the design stand out in relief. Use the broad end of a modeling tool and press firmly near the cut, working back and forth.

6   Metal saddle stamps may also be used to depress the background areas. See steps 1 and 2 under Stamping the Leather. If the impressions are stamped as close together as possible, a solid effect is produced. The raised areas contrasting with the depressed ones give a carved-out appearance.

DYEING

Color may be added to the surface of the leather with a brush, dauber, atomizer, or spray gun, or the leather may be dipped in a dye bath. If the piece is small or only partial areas are to be covered, brushing is the most convenient method. Leather is usually dampened before it is dyed; however, dye may be applied to dry leather. Dyes especially prepared for leather are available. Stains, inks, water colors, shoe polish, and food coloring may also be used. It is recommended that they be tried on scrap pieces first.

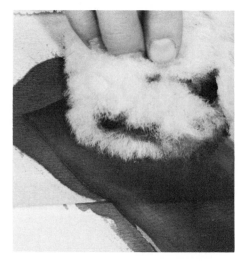

1 Dampen the leather if desired. Work directly on a masonite board, or use old newspapers as a protective work surface.

2 Apply dye or paint to the leather surface with a brush, spreading it quickly before it dries and forms streaks. A swab made of lamb's wool may also be used.

3 Apply additional colors to specific design areas to bring out the pattern.

4 To dip the leather in a dye bath, use a shallow pan wide enough to hold the piece. Use the dye in its concentrated strength or dilute with water for lighter shades. Immerse the dampened piece quickly so that it is entirely covered with the dye. Remove and lay it on a clean surface to dry. Rubber gloves may be worn to prevent dye stains on the hands.

5 Use an atomizer or spray gun to spray dyes or paints on dampened leather. Protect the work surface from excess spray with newspapers. The leather may be left in a flat position or held upright for work. Hold the atomizer about a foot or more away from the leather and spray the color quickly over the entire surface. If the atomizer is held too close, the color will run in streaks.

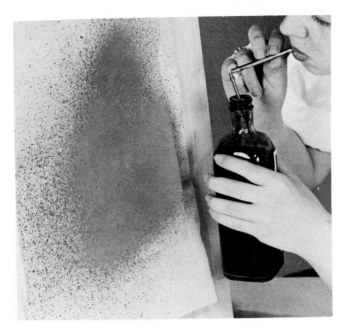

PUNCHED HOLES IN LEATHER

Openings can be made in leather for decorative purposes as well as for lacing. Holes are punched with various kinds of tools. To space holes for lacing, a light mark is made with an awl or pencil about ⅛ inch from the edge. If the holes are too close to the edge, they will be torn out; and if too far, the lacing will appear awkward. The distance between holes is marked with a pair of dividers or a ruler and pencil. To determine the space needed between holes, punch several holes of the size selected in scrap leather. Some prefer space about the width of a hole between the holes, while others allow 3/16 inch. A space marker can also be used for marking holes for lacing.

1 To make a hole with a round drive punch, place the punch over the marker and strike it with a mallet. Drive punches are available in a number of different sizes. They are useful for punching holes that are too far from the edges for the revolving punch to reach.

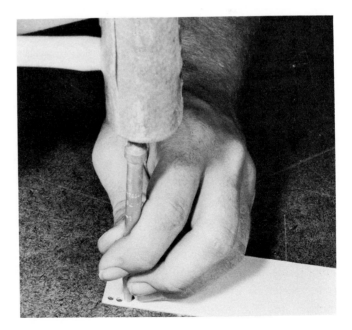

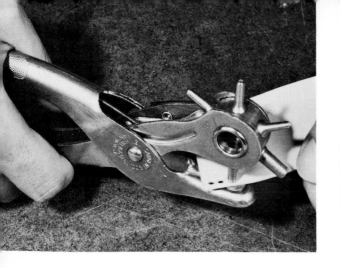

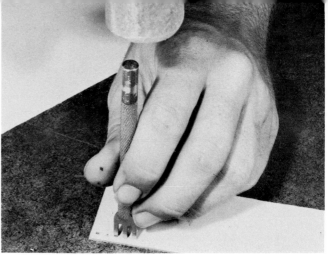

2 *Various sizes of holes can be made with the revolving punch. Select the size of tube needed, place it over the mark, and punch the hole. Try the size first in scrap leather.*

3 *For making narrow slits, use a thonging chisel with three or four prongs. Place the chisel on the drawn line and tap with a mallet. To space the slits evenly, lift the chisel, put the end prong in the last slit, and hold in position while new slits are punched. Continue putting the end prong in the last slit made until all are punched. To round a corner, use a one-prong chisel and place one slit at an angle. If difficulty is incurred in pulling the lace through the opening, open the slit wider with an awl or a fid, which is similar to an awl but has a flattened point.*

LACING TECHNIQUES

The purpose of lacing is to join together two pieces of leather as for a purse or billfold; however, it is designed to serve as decoration also. To line up the holes in the two pieces to be laced together, punch one piece first, then put the other underneath and mark it through the holes in the first piece. To prevent slipping, hold them together along the edge with rubber cement.

Lacing is made of calf or goat and comes in an assortment of colors. It is sold either by the yard or by the spool. A 3/32-inch width is most generally used, although a 1/8-inch width is best on large projects. The amount of lace required in the process depends upon the style of the method selected. For the simple whipstitch, three times the length of the distance to be laced is needed; for the single buttonhole stitch, five times; and seven times is required for the double buttonhole stitch. The amount of lace needed may be measured out ahead of time. Since it is difficult to handle a piece much more than a yard in length it is advisable to add lace as it is needed. To splice a new piece to the first one, skive the top or grain side of the first about 1/2 inch or more at the end, and skive the underside of the new strip. Overlap and glue or cement them together.

When lacing is completed, tuck 1/2 inch or so of the end back under the last few stitches.

Needles for lacing have a tiny hook near the eye where the end of the leather lace can be attached. If a needle is not used, make the end of the lace pointed by cutting it at an angle, and stiffen it with glue.

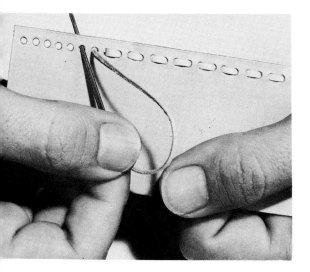

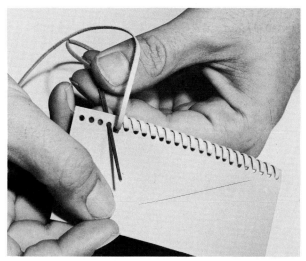

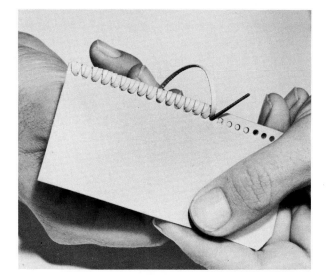

1 To make a running stitch, push the needle through one hole and out through the next, continuing until the end is reached.

2 To make the whipstitch put the needle through the end hole, over the top edge, and back through the next hole.

3 For the double whipstitch, follow the directions for step 2 but go through each hole twice.

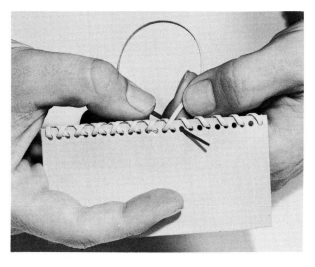

4 For the cross stitch, follow the directions for the whipstitch but go through every other hole. When the end is reached, change directions and repeat to fill in the holes that have not already been laced.

5 To begin the single buttonhole stitch, (a) start at the left end. Push the needle through the first hole, leaving a tail of about an inch. Bend the tail upward so that it projects above the edge of the leather, and hold it in position with the thumb. (b) Bring the lace across the front of the tail, moving from right to left; encircle it, and (c) push the needle through the second hole from front to back. (d) Bring the lace over the top edge and turn back under the loop already formed. This is the step demonstrated in the illustration. Repeat the process. Although the stitch appears complicated it goes very easily once the idea is grasped.

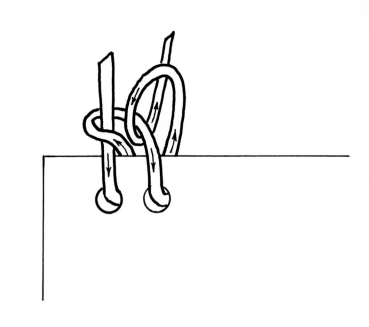

6 Directions for the double buttonhole stitch are the same as for the single buttonhole stitch, except that the needle is put under two loops instead of one. Notice in the illustration (step 5) that the needle is going under one loop. In the double buttonhole stitch the needle goes under both loops.

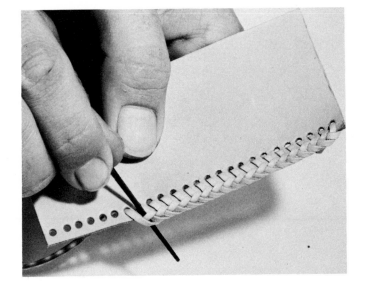

SEWING PROCEDURES

Sewing is used for joining pieces of leather together or adding parts such as pockets, inserts, tabs, or zippers. Pieces should be cemented first to be kept from slipping. If the sewing is done on a machine, a larger needle is used and the stitch is adjusted for wide spacing. Glover's needles (available at notions counters) or harness needles are suitable for hand sewing. Waxed linen, nylon, or heavy cotton thread may be used for this work. Holes for sewing are marked with a spacer and then punched with an awl, or slits for sewing are made with a thonging chisel. If the leather is thick, a drill can be used for making the holes.

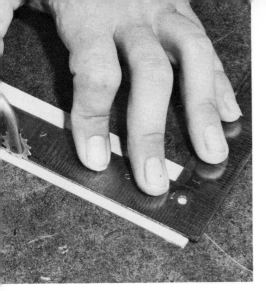

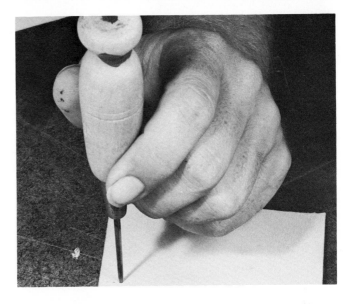

1   On the grain side of the leather, mark a light line with a pencil or awl ⅛ inch or less from the edge of the leather where it is to be sewn.

2   To mark the points for the stitches, roll a space marker along the line with the use of a guide.

3   Puncture the marks made for the stitches with an awl.

4   The awl may be held upright on a masonite board and tapped with a mallet.

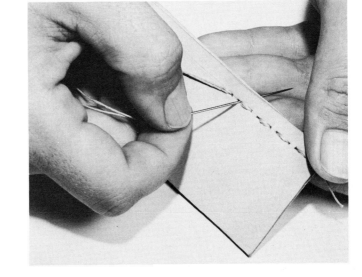

5   Make a running stitch and then reverse the direction, filling in the spaces between. The straight running stitch can be used for thin leathers. For heavier leathers two threaded needles may be used at one time. They go through the same hole from opposite sides of the leather, exchange positions, and return through the next hole. This process fills in all spaces between the holes.

LEATHER   275

6 *Pieces can be added for reinforcement or decoration. Cement pieces to hold them in place. Make slits with a thonging chisel or awl, and sew.*

PUTTING IN A LINING

Linings of lightweight leathers such as skiver and suede are sometimes used in items like purses and key cases. They are attached with an adhesive such as rubber cement, paste, or glue. Linings are put in before lacing or sewing.

Apply cement to the flesh side of the leather and lay the lining piece on it. Rub well with a clean cloth until the two pieces adhere.

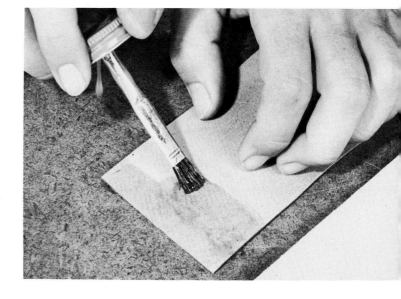

SETTING SNAPS

Snaps are used to close purses, key cases, or any other object with an overlapping closure. There are two kinds of snap setters: the segma and the birdcage. The button set must correspond with the setter used. Snap setters are composed of a metal strip with a small knob projecting at each end and one in the center, and accompanying metal cylinder posts. Directions for using different kinds of snap setters are enclosed with purchased sets.

The snap sets are composed of four parts: the button, the socket that fits into its concave opening, and the eyelet and stud, which fit together to form the part that snaps into the button.

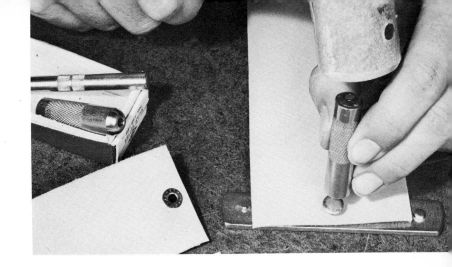

1 First determine the size of hole needed for the button by trying punches on some scrap leather until one that fits is found. With this punch make the hole for inserting the button.

2 To find the location of the stud, close the flap and mark through the hole punched for the button.

3 Lay out the four pieces for a segma snap.

4 Punch the two holes needed for inserting the two snap units.

5 Put the socket that fits in the button on the center raised portion of the segma metal strip.

6 Fit the piece of leather over the socket through the punched hole, with the grain side up. If the hole in the leather is too tight, stretch it with an awl.

7 Put the button cap over the socket and cover it with the metal post that has the wide concave area at the end. Hold it perpendicularly so that it does not slip, and strike it with a mallet to set the parts.

8 To set the other two pieces, place the eyelet over one of the knobs at either end of the metal strip, depending upon which size is needed. Put the leather over the eyelet, grain side up, pushing it through the hole made for this purpose. Put the stud over the eyelet, cover it with the hollow end of a metal post of the correct size, and strike with a mallet to set it. Try the snap to see if it works. Sometimes it can be adjusted with pliers to make it fit. If the setting was not successful, the parts will have to be removed and the process repeated with a new set.

FINISHING THE LEATHER

Color and other decoration such as tooling and stamping is easier to add to leather that does not have a dressing or finish already on it, since the water necessary in these operations cannot penetrate an oiled surface. After the leather has been decorated, it can be treated in a number of different ways. Saddle soap is used to remove light soil and fingerprints and to help soften the leather. It may be put on before dyes or lacquers are applied. Care should be exercised not to soil or disfigure leather any more than necessary. Metal, such as steel squares or the edges of rulers, will leave stains on damp leather. A special leather lacquer is the best all-round finish to use, and it can be thinned with a lacquer thinner when necessary. It preserves the color and protects from soil. Antique finishes that produce highlights and shadows are available in a number of colors. Waxes in liquid, paste, or cake form, may also be used as a finish and protective coat. When leather is to receive hard use, neat's-foot oil, which will darken and waterproof natural leather, is recommended.

KEY CASE

A key case consists of a leather cover, a key frame with hooks, and a snap. The cover may be dyed and decorated with modeling, stamping, and carving tools. Key frames are available in many sizes. The key frame may be attached directly to the cover, or to the lining before the lining is glued to the cover, or to a tab that can be laced, sewn, glued, or riveted to the cover. The purpose of the tab is to conceal the attachment of the key frame or to give more body if the cover is soft. The snap provides a closure for the case. It may be attached to the cover flap or to a small tab. More than one snap may be used. The edges of the cover may be laced to attach the key frame tab or to give additional decoration.

MATERIALS

1. Leather
2. Key frame
3. Rivets
4. Snaps
5. Snap setter
6. Leather lace
7. Lacing needle
8. Knife
9. Skiving knife
10. Steel square or ruler
11. Mallet
12. Dye
13. Modeling, stamping, and carving tools
14. Brush
15. Space marker
16. Thonging chisel

1 *To make the pattern for the key case, use paper to plan the shape and size of the cover so that it will easily encompass the key frame. Allow enough space for the keys.*

2 *Place the pattern on the grain side of the leather. Carefully cut the leather, using the pattern as a guide.*

3 The edges of thick leather may be made thinner by skiving.

4 Leather may be scored to facilitate folding. To score with a knife, press gently along a straightedge on the flesh side until a permanent crease is formed.

5 To decorate the leather with an eraser stamp, stamp a pattern with dye on the grain side. The cover may also be tooled, stamped, or carved.

6 The inside of the cover may be left plain, it may be dyed, or a lining may be inserted.

7 If a lining is to be used, cement the lining to the inside of the cover. Apply rubber cement to the entire surface of the flesh side of each piece and press the pieces together with the use of a bone folder or a clean cloth.

8 Cut a tab wide enough to hold the key frame. It may be the same length as the cover or shorter.

9 Hold the key frame in place on the tab, and mark where the rivet holes are to be punched.

10 Punch the rivet holes.

11 Attach the rivets.

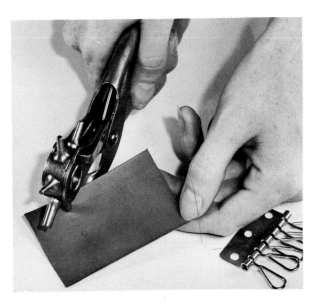

12 If the tab is to be laced rather than glued, riveted, or sewn to the cover, first lay the tab in place on the inside of the cover and secure it with a little rubber cement. Then mark the edge of the cover for lacing, using a straightedge and space marker.

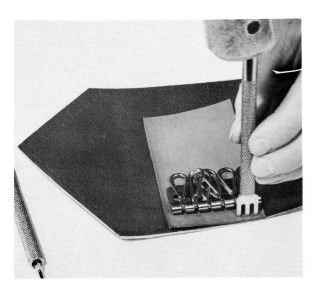

13 Punch the lacing holes with a three-hole thonging chisel.

14 Use a single-prong chisel to turn the corner.

15 Lace the edges of the cover. The key tab is held in place by the lacing.

16 Punch a hole for the snap on the flap side of the cover.

17 Attach the snap.

LEATHER BELT

The type of leather used for a belt is determined by its purpose. Leather for belts may vary from soft suede to heavy cowhide. Light leathers can be cut with shears, but heavier leathers must be cut with a sharp knife, with a head knife that has a semicircular blade, or with an adjustable draw gauge for very thick leathers. Unless one has the right tools and the skill to use them the problem can be solved best by purchasing the heavy leathers in precut belt straps.

The belt may be left square on the end, shaped by rounding, or made pointed. The edges may be beveled with an edge tool so that they slope; also, a line may be tooled near the edge with an edge creaser.

There are various ways to decorate belts. The surface may be left plain, dyed in whole or part, tooled, stamped, or carved. Holes may be punched to form a decorative pattern. Attachments can be added by gluing or sewing. Belts may be fastened with buckles, snaps, or various other means (refer to the fastener in the section on Making a Leather Purse).

MATERIALS

1. Leather or precut blanks
2. Cutting tools—leather-cutting shears, knives, adjustable draw gauge
3. Steel square
4. Adhesives—rubber cement or glue
5. Decorating tools—modeling, stamping, and carving tools, punches
6. Dyes
7. Fasteners—buckles, snaps, rivets, eyelets

1 *To make a belt, cut or purchase a precut strip of leather the desired width and length.*

2 *If color is to be used, dye the surface of the strip with the swab from the dye bottle or a piece of lamb's wool. Refer to the section on Dyeing Leather, p. 270. Edges may also be dyed.*

3 *To attach a buckle to thick leather, skive a section about 4 inches from one end of the flesh side, to permit easier folding. If the leather is thin enough to fold easily, it need not be skived.*

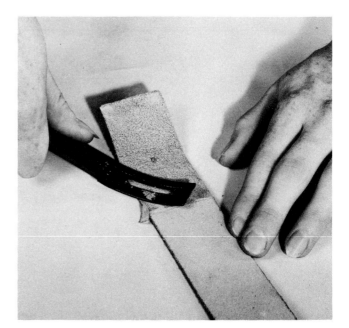

4 Punch a hole or cut a slot in the center of the skived section.

5 Insert the tongue of the buckle through the hole and fasten the edge of the folded strip with rivets, eyelets, button snaps, or by sewing.

6 If a loop is needed to hold the belt end, cut a narrow strip of leather to encircle the belt strip. With a belt staple or by sewing, fasten this strip underneath where it overlaps. This attached strip may conceal the stitching or other attachment that holds the buckle, as well as provide a loop to hold the belt end when it is fastened.

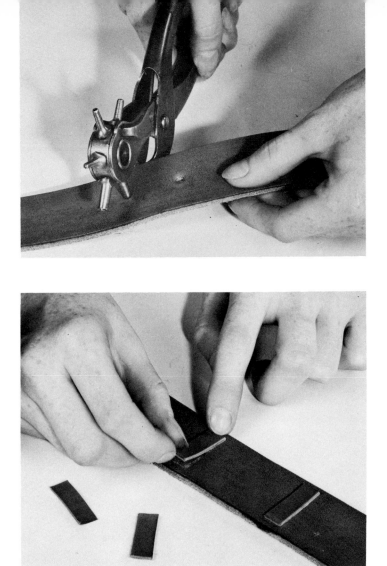

7   Punch evenly spaced holes in the other end of the belt strip to fasten the buckle.

8   Decorate the surface of the leather by attaching small pieces of leather with cement. These may be of the same or a different color. Tooling, stamping, or carving may be done either before or after the buckle is attached.

9   To finish the belt, touch up areas that need more dye. Also add color to any specific places where it is needed in the organization of the pattern.

LEATHER PURSE

Purses or bags may be designed according to the size and shape desired. They may be cylindrical with a circular bottom, or rectangular with gussets inserted on the sides to provide width. Coin purses may be folded flat. A paper pattern is always cut first to establish the size and proportions of the shape, and to help determine the amount of leather needed.

The leather may be decorated with tooling, stamping, carving, appliqué, inserts, pieces sewn together, and with various attachments such as fringe.

Tabs and fasteners, like button snaps and metal locks, are attached according to the type used. If a lining is used, it is cemented in after the leather is decorated and attachments secured, but before the parts are secured or laced together.

MATERIALS

1. Leather for the purse and for the lining
2. Cutting tools—knives, shears
3. Steel square
4. Modeling, stamping, and carving tools
5. Dyes
6. Adhesives—rubber cement or glue
7. Fasteners, button snaps
8. Linen thread
9. Leather lace
10. Needle

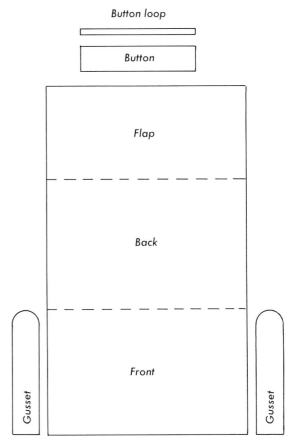

1 Cut a paper pattern for all the parts needed.

2 Lay the cut-out pattern on the leather. Using a straightedge and sharp blade cut out the rectangular piece, or mark around the piece and cut with shears or knife.

3 Glue lining leather to the leather to be used for the gussets. Allow the glue to dry. Then cut out the two gussets for inserts on each end of the purse, using the paper pattern as a guide. The liner may be glued to the gusset leather before it is cut in this case, because the gussets will have no added decoration or attachments.

4 Decorate the outer surface of the leather with metal stamp tools, or with any other means desired.

5 Dye the leather surface. Refer to the section on Dyeing Leather. Add color to special areas where needed to complete the pattern.

6 Cut a strip of leather to serve as a loop for the fastener. Glue the ends of the loop to the inside of the flap for smoothness and support. Cover the loop attachment with a thin glued piece of leather. This loop and its support must be put in before the lining is attached to the main body of the purse.

7 To make a rolled fastener, cut a strip of leather long enough so that when it is rolled it will easily pass through the loop on the flap.

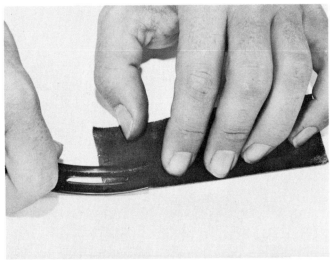

8 Cover the strip with cement or glue, and roll tightly, completing the roll with the skived end.

9 If the ends of the rolled strip are uneven, trim them with a razor blade when the glue is dry. This method can be used to make spirals for buttons and decorations.

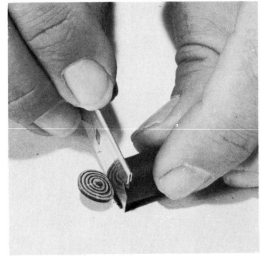

10 Dye a length of linen thread the same color as the purse. Bind the rolled fastener tightly around the middle with several wrappings of this dyed linen thread.

11 After deciding the position of the fastener in relation to the leather loop previously attached, poke two holes through the front of the purse with an awl.

12 Attach the fastener with a double strand of the dyed thread.

13 Line the main body of the purse. The lining may be cut from the paper pattern and then glued to the body of the purse; or the lining leather may be glued to the body, allowed to dry, and then trimmed to fit.

14 To mark the places for the stitches, use a space-marker wheel. Refer to step 2 under Sewing Procedures. Mark the gussets on the sides and bottom but not across the top. Mark the edges of the purse from the front to the back a distance equal to the length of the parts of the gusset to be sewn. Do not mark the flap.

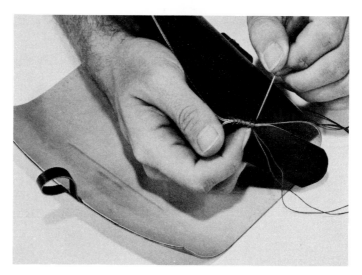

15 Line up the gussets evenly with the top edge of the purse on the side where the fastener is sewed. Attach them to the purse with the dyed linen thread, using an overcast stitch.

16 The completed purse.

LEATHER-COVERED BOX

Sturdy boxes of various sizes, which can be covered with leather, are available from craft supply sources at a reasonable cost. Other types such as cigar boxes may also be used. Almost any type of leather can be used. A pattern is cut of paper and traced onto the leather, and the leather is cut out. The pieces are cemented or glued to the box. One long strip of leather may be cut instead of sections for covering the sides. Corners must be closely joined so that no part of the box will show between them.

The leather may be dyed and decorated with modeling, stamping, and carving tools, with inlay, onlay, mosaic, and embossed or pressed forms. Leather-covered boxes can be further decorated with enameled inserts.

MATERIALS

1. Boxes
2. Leather
3. Cutting tools—shears, knives
4. Objects for decoration—modeling, stamping, and carving tools
5. Dyes
6. Adhesives—rubber cement, glues

1 Obtain a box for covering and plan a design appropriate for the shape.

2 Select the leather and, if color is to be used, apply dye. Refer to section on Dyeing Leather.

3 Cut paper pattern strips to fit the sides of the box.

4 Lay the strips on the leather, mark around them or use them as a pattern, and cut the leather with scissors or a sharp knife.

5 Cement the strips to the sides of the box, making certain that the corners meet. Rub the leather carefully to make it adhere.

6 Cut to exact size and glue the leather for the bottom of the box. This may be the same leather that was used on the sides, or it may be soft suede or some other suitable material.

7 Cut a paper pattern for the lid of the box to cover the top and sides. The pattern may be cut in separate pieces to fit all sides of the lid, or it may be cut in one piece.

8 Place the pattern for the lid on the leather, trace, and cut out.

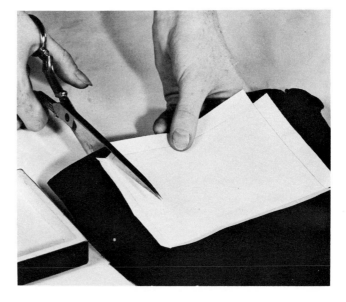

9 If a mosaic pattern of small pieces of leather is used on the lid, cut out the center portion of the leather, leaving ½ inch or so around the edge.

10 Cement the leather to the lid of the box.

11 Cut small pieces of the same leather and dye them according to the color plan desired, or use pieces of leather of different types.

12 Cement the small pieces close together to form a pattern.

LEATHER 289

13 *Leather-covered box with design pressed into the leather by means of a pattern cut in relief on a linoleum block. Pressure was exerted with an etching press. Color has been applied to small areas with a brush.*

Memo Pad Cover. 1955. Combination of tooling and stamping on leather. Height 6". Adult student.

Leather Bag. Leather-covered Boxes. Adult students, University of Washington. Steven Fuller, Instructor.

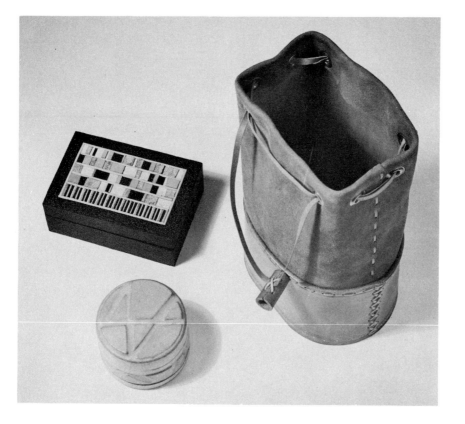

ADDITIONAL SUGGESTIONS FOR LEATHER

Working with leather has more appeal to older students, for they are fascinated both by the manipulation of the tools in making impressions on the leather surface, and by the resulting product as something they can wear or use in some way. However, since interest in the product sometimes overshadows the need for preparation, the teacher must emphasize that there is no purpose in construction that is poorly conceived and carelessly executed. He must strive to get the students to see that planning is essential, and that an object must be well designed before it is made. So many articles made of leather have stereotyped designs, and so many available patterns set poor standards, that the student becomes confused because he has little to guide him in developing taste and judgment. Therefore, it is important that the student experiment with pieces of scrap leather, to try out colors and repetitive patterns.

The beginner can plan designs by cutting geometric shapes from paper and arranging them in formal repeats or other types of organizational plans. Or a lettering pen with a small round nib can be used for planning patterns that combine lines and shapes in design units. Beginners will be more successful if they stick to abstract units before trying anything pictorial.

The student can be challenged to take small pieces of leather and find ways to use them. He can fit them together to form belts or bags, use them in mosaic patterns on a box or book cover, or apply them over larger surfaces of leather as onlay or appliqué.

The luggage tag, which does not require much material, is a good problem to begin on. The key case may involve practically all leather techniques and is also a good learning problem. Students may choose from a number of projects in addition to those mentioned, including wallets, hats, sandals, boxes, and cases for cameras or glasses. They should never try to imitate or copy commercially made products, for there is no value in such procedure.

Careful craftsmanship and pride in doing a job well should always be encouraged. After a student has once made a successful item and received praise for his efforts, he will begin to appreciate the importance of good design and technique. He will also have more respect for the material and be less wasteful of it. There is nothing more discouraging than to see a beautiful, expensive piece of leather insensitively handled.

CLAY

Peter Voulkos: *Butte Divide*. 1958. Ceramic, 4½' high. Pasadena Museum.
Photograph courtesy of the artist.

CLAY

The use of clay for aesthetic and practical purposes is probably coeval with the development of human culture. The world over, in ancient and modern times, this common material has been molded or cast into forms both expressive and functional: bricks and tile for architecture; great sculpture; children's toys; bowls and vessels for storing and mixing grains, honey, water, wine, and oils, for bringing food and drink to the lips, and for holding the remains of the dead.

Clay is plastic when it is wet. It can be pinched, pulled, stretched, rolled, joined, cut, kneaded, and pushed into shape by the craftsman's hands. It can be dug away and added to while the work is in process. If enough water is mixed with it, it can be poured into forms. When it has dried it can be fired or baked to great hardness and strength for usability and permanence.

There are many kinds of clay, and each will result in a different appearance of color, texture, and even shape. The clay used to make porous low-fired earthenware is very different from the fine-grained clay used in making high-fired translucent porcelain. Within the molecular structure of the clay itself are the qualities that determine the limitations, possibilities, and necessary processes for its use. Through experience, the craftsman learns the "feel" of his material; he learns to respect its limitations and to utilize them to build expressive forms.

There are eight basic processes in working with clay: modeling from a lump, pinching, piece mounting, building with slabs, building with coils, throwing on a wheel, slip molding, and press molding. The first five are known as *hand building techniques* because they require no special tools or equipment. Essentially, the methods used by modern potters and sculptors in hand building are the same as have been used since primitive times. Each of these processes imparts its own particular characteristics to the shape and finish of the final products, and in large part its limitations and possibilities determine the form of the work. A skilled designer does not need to conceal his methods. The touch of the potter, the mark of his tools, the qualities of the clay, and the direct expressiveness of each process are all prized in the finished work if they are sensitively handled and integrated into the design of the whole. The hand building processes all offer potentials of form not possible with machined products. Each piece can be individually expressive, limited only by the ability of the craftsman who made it.

Modeling from a lump of clay is the simple beginning for solid three-dimensional forms. Starting with a small ball of material, the clay is shaped by pressing, pulling, adding on, or cutting away. Small bits can be added a little at a time to build out to a desired contour, or sections can be dug out wherever needed. Rolls of clay can be attached to the original lump. The material yields easily to the fingers and can be shaped and reshaped until the artist is satisfied and his form is complete. In this way the famous little

Egyptian, from the Tomb of Senbi: *Figure of a Hippopotamus.* XII Dynasty. Ceramics, Faience, 7⅞" x 4⅜". Courtesy of the Metropolitan Museum of Art. Gift of Edward S. Harkness, 1917.

Chinese, Late Chou Period: *Group of Four Mourners.* Fourth—third century B.C. Black pottery, 3" to 4" high. Seattle Art Museum, Eugene Fuller Memorial Collection.

ancient Egyptian hippopotamus was made. His generously rounded form is characteristic of the material, which readily lends itself to curved surfaces. The artisan has simplified his subject in order to heighten the sense of volume and the relationship of curved shapes. The legs are stout to support the body above, as necessitated by the material. In the same way, from small lumps or rolls of clay, ancient Greek children's toys and votive figures were formed. Simple, expressive of volume, rhythmic in line and shape, the clay has been used to express its own qualities as much as to represent the figures and creatures that delight us. The Chinese *Group of Four Mourners,* the Southwest American Indian *Horse,* and the Mexican folk art pieces were built with the same process. Adding bit by bit, taking away, pushing, pressing, changing the basic form until its contours and volumes took shape, these artists have made their works strikingly expressive of the material from which they were formed; these works show the complex development possible with this simple method.

Greek: *Figure Seated in an Armchair.* Eighth century B.C. Terra cotta, 4⅞" high. Courtesy of The Metropolitan Museum of Art, Fletcher Fund, 1931.

Greek, Boeotian: *Figure.* Eighth century B.C. Terra cotta, 11⅞" high. Courtesy of the Museum of Fine Arts, Boston.

Southwest American Indian: *Horse.* Twentieth century. Fired clay with horsehair mane and tail, 10½" high.

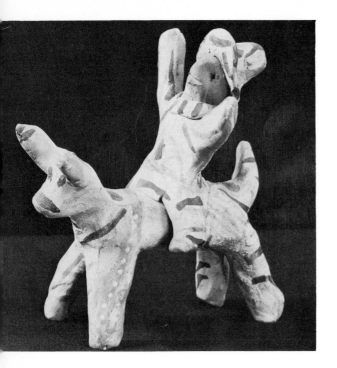

Mexican: *Donkey and Rider*. Twentieth century. Fired clay, painted decoration, 5½" high.

For making pots, the simplest hand building process is *pinching*. The potter begins with a ball of clay, and with his thumbs makes a depression or hollow in it. He then pinches and works the clay until the hollow has developed and the clay has been shaped into the even thickness of a pot wall. The marks of the potter's fingers can be an integral part of the form, indicative of the process with which it was shaped. Pinch pots are usually small enough to be held easily in the hand, for larger shapes are difficult to manage.

Piece mounting is closely related to pinching. In this method, the craftsman develops the work by adding clay a bit at a time, pinching it firmly to the clay before, until the piece is shaped. With this process a greater variety of forms is possible because the craftsman is not limited to a size or shape he can derive from a ball of clay he can hold in his hands, and as the work grows in small increments, complex forms can be made.

The slab process is begun by pressing or rolling the clay into slabs or sheets. These are cut into flat tiles or into strips that can be decorated as individual tiles, or combined for wall or other surface decoration. For three-dimensional forms, these flat slabs can be joined to make pots or sculpture. Rectangular or cylindrical forms naturally result, the shapes determined by the process. The Peruvian folk art *Cathedral* is a clear example of form derived from the slab process. The basic shape, composed of rectangular solids, is varied with the addition of figures and ornaments, and red and brown decoration painted on the sides. Although the simple shape is satisfying in itself, the design, with its varied rhythmic elements and space-filling qualities, greatly enhances the appearance of the work.

The coil process, like piece mounting, offers a wide development of forms and shapes, because the pot builds slowly, allowing many changes in contour as it grows coil by coil. With the coil method, both very small pots and giant pots may be constructed. In the Mediterranean area, potters make jars for olive oil storage so large that two men work on them at once, one man inside the pot to attach the long ropes of clay coils which are prepared and passed to him by his assistant outside the pot. Such huge pots could not be thrown on a wheel. The possibilities of shape are equally varied, ranging from simple bowls, cups, bottles, and pitchers to complicated pots representing human and animal forms— pots that approach sculpture in their free use of shapes, contours, and volumes.

The coil method is actually very simple. First, a flat disc of clay is prepared; then on this base the potter begins to build his form by attaching coil after coil. He makes the coils by rolling balls of clay with steady even pressure under his hands until they are long cylindrical shapes. The coil is then attached to the flat base and wrapped around the circumference, overlapping itself.

Mexican: *Figure and Animal Group.* Twentieth century. Fired clay with painted decoration, 16½" high.

Jane Dickerman: *Tile.* 1954. Glazed tile with stamped decoration, 6" x 6".

Upper right: Rut Bryk: *Decorative Wall Plaque.* 1957. Porcelain and ceramic colors, 12" x 19⅞". Courtesy, Wärtsilä-Koncernen Arabia, Finland.

Mexican: *Tiles.* Twentieth century. Fired clay, glazed decoration, 6", 4", 4".

Persian, Kashan Style: *Tile, Six-pointed Star*. Thirteenth or fourteenth century. Clay: soft, white. Glaze: cream white. Decoration: painted brown luster on white ground, 5⅝″ x 5″. Courtesy of the Smithsonian Institution, Freer Gallery of Art, Washington, D. C.

Peruvian: *Cathedral*. Twentieth century. Fired clay, engobe decoration. 12½″ high.

Miró and Artigas: *The Wall of the Moon* for UNESCO House in Paris. Ceramic tile. Courtesy of UNESCO, Photograph by Pablo Volta, 1958.

Left: English (Staffordshire): *Pew Group.* c. 1745. Salt-glazed stoneware. Courtesy of The Metropolitan Museum of Art. Gift of Carleton Macy, 1934.

Acoma Pueblo, New Mexico: *Pottery Jar, abstract style.* Fired clay, 10¼" high. American Museum of Natural History.

Mexican, Tarascan: State of Nayarit: *Figure.* Terra cotta, 10¾" high. Portland Art Museum.

Each coil adds to the height of the growing form. As the potter builds, he may alter the shape with great freedom, causing the walls of the pot to enlarge or diminish in size in order to vary the contour or suggest subject matter in the form he is making. As the potter attaches each coil to the one beneath it, he may smooth the surface carefully so that the method of construction is skillfully concealed, or he may prefer to let the coils show, welding them together only on the inside. Then the coils provide a surface pattern that is automatically integral with the form.

Some of the possibilities of the coil method can be grasped by examining a few of the pots made in pre-Columbian America. In the southwestern United States, many Indian peoples developed the art of potting to a high degree. The Navajo, Hopi, Pueblo, Acoma, and Zuñi potters made pots of great vitality and sensitivity, pots with graceful contours and close detail, ornamental pots with rich pattern designed to increase awareness of the sense of volume and shape. Such a pot is the Acoma *Jar.* Although the shape is simple, the line of the edge is a subtle combination of arcs, leading the eye easily around the form. The surface design is a carefully thought-out pattern of darks and lights, so skillfully balanced and arranged that the positive and negative shapes of the design seem to alternate, the background becoming foreground in a surprising exchange. The placement of the pattern on the pot and the choice of line direction serve to point up the beauty of the contour and to pull the eye around the form.

Many peoples over the world have made pots with human or animal shapes for ritual use or for the pleasure of the design and the skill involved. The pre-Columbian potters of Peru and the Tarascan potters of Mexico excelled in the use of these forms, creating an enormous variety of pot shapes derived from subject matter. The Tarascan *Figure* and *Dog* pots illustrate the sensitivity of their design and their keen observation

of life. In each case, however, the potter has not forgotten that his primary purpose was the making of a pot, and these works express all the qualities we expect to find in a well-designed pot. Especially pronounced is the feeling that each of these pots is a container, with a satisfying interior space. We might say that they are pots first and figures or animals afterward. The hollow legs are too big in comparison with their living counterparts, but necessarily so to support, both physically and visually, the bulk of the body above. The sense of interior volume is everywhere stressed in the easy, flowing contours. The superb Peruvian *Deer* and *Fish* are examples of the skilled use of negative space. Rhythmic lines, patterns, and volumes combine with varied openings to produce subtle form. The pre-Columbian artisans united the container's purpose with fanciful subject matter in an easy, gracious way, with a knowledge of design and method. The Japanese Haniwa *Horse* and the monumental Etruscan-style *Warrior* indicate the

Peru (Early Nazca): *Pot in the Form of a Fish.* c. Sixth century. Pottery, painted grey, black, yellow, red, white, 5¾″ x 8½″. The Minneapolis Institute of Arts.

Mexican, Tarascan; from State of Colima: *Dog.* Clay, 10⅝″ x 16⅛″. Portland Art Museum.

Japanese, Tumulus Period: *Haniwa Horse*. Third–sixth century. Orange-red low-fired earthenware, 26½" high. Seattle Art Museum, Eugene Fuller Memorial Collection.

Etruscan: *Mars or a Warrior*. (Recent copy after early Etruscan work.) Terra cotta, 8′ ¼" high (total). Courtesy of the Metropolitan Museum of Art, Kennedy Fund, 1921.

Mexican: *Calypso*. Twentieth century. Black Oaxaca clay, 13″ high. Traditional Mexican folk-art form.

Greek: *Black-figured Kylix;* painted by Xenokles. Third quarter of sixth century B.C. Painted earthenware, 4″ high; diam. 7″. Seattle Art Museum, Norman Davis Collection.

Etruscan: *Trefoil Mouthed Oinochoë*. About 520 B.C. Painted earthenware, 11¾″ high; 20″ girth. Seattle Art Museum, Norman Davis Collection.

potentials of size and excellence of sculptural design possible with simple clay techniques.

The Greek potters are especially famed for the precision and carefully planned design of their work. Each of the pot forms developed by Greek craftsmen was based on a specific function and was built to serve that function. The *krater* for mixing wine and water, the *oinochoë* for pouring, the *amphora* for carrying water, the *kylix* for drinking—all have individual shapes adopted for their use. The kylix, with its subtle lines and beautifully proportioned handles and foot, illustrates a fine sense of geometric symmetry, graceful contour, thoughtful surface pattern placed with skill to accentuate the volumes, and a functional form treated as a work of art. Interior volume is handsomely expressed in the amphora (page 19), built around an egg-shaped void. The wide mouth permits easy access to the contents, the broad foot ensures stability, and the large open handles provide a good grasp.

Visually, these parts also function as elements in a design of great strength. Observe how easily the eye moves from handle to body with the gentle transition at the point of contact; how the size of the neck complements the breadth of the foot and the opening of the two handles; and, too, how the black-painted design combines pattern and subject matter to blend surface and volume into a continuous unity.

Throwing on the wheel is a technique that introduced a new tool to the craft of potting, a tool that provides a whole new vocabulary of forms and potentialities of structure or design. The technique of using a wheel imparts its own characteristic shapes, surface textures, and details to the form of the pot. The wheel is a rotating disc on a shaft, turned either by the foot or by machine. To make a pot the potter first must carefully prepare his clay, wedging or kneading it to remove completely all air bubbles and to work it to the right consistency. Then a lump of this clay is thrown or *centered* in the exact center of the disc. This must be done with precision, for an off-center, unbalanced beginning is difficult to control. The clay is kept moist so that it will slip easily under the hands that shape it. As the wheel turns, pressure is applied to the mass, pressing it in and up. Then, with his thumbs, the potter makes an indentation in the center of the mass, pressing down almost to the base. Into this opening, he places the fingers of one hand and, with gentle support from the outside, pulls out the wall of clay, opening up the interior space. Now with the side of the index finger on the outside and supported with the other hand on the inside, he draws the wall of clay upward to the height he wishes. With further pressure, pushing and pulling, or with tools and templates, the pot walls may be shaped further into bottles, bowls, plates, pitchers, and jars. The possibilities of form seem almost unlimited. After the pot is removed from the wheel, while it is still plastic, the clay can be bent and shaped

into spouts for pitchers; or indentations can be pressed for design, handles can be added, or two or more thrown pieces, such as a bowl and its separately thrown foot, can be joined.

Press molding and *slip molding* are methods especially useful for the production of many identical pieces. In any technique that employs a mold, the quality of the finished piece is almost entirely dependent upon the quality of design of the mold itself. Either the mold is cast around a work or the form is carved directly into the mold material. The piece to be molded should be designed so that it can easily be pulled free from the form without any of its projections breaking off. The process dictates very strongly the nature of the design. The press-mold piece is made of plastic clay pressed into the mold. Sometimes, especially for complex works, the potter must make the mold in several parts that he can easily assemble and disassemble without ruining the clay form within. The mold may then be removed, or the clay may be allowed to dry before the mold is opened. Then the process is continued until the required number of pieces has been cast. The slip mold, a more recent development, is made of plaster. Into the negative or female form, *slip* or liquid clay is poured. The plaster quickly absorbs the water from the clay, which begins to dry around the inner surface of the mold. When the dried clay has reached a sufficient thickness, the excess slip is poured from the center of the mold. After an interval the mold may be opened and the piece removed.

Ancient Greek artisans, who enjoyed a lively trade in small sculptures of household gods called *Tanagra* figures, employed the press mold to keep up with the demand. These sensitive, well-designed works achieve the aesthetic level of fine sculpture with their carefully conceived volumes and imaginative treatment of drapery and gesture. Also with the press mold small details may be formed and added to pots made with other processes. This technique, called *sprigging,* is used by many potters the world over to embellish simpler forms.

However the pot is made, its quality depends upon the design of its basic shape and the way the potter has utilized his tools and processes. A well-made pot can derive its beauty from its form alone—the satisfaction of its volumes and voids and the interest of the marks of the tools and methods of its making are often sufficient in themselves. For variety, there are many ways to add to the design, such as incising, adding parts, and decorating the surface with engobes and glazes. Incised design is carved into the clay while it is still plastic. The potter may cut thin lines, large masses, or even holes into the clay, creating a pattern of surface levels. He may also press bits of clay onto the surface or attach them with slip to develop a raised pattern, as in sprigging. On the pot surface, varied colored clays in liquid form, called *engobes* or slips, may be applied to make designs. Engobes may be brushed, applied with a stencil, sprayed, dripped, or trailed onto the surface. When the slip is trailed from a syringe, slightly raised lines result, which accentuate the pattern. A technique called *sgraffito*—covering the surface of the pot with a thin layer of engobe and then scratching through to reveal the original clay color beneath—gives a quality of line and mass completely different from similar areas done by direct painting with the brush. Clear and crisp, the cutaway areas stand out in strong contrast heightened by the slight variation in surface texture caused by the scratching tool.

Until the invention of glazes in the ancient Near East, the potter depended solely upon the possible variations in color of clay itself for his surface decoration. With the introduction of glazing materials, the variety of colors and textures of pottery was greatly increased; and, because glazes provide a watertight surface, the usefulness of low-fired ceramic utensils was

Greek: *Tanagra Figure.* c. 200 B.C. Terra Cotta 13½" high.

Korean, Late Silla Period: *Footed Bowl.* 668–935 A.D. Unglazed grey stoneware. M. H. deYoung Memorial Museum, San Francisco.

Korean, Early Silla Period: *Covered Stem Cup.* Third to fifth century A.D. Stoneware, 9¼" high. Seattle Art Museum, Eugene Fuller Memorial Collection.

Chinese, Sung Dynasty: *Pillow.* c. 960–1279. Porcelaneous ware, iron oxide scroll decoration, 10½" wide. Seattle Art Museum, Eugene Fuller Memorial Collection.

Chinese, Late Chou Period: *Bell.* Sixth to fourth century B.C. Earthenware, 12⅜" high. Seattle Art Museum, Eugene Fuller Memorial Collection.

Opposite page: Chinese, Sung Dynasty: *Tz-u Chou Ware Vase.* c. 960–1279. Stoneware, 9½" high. Seattle Art Museum, Gift of Mr. and Mrs. Herbert Brink.

Upper left: Pennsylvania German: *Plate, Washington on Horseback.* 1805. Pottery, sgraffito design. The Continental soldier is thought to be General Washington. The translated inscription reads, "I have been riding over hill and dale and everywhere have found pretty girls." Philadelphia Museum of Art.

Upper right: Pennsylvania German: *Dish.* 1769. Common clay pottery plate, slip decoration of conventional tulip design. Philadelphia Museum of Art.

Pablo Picasso: *Plate.* 1952. Earthenware. 3" high, 17" diameter. Courtesy of Elena M. Netherby, Mills College.

Gertrud and Otto Natzler: *Bowl.* 1959. Ceramic bowl, hand-thrown. Tan and black crater glaze, 4″ high, 8½″ diameter.

John Fassbinder: *Garden Pot.* 1960. Fired clay, 24″ high.

improved. The glaze in liquid form is applied to the pot by dipping, brushing, or spraying. Pattern and color change can be achieved by combining different glazes. The range of color is enormous—from the subtle deep browns and plum hues with rich depth and delicately modulated or mottled color of ancient Oriental pots to the intense reds, oranges, yellows, and greens of modern ceramic engineering. Texture also varies from soft, eggshell-like mat surfaces to those of glossy brilliance, or coarsely puckered, lava-like textures. In glazing their ware, many fine Oriental potters like to leave part of each piece with some of the unglazed clay exposed to remind us of what the material is like underneath the smooth glaze, and to offer a rich variation in surface texture, a poetic and sensitive use of the materials.

As with many products of our contemporary scientific age, the raw materials from which glazes are made are highly refined and precise; therefore, the glazes made from them are uniform, even, and clear of defects. Most ancient potters gathered their own glazing materials; burned their own woods for wood ash, an essential ingredient in many glazes; sifted the colored earths by hand, often with some difficulty; and, with an alert eye for the results of any happy accident, mixed their own glazes. Because complete accuracy was not possible, and because the ingredients were never pure, the glazes were rich with subtle variations in color and texture. Many modern potters, who feel that scientifically prepared materials overpurify and remove any element of chance, have returned to the older, less certain methods. Combined with underglaze decoration of slip and engobes, glazing offers the potter almost numberless combinations of color, texture, line, and value from which to build his design.

Firing the clay is the last step in making a pot. Primitive man probably discovered this technique by accident. Possibly some earthen vessel

Left: Maija Grotell: *Bowl*. 1959. Stoneware with decorative glaze. *Center*: Charlotte Malten: *Sculptured Vase, Five Spouts*. 1960. Dark brown grogged clay, slip glazed, 10″ x 12″. *Right*: Marie Woo: *Covered Jar*. 1960. Stoneware, 11″ high.

Robert Sperry: *Multi-spouted Fountain*. 1960. Ceramic, decorated with black glaze on brown textured surface. 36″ high.

used for cooking was left too long on the fire (or perhaps fell into the hot coals and ashes where it lay forgotten overnight), and its user found that it had undergone a remarkable change. The overheated clay became stronger and harder, and would no longer dissolve in water. Primitive peoples still fire their pots in a similar fashion. The simple process is begun when the pots are placed in hot embers for an hour or two to dry them thoroughly; then they are piled up over the bed of a fire, which is then ignited. After the initial burst of flames, grass, twigs, dung, or other combustibles are thrown over the burning mass, covering it and keeping in the heat and smoke. The color of the pot will depend on how near it is to the direct flame or on how much smoke it gets during the firing. Different woods and grasses will color the clay differently, and among many primitive potters firing secrets are as jealously guarded as any secrets of the potter's craft. Firing is the most suspenseful part of pot making. Up to the point where the pot goes in the kiln, the potter has his work pretty much under control. But when the kiln door is closed he can only hope that all goes well, and steal an occasional peek through the spyholes provided for that purpose. Especially in wood kilns, the variation possible in the temperature of the kiln and in the chemical environment inside the chamber provides an element of chance. Even the modern gas and electric kilns are not thoroughly predictable. When the firing is begun, many terrible or wonderful things that the potter did not plan may happen to the pot. Under the extreme heat, the pot shrinks as the remaining moisture is removed from the clay. Glazes may change color for better or for worse; they may run off the surface, pucker, burn off, or puddle. Upon opening the kiln, an exciting event fraught with anticipation, the potter can see what has actually happened during the hours when he could not look in on his work. In many Japanese folk potters' com-

munities, opening the kiln is a regular ceremony. When the hour of the kiln opening is near, the townsfolk gather at the kiln door. Then the door is opened, and the ware is removed, not yet even thoroughly cooled, so that it must be handled with gloves or pads. As each piece is examined and set aside, an onlooker may see a pot he particularly admires. He may write a note on a bit of paper and leave it in the pot of his choice: "If you can bring yourself to part with this pot, I would like to own it." To avoid vulgarity he does not mention the price. In such a ceremony, the potter's anticipation of opening the kiln is shared with the townsfolk.

Each clay body has a firing temperature that will bring out its best qualities of appearance and function. Very low-fired earthenware may be fired from 600° to 700° C. At these temperatures the clay remains somewhat porous, and, unless it is glazed, water will seep through the clay body. At stoneware temperature, from about 1140° to 1320° C., the fired clay becomes vitreous and impervious to water, and needs no glaze. Very high-fired clay bodies such as porcelain may be fired up to 1400° C. to bring about the subtle translucent qualities we associate with such clay ware. Instead of using a thermometer to check the temperature, the potter employs small test pieces called cones to determine the correct firing temperature. The cone is designed to melt at certain temperatures. Cone .04, for example, will melt at 1020° C., cone 6 at 1200° C. The higher the number, the greater the heat necessary to melt the cone. When the potter loads the kiln with ware to be fired, he presses a cone in a bit of soft clay so that it will stand nearly upright and places it on a shelf in the kiln where he can see it through a spyhole. Then as the kiln is fired, he looks in at the cone from time to time until he observes that it is beginning to sag. This indicates that the proper temperature has been reached, and the fire may be slackened or the kiln shut off. Some modern kilns are equipped with pyrometers, which automatically turn off the kiln at the proper temperature, thus simplifying the operation of firing. After the desired temperature has been reached, the kiln is allowed to cool slowly before the pots are removed to avoid too rapid a cooling off, which might shatter the ware.

Throughout the process of building a pot, the good potter keeps two things constantly in mind: function and design. Each aspect of the form springs from the need for which it is designed. The positive and negative spaces must be equally considered and equally satisfying. Even when a pot is so refined in shape and so handsome that it will never be used except to look at, the possibility of its use underlies and supports its visual appearance and its aesthetic value. The design of the negative volume is the core around which the structure is formed. The clay wall should reveal the quality of the void within, echo its contours, strengthen its form. Any parts added to this basic unit must relate visually to its character and add to its purpose. Any decoration applied to the surface must be integrated into the design so that it becomes a part of an organic whole, not just stuck on haphazardly. Even a small acquaintance with pots from many cultures the world over brings us a new awareness of form and new concepts of design and beauty. Each potter, when his hands are in the clay, experiences some of the excitement of creation, of adventure in shape and texture and color, which has always been the most important part of pot making.

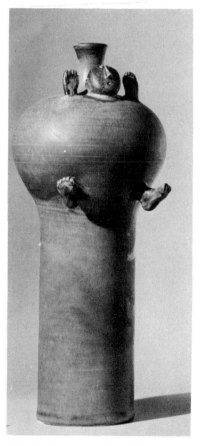

Stig Lindberg: *Bottle*. 1960. Stoneware, green and black. C. B. Gustavsbergs Fabriker.

Antonio Prieto: *Container*. 1960. Fired clay. Photograph by Margaret Dhaemers.

CLAY PROCESSES

There are many different kinds of clay, each suitable for different purposes. For jewelry and fine work, a smooth clay body that matures at a low temperature, permitting the use of high-color glazes, is preferable. A clay body for sculpture and hand building should be firm and plastic enough to mold, but strong enough to support itself without sagging. Pottery clay or earthenware with about a 10 per cent addition of sand or grog provides a clay of this quality, or a stoneware clay may be used. The addition of sand or grog to a clay body strengthens it for working and ensures less shrinkage.

Clay may be purchased in the wet pug state, or in a dry powder form, and in some localities may be dug directly. The most convenient method is to buy the clay pug wet, packed in plastic storage bags. This commercially prepared clay is free of lumps and foreign material, and is easy to handle; it is the proper consistency and may be kept indefinitely in the plastic sacks. Dry clay may be stored in powder form and mixed in large or small quantities when needed. The mixed clay can also be stored in plastic sacks or other suitable closed containers. Clay is easier to handle if it has aged or mellowed for at least a week (the longer the aging period the better). It must, however, be kept in airtight containers to prevent drying. Clay that is too moist to use may be wedged or rolled on a dry table or plaster bat, and clay that is too dry may be rolled or wedged on a damp surface, or left on a wet plaster bat and covered with a wet cloth or paper towels. Leather-dry clay may be cut in strips and soaked in water until it is plastic enough to knead and be wedged again. Even completely dried clay may be re-used after it has been soaked in water, drained, dried to working consistency, and rewedged.

Clays fire at different temperatures; earthenware fires much lower than stoneware, and, although it is sturdy, it is less strong and impervious to water than stoneware, which is watertight without the addition of glaze. In general, the lower the firing temperature of a clay, the more fragile and porous it is. High-fired, fused clay bodies are very strong and moisture resistant. Therefore, a very low-fired unglazed clay would not be suitable material for a cream pitcher, but might be excellent for a necklace or a tile.

CLAY MIXING

Clay can be mixed in small quantities for immediate use.

MATERIALS

1. Clay powder
2. Water, warm if possible
3. Pan, coffee can, or plastic sack
4. Sand or grog (particles of prefired clay)—optional

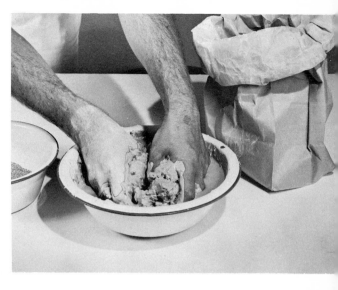

1   *To mix a small quantity of clay in a pan, partially fill the pan with water and sift the powdered clay into the water. Mix it with the fingers until the mass can be manipulated into a ball with the hands. Add more clay or water if necessary. When mixed, the clay should be plastic but not sticky. When properly plastic, a small roll of clay can be bent without cracking. Sand or grog can be added for hand building.*

2   *A plastic sack may be substituted for the pan as a mixing container. The powder and water are combined in a plastic sack, which, when tightly closed, can be kneaded with the hands until the clay mixture reaches the proper consistency.*

TO PREPARE A LARGE QUANTITY OF CLAY

Clay prepared in large quantities can be stored in closed containers, ready for use when needed. This allows it to age, and thus improves its consistency and workability.

MATERIALS

1. Clay powder
2. Covered container such as crock, garbage can, or plastic bucket
3. Water, between 3 and 4 gallons for 100 pounds of clay
4. Sifter screen
5. Stirring stick

CLAY   **313**

1 Clay powder can be added to the full quantity of water. Pour the water in the container. Sift the clay into the water with the screen, or with the hand. Another method to mix large quantities of clay is to fill the container with alternate layers of clay and water.

2 Remove any lumps by stirring. Stirring will assure an even distribution of the water. A long, stout stick forced to the bottom of the clay mass can be rotated from the top to stir the mixture.

3 Allow the mixture to stand until the water works its way through the clay and the mixture has dried to proper working consistency. If the first method is employed and the clay is too damp, it will thicken if it is allowed to stand long enough for the water to evaporate. Wet clay may also be poured into plaster forms or bats to hasten evaporation. All clay mixed in large quantities should be allowed to ripen at least a week.

PREPARING CLAY

WEDGING

Wedging removes air pockets from the clay and improves the consistency, ensuring more successful handling and firing. The potter wedges the clay by forming it into a rectangular shape, cutting it into two parts with a wire, inverting the ends, and then vigorously throwing the parts onto a solid surface such as a wedging table or floor. This process is repeated about twenty times.

The potter can wedge the clay also by kneading it in a circular fashion, forming a shell-like shape, and rolling it into a cylinder. This may also be done either on a table top, bench, or floor. The body movements and the rhythms of wedging are difficult to describe successfully. Traditional clay-wedging techniques involve a sequence of ordered motion verging on the dance that is a pleasure to observe.

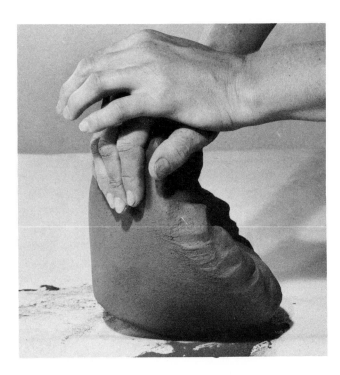

SHELL METHOD

1 Shape the clay into a ball. Start kneading in a circular motion with the hands overlapped and the palms down.

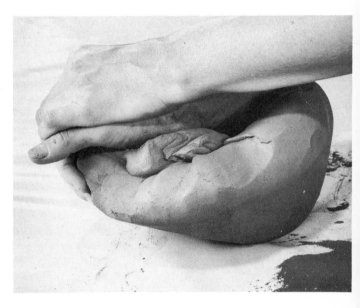

2 *The pressure of the hands moves a portion of the clay from the edge toward the center of the mass, creating a series of overlaps. As pressure is applied, the clay mass rotates under the hands.*

4 *Pull the mass back into position for the next stroke.*

3 *Grasp the outer edge.*

5 *As this action is repeated, the shell-like form develops. Continue until the clay reaches a good working consistency. Practice is necessary to acquire wedging skill.*

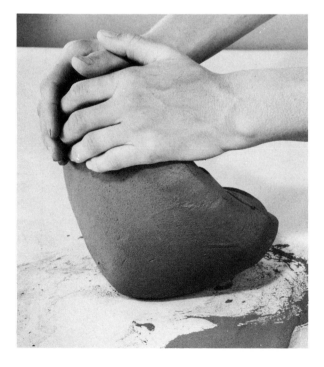

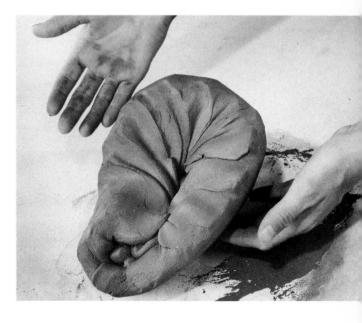

MAKING A PLASTER BAT

A plaster bat is required for many clay projects. Bats can be used as a work surface for hand building processes or throwing on the wheel. Wet clay dries quickly when it is spread thinly over the surface of a dry plaster bat, which absorbs the excess moisture from the clay body. Clay in liquid form can be poured into large tray-shaped plaster bats and left to dry. A large flat bat can be used for wedging. Cast plaster shapes may also be used for press molds and slip molds.

MATERIALS

1. Plaster of Paris
2. Mixing bowl
3. Pie tin
4. Water

1 *Put water in the mixing bowl. Slowly sift the plaster into the water. Avoid splashing; it may carry air into the mixture.*

2 *Continue to sift until the plaster level rises to the surface of the water and the surface takes on the appearance of buttermilk.*

3 *Carefully introduce the hand into the plaster from the edge of the mixing bowl, fingers together to avoid carrying air into the mixture. Stir by gently moving the hand back and forth across the bottom, disturbing the surface as little as possible. Withdraw the hand.*

4 Pour the plaster immediately into the mold. Allow it to harden completely before moving. If the plaster is disturbed, the cast may be damaged.

5 Remove the mold from the finished bat.

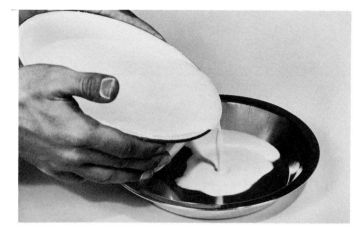

6 Clean the mixing bowl immediately after use. Do not allow any plaster to go down the drain or get into the plumbing, because it will harden in the pipes and necessitate extensive plumbing repair. Empty excess plaster into papers and throw in refuse. Clean the pan carefully with paper before rinsing. Even the small amount of plaster left on the hands after mixing could damage plumbing fixtures.

7 A pie tin makes a very satisfactory mold for this type of bat. Plaster can also be cast in cardboard boxes or other containers for other shapes.

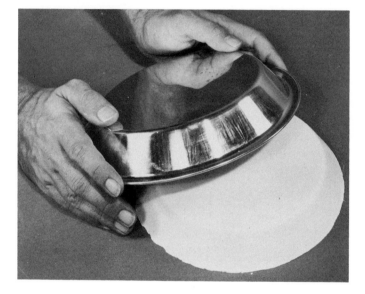

WORK AREA

Although a special work area is desirable for clay work, it is not necessary if a few simple precautions are taken. The worktable can be covered with oilcloth or plastic film. Space must be provided for safe storage of pieces that are drying or waiting to be fired. Clay storage and glaze storage areas should be convenient to the work area. Access to running water makes working much easier.

GENERAL HAND BUILDING TECHNIQUES AND CARE OF POTS: BUILDING, DRYING, AND STORING

Pots can be built on plaster bats, small commercial turntables, can lids, pieces of masonite, or any kind of rigid surface that enables the piece to be turned without its having to be picked up. This rigid surface also provides a portable base to be moved about for drying and storing pieces between work sessions. Clay construction requires care and concentration. Improperly built pieces may not survive the drying and firing processes. They may warp, crack, or explode in firing. To ensure good construction, care must be taken to weld all joints properly, and to keep the thickness of the walls and parts consistent. Thin parts dry much faster than thick ones and can cause stress and cracking. An appendage more than ½ inch thick should usually be constructed hollow, or be hollowed after building.

If pots are to remain plastic between working sessions, they must be kept moist. They will stay moist if they are stored in airtight cupboards or wrapped in plastic film. If the period between sessions is long, or the weather dry, damp cloths or wet paper towels may be wrapped around the piece. Trimming and finishing may be done after the pots have dried until they are leather hard. Sometimes knives or wooden tools are useful in the final shaping of the pot, and the surface areas can be polished down with a smooth stone or the back of a spoon.

Finished pots should dry slowly and evenly. As soon as a pot is firm enough to stand on its rim, it can be turned over to ensure even drying. If a pot has many projections, storage under a loose cover helps prevent uneven drying. The final drying should be done in the open air. Clay should be bone dry before it is fired. Some potters find it beneficial to lengthen the drying process over a period of several days to ensure drying. The damp ware is kept securely wrapped in plastic film, kept in an airtight cupboard, or stored in a damp room during this period.

Greenware, or dry unfired pottery, is extremely fragile. Many potters have special storage areas to protect their greenware.

PINCH POT

This ancient method of making pots serves as an excellent introduction to clay. The size of the pot is determined by the amount of clay that can easily be held and worked with the hands.

MATERIALS

1. Clay
2. Tools for smoothing and polishing if desired

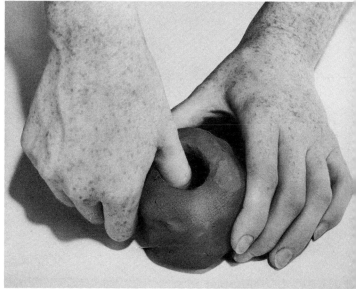

1 Roll the clay into a ball, one that can be held easily in the hands.

2 Hold the clay in both hands and press the thumbs into the ball, making a center depression.

3 Slowly pinch the clay outward, forming the walls of the pot.

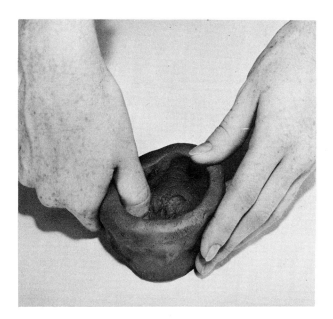

4 Pinch the wall until it is of even thickness.

5 Smooth the pot with the fingers or a wooden tool until its surface has a uniform quality. The finger pattern need not be smoothed away but may be retained as a part of the design. The even, regular pattern of the finger marks on the surface is traditionally prized as characteristic of a fine pinch pot.

PIECE MOUNTING

Piece mounting consists of building the form by adding small amounts of clay at a time and pressing them into place as the work progresses.

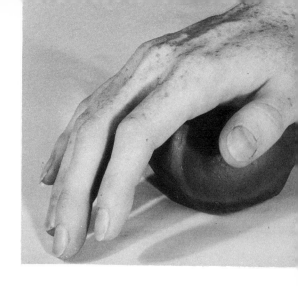

MATERIALS

1. Clay
2. Tools for smoothing and shaping if desired

1 *Flatten a ball of clay to about finger thickness.*

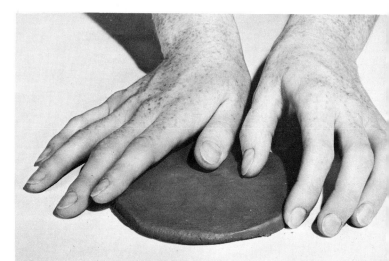

2 *Shape it to form the base of the pot.*

3 *Begin to build the wall of the pot by pressing small pieces of clay around the edge of the base. Maintain a constant thickness of the clay wall. The clay wall may begin to sag as it is built up, at which point it may be necessary to wait to continue until it is firm enough not to sag. This time may be used to smooth and shape the portion already completed. Lumps may be pinched out and hollows filled with small bits of additional clay.*

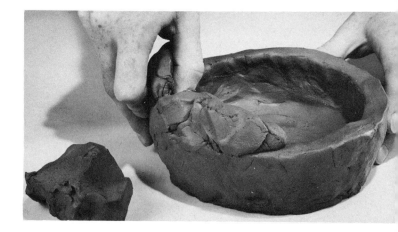

4 *When the wall is complete, smooth the surface.*

SLAB PROCESS

A slab pot is built with flat pieces or slabs of clay, which are assembled and joined to form a container. A slab construction may be planned by cutting heavy paper or cardboard patterns to be used as guides for cutting the clay parts. A straightedge is necessary for accuracy.

MATERIALS

1. Cardboard
2. Scissors
3. Clay
4. Rolling pin
5. Strips of wood
6. Knife
7. Water
8. Pan for slip
9. Piece of cloth
10. Straightedge

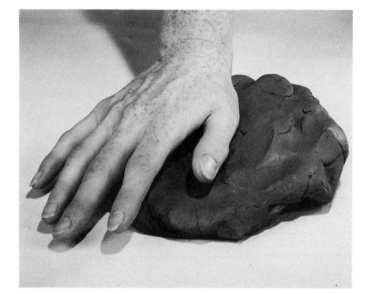

1 *First flatten a ball of clay by pressing it with the hands or rolling it with a rolling pin.*

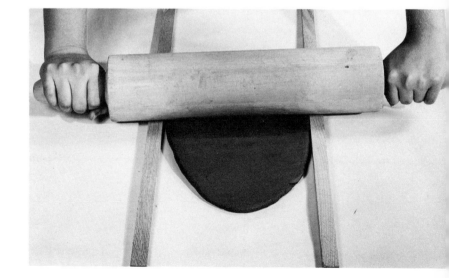

2 *Level the slabs by rolling them on a cloth-covered surface. To ensure even thickness, roll the clay mass in a form made from two wooden strips of the same thickness, placed on either side of the clay. Avoid air pockets.*

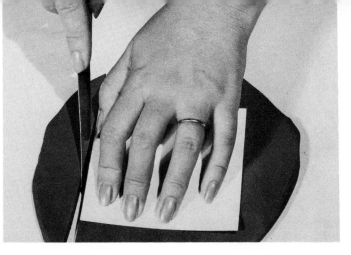

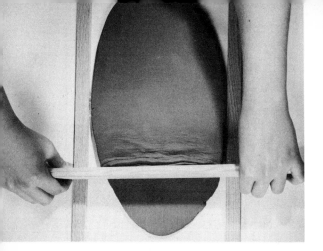

3 Clay flattened by hand or rolled with a rolling pin can be further leveled by drawing a screed across the surface, resting it on the wooden side supports.

4 Cut the parts of the pot from the slab with a knife, using a straightedge or the cardboard pattern as a guide. Set aside the individual pieces so that they can dry and stiffen before assembling. Each piece should have clean-cut, unbroken edges.

5 To assemble the pot, score the edge of each slab with a knife.

6 Spread the scored edges with slip made by mixing clay with water to a heavy cream-like consistency. Prepare a small roll of clay the same length as the side of the pot.

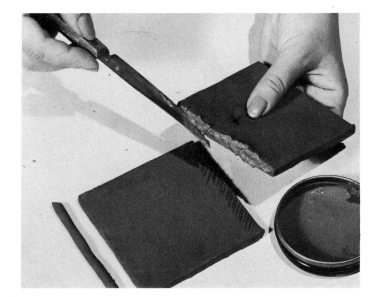

7   Join the side onto the base. Then spread the joint with slip on the inside of the pot.

8   Press the small roll of clay into the joint.

9   Smooth the joint.

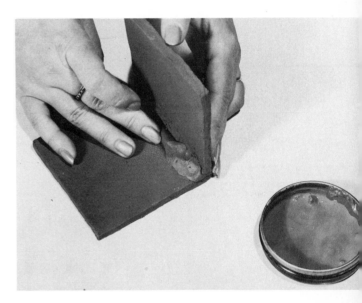

10   Continue the process with each side, spreading slip on the joints and adding small rolls of clay.

11   Smooth the pot inside and out with the fingers or a wooden tool.

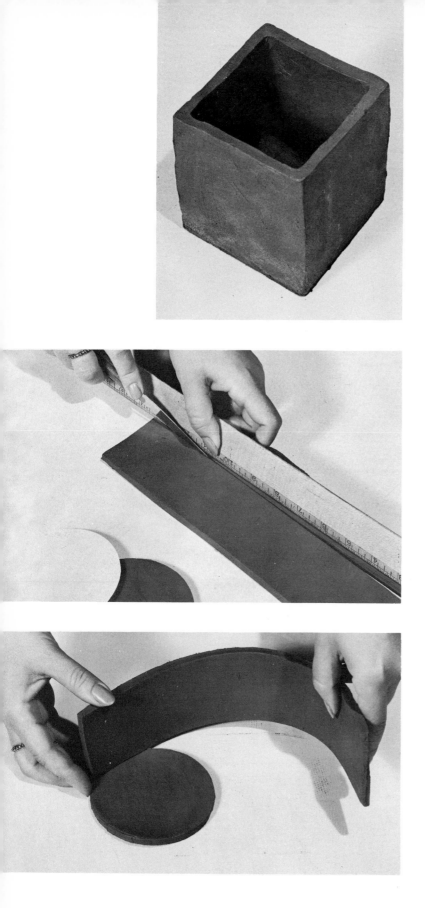

12 *Finished slab pot.*

13 To make a cylindrical slab pot, cut a circle for the base. Cut a slab for the wall the length of the circumference of the base.

14 Join the side to the base and fasten the ends together as described above.

15 *Finished cylindrical slab pot.*

MAKING A TILE

Tiles are made in the same way that the slabs are cut for the slab process. To keep the tile from warping while drying, cut grooves in the base of the tile. Let it dry between two plaster bats or turn it frequently while drying to permit equal evaporation of moisture from both sides. Tiles can be made in many sizes, depending upon their use. Single tiles, the backs protected with felt, can be used on the table; or tiles can be combined to make table tops or wall decorations. Small tiles can be made for mosaics.

The tile can be decorated by incising, stamping, adding clay, painting, glazing (see pp. 341-352).

COIL PROCESS

Coil pieces may be constructed to follow a preconceived design, or the form may be developed as the piece is built. A template, made by drawing and cutting a planned profile of the pot from a piece of cardboard (or wood or tin), can be used as a reference during the building process.

MATERIALS

1. Clay
2. Water
3. Modeling tools
4. Knife
5. Sponge
6. Plastic sheet
7. Small piece of masonite

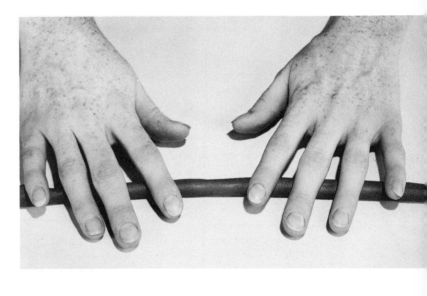

1 *A base may be made of coils, or may be pressed out as illustrated in steps 1 and 2 of Piece Mounting. To roll a coil, gently roll a handful of clay between the flat palm of the hand and a smooth working surface. As the coil length develops, use both hands. For a round regular coil, roll from the tips of the fingers to the base of the palm with even pressure.*

2 *To form the base of the pot, wrap the coil in a spiral.*

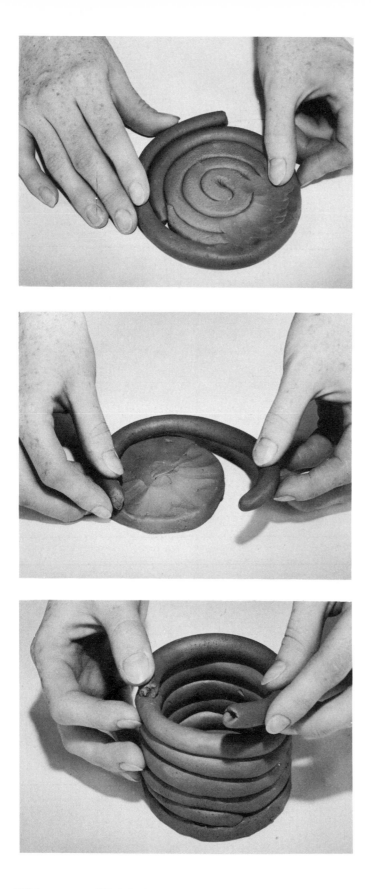

3 Smooth the coils. Weld each coil to the adjacent coil by pressing some of the clay from a coil with the thumb until it overlaps its neighbor. Mere smoothing will not suffice to bind the coils to one another. A joint must actually be made with the clay. Turn the base over and repeat the process.

4 To begin the walls of the pot, first roll a coil. Lay it in place on the base of the pot. The coil may be cut to fit the circumference of the base; or a longer coil may be used, in which case the wrapping is continued until the end of the coil. If the clay is not sufficiently moist to join readily, the coil may be scored and moistened with slip before it is put in place. This will ensure a tight bond.

5 Continue to wrap the coils, building the wall of the pot to the desired height. Join the coils together as described in step 3 above. This joining must be done at intervals during the building, finishing each section before proceeding upward. If you wait until the pot is finished to smooth the clay, it may become too firm and the inside may be difficult to reach. Take care to keep the thickness of the walls consistent.

6 You may vary the shape of the pot by gradually increasing or decreasing the circumference of the top opening. As mentioned before, a template may be used as a guide in the final shaping of the contour of the sides, although the eye is always the final judge. To complete the pot, finish the smoothing with the fingers or a wooden tool. Do not try to smooth by adding water to the surface either with the fingers or with the sponge. If the clay is too dry, water must be

Do not be dismayed if the pot appears clumsy in its initial stages. As skill is acquired in making controlled regular coils, the pattern of the coils and the joining can become an integral part of the design and may not require a final smoothing operation. added by kneading it into the clay mass before it is worked into coils. Water applied to the surface actually washes away the fine particles of clay and leaves a coarse, grainy surface that cannot be smoothed.

7 Another way to make coils is to roll a coil as thick as the thumb, lay the coil on a flat surface, and make it into a wedge shape by pressing along one side with the thumb.

8 Then score along one side of the wedge with a knife or wooden modeling tool.

9 Moisten the scored side of the wedge with a damp sponge or with slip. When wrapping this type of coil around the pot, always put the scored side down with the thin side of the coil toward the inside of the pot. The dampened edge makes a firm bond with the coil beneath. This method is especially useful if the clay is a little dry, or if the potter desires to leave the coil pattern as part of the design without making a joint or smoothing the surface.

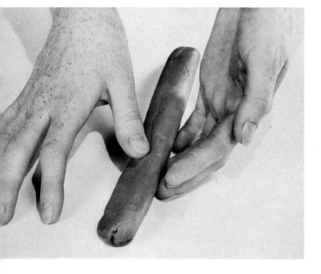

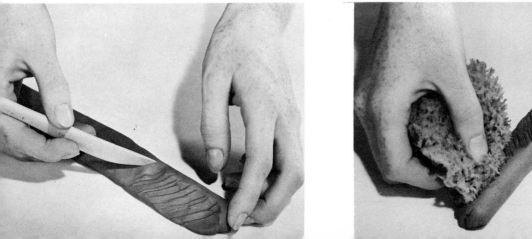

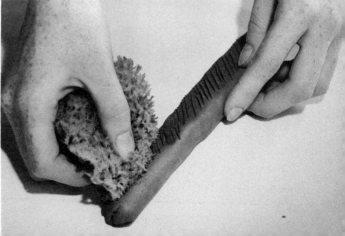

COIL-SLAB PROCESS

The coil-slab method combines advantages of both coil and slab techniques. With skill, you can build the pot more rapidly using this process.

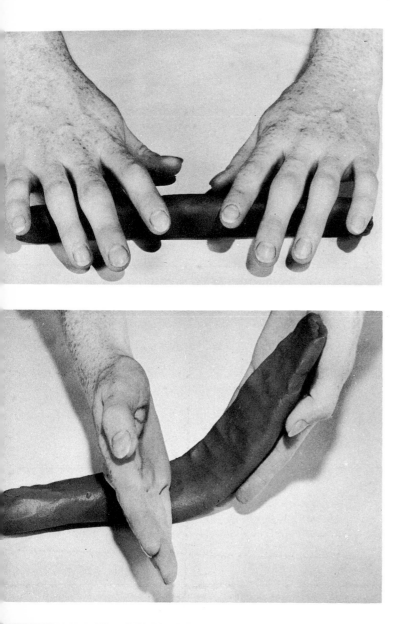

1 Roll out a fat coil 1½ to 3 inches in diameter.

2 Flatten the coil with the side of the hand. Use a regular striking motion. As the action proceeds along the coil, the pressure of the hand increases the length of the coil. Lift the end as you strike to allow the coil to expand.

3 Lay the coil-slab in place on the base. Trim to size, join the ends together, and make the joint with the base. The joints may be moistened with water or slip.

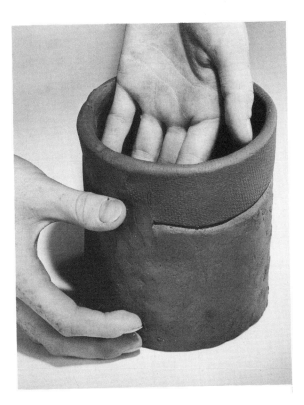

4 Continue to build, joining each slab to the one below as it is added.

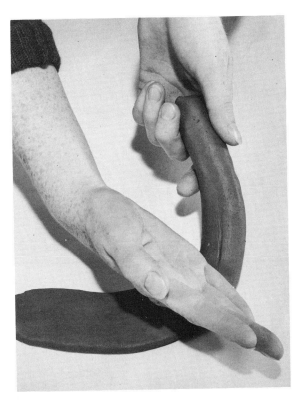

5 To make a coil-slab that will either increase or decrease the circumference of the pot, lay the coil in an arc before striking it with the side of the hand. The resulting slab will be curved, not straight.

6 Lay the curved coil-slab in place. In the illustration, the coil-slab is being placed so that it will diminish the circumference of the pot.

7 A pitcher built with the coil-slab process.

PRESS MOLD

A mold is especially useful to make more than one copy of a particular piece. The mold can be made of plaster of Paris or of fired clay. The quality of the mold determines the quality of the finished piece. The press mold illustrated in the following steps was designed for a decorative wall tile, but the same process could be used to make plates, bowls, or design motifs for sprigging.

MATERIALS

1. Clay or modeling clay
2. Cardboard box
3. Equipment for mixing plaster
4. Petroleum jelly or green soap
5. Plaster

1 *Design the model with clay or modeling clay. Plan the design so that any raised area slopes outward as it approaches the base to avoid undercuts, which would make it impossible to remove the finished product from the mold.*

2 *Place the model in a cardboard container at least 1 inch deeper than the height of the piece and 2 inches wider. Cover the model with a thin coat of petroleum jelly or green soap. Be certain to cover all of the surface, even small openings. Mix the plaster (page 316) and pour it into the box.*

3 *Allow the plaster to harden. Remove the box from the finished plaster mold. Wash the mold carefully with soap and water to remove the jelly or soap. Allow the plaster mold to dry thoroughly before proceeding.*

4 Press soft clay firmly into the mold. Avoid air pockets. Permit the clay to dry.

5 As the clay dries it will pull away slightly from the mold, permitting it to be easily removed. Finish the tile by trimming the edges with a knife or wooden tool. The design may be touched up if necessary. Any imperfections in the mold can be trimmed or carved out with a knife or carving tool before the next piece is pressed. This same mold can be used as a slip mold. In this case, slip or liquid clay is poured in the mold and left to dry as above.

WHEEL THROWING

There are many different kinds of potter's wheels. The kick wheel and the treadle wheel are turned by man power. Electrically powered wheels are also available. A lump of clay is centered on the revolving wheel and shaped as the wheel turns. The act of centering is a skill acquired with practice. After the clay is cen-tered, the potter begins forming the walls of the pot. He may develop the shape as he goes, or he may work toward a preconceived shape, using a template if he desires.

The wheel is best adapted to the production of symmetrical forms, although the forms can be altered after they are thrown.

MATERIALS

1. Potter's wheel
2. Wedged clay
3. Plaster bat
4. Water pan
5. Sponge
6. Tools—pear pitter, needle, wire, wooden shaping tools

1 *A plaster bat is often attached to the wheel to facilitate the removal of the thrown piece. To attach the bat, take a little soft clay on the fingers and smear it on the wheel. Add a little water with a sponge.*

2 *Now place the bat on the center of the wheel. Press it into place. Spread the clay beneath it for firm attachment by sliding the bat back and forth under pressure until it seems to adhere.*

3 Pat a lump of wedged clay into a hemispherical shape, moisten the bottom, and place it firmly on the center of the bat. Wet down the clay mass by squeezing a water-filled sponge over it.

4 Start the wheel. With the thumbs interlocked to steady the hands, begin to center the clay. Apply steady pressure to the mass as it rotates, until it is revolving evenly under the hands. The elbow can be supported against the abdomen if necessary to sustain the required pressure.

5 Bring up the clay by applying pressure with both hands to the base of the mass. Occasionally wet down the surface of the clay so that it will turn freely under the hands. If the clay is not sufficiently wet, it will grab and break the even turning.

6 With pressure from above, push down the clay with the palm and heel of the hand. Support the sides of the mass with the fingers to prevent a lip from forming. This process is a final aid to centering and may be repeated until the clay is completely centered.

7 Wet down the surface of the clay frequently with water from the sponge.

8 With the thumbs together, slowly press an opening in the center of the clay mass. Opening the mass must be done carefully to avoid decentering the clay.

9 With one hand in the opening and the other hand supporting the clay wall, carefully widen the hole by pulling the clay wall outward with steady pressure.

10   To raise the clay wall, hold the knuckle of the right hand on the outside base of the piece, supporting the clay wall with the other hand, with the tips of the fingers inside the pot slightly above the knuckle on the outside. Apply pressure to the clay wall with the right knuckle. A little roll of clay is formed over the knuckle and is moved upward by pressure from the right hand. The other hand carefully steadies and supports the clay wall from the inside while moving upward. Bring the two hands up together, the left hand slightly above the right.

11   Continue raising the cylinder. Repeat step 10 until the desired height is reached.

12   If the top is uneven, level it by cutting off a strip of clay. While the wheel is in motion, insert the needle through the wall of the pot a short distance below the lip. Hold the cutting needle at a consistent level. Keep the left hand on the lip while cutting.

13   When the cut is complete, lift the sliced-off ring of clay. The wheel need not be stopped.

14 To smooth the lip of the pot while the wheel is in motion, gently hold the lip between the thumb and forefinger of the left hand. Place the right index finger directly on the edge and brace it with the fingers of the left hand. The clay wall, revolving under this **H** form, will be smoothed by gentle pressure of the fingers.

15 Every form thrown on the wheel begins as a cylinder, which can be subsequently shaped into other forms. To press the wall outward, a wooden shaping tool is sometimes used. Dip the tool in water to lessen the drag before it is applied to the clay. The tool is held gently against the inside wall, and with firm, steady pressure the form is carefully opened. Use the other hand to support the outside wall. Any tools brought in contact with the clay while it is in motion must be applied and removed gradually and carefully so as not to damage the clay structure or set it off balance.

16 Continue the opening process until the bowl is shaped.

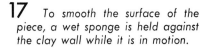

17 To smooth the surface of the piece, a wet sponge is held against the clay wall while it is in motion.

18 Excess clay is removed from the base of the pot with a wooden tool while the pot is in motion.

19 To remove the piece from the plaster bat, cut underneath the base with a wire. Stretch the wire taut and slide it underneath the pot. With deft handling the pot can now be lifted from the bat.

20 Another way to remove the pot, which involves less risk, is to lift the bat from the wheel by carefully prying it up with a spatula, leaving the pot attached to the bat. Place it aside to dry. As it dries, the pot separates from the bat and can be easily removed when it is leather hard.

21   *If a pitcher is being made the cylinder is first formed into an appropriate shape, and the pouring spout is made before the form is removed from the wheel. Stop the wheel. Place two fingers of one hand on the outside of the rim. Place the index finger of the other hand inside the rim through the two fingers. Supporting the rim with the two fingers, with the other finger gently pull the clay outward into a pouring spout.*

PULLING A HANDLE

Handles and other attachments for pots can be made by the coil method or by pulling. Roll out the coil and shape it to fit the pot. Before final placement the ends of the handle and the areas on the pot where it will be attached should be scored and buttered with slip. The shaped handle should be allowed to become firm before it is attached, to prevent sagging. For either method, the size and shape of the handle should be considered in relationship to the total design of the pot. The handle should be comfortable to hold, and the space between the handle and the pot should be adequate. This negative shape should also be planned as part of the design.

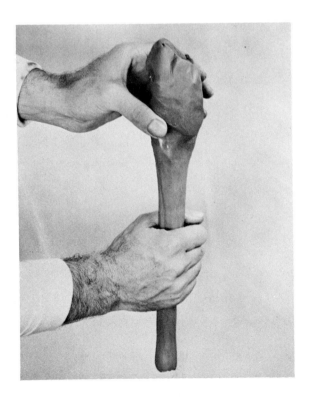

1   *To pull a handle suspend a short roll of clay from one hand. Grasp the clay and, keeping the clay thoroughly wet, slide the other hand down the coil with gentle pressure. Each stroke will slightly extend the shape. Continue this process, wetting the clay between strokes, until the desired length is reached.*

2 *Invert the pulled clay and allow it naturally to assume a curved shape. This shape can now be cut from the mass and attached to the pot.*

3 *Another method of pulling the handle is to start by attaching the short roll of clay to the pot. Attach it to the side of the pot with slight pressure, supporting the inside of the pot with the other hand. Then hold the pot on its side so that the clay can hang free while it is being pulled. Pull the handle as in step 2 above. Set the pot on its base, allow the handle to assume its natural curve, and attach the lower end to the pot. Trim off excess.*

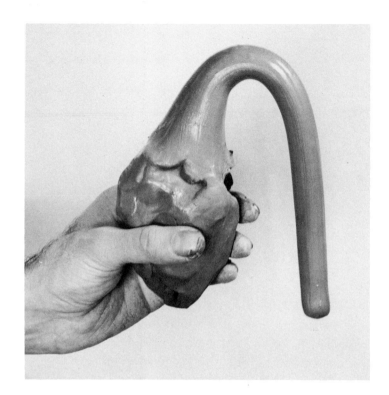

TRIMMING THE POT

As soon as the clay is leather hard the pot can be trimmed. Those parts of the pot that could not be perfected while it was being thrown can now be finished. If the base is too heavy, trimming can bring it to a thickness consistent with the walls, assuring better drying and firing.

1 *To trim the foot, center the leather-hard pot on the wheel. Hold it in place with wads of clay.*

2 *Start the wheel and with the pear pitter cut out excess clay from the foot. Start from the center and move outward to the edge describing a spiral.*

3 *The finished foot.*

DECORATING AND GLAZING

After the basic form of the pot is achieved, it can be decorated and glazed. Decoration or surface treatment may enhance the basic design quality of the piece, and glazing increases its utility by adding a nonporous surface to the clay.

Many pots do not require decoration, but those designed to hold liquid should be glazed at least on the inside. Techniques for decorating and glazing include: first, modifying the surface of the pot by incising or pressing design into the clay or adding clay to the surface; second, using engobes or slips; third, using glazes; or, fourth, using combinations of these techniques.

MODIFYING THE SURFACE

An endless variety of surface designs may be obtained by taking away from, pressing into, or adding to the surface of the clay while it is still plastic. Remember that all work with unfired clay must be very carefully done, for the pots are still in a very fragile state. These methods of modifying the surface can be used singly or in combination. The quality of the textured surface may be intensified with engobes or glazes. The bumps and hollows collect the glaze, adding further variety.

INCISING

Incising is done by carving out or scratching away the surface of the clay. Small or large areas can be cut away according to the needs of the design. Incisions may be deep or shallow. Many tools can be used: knives, carving tools, wooden sticks, or anything that lends itself to carving or scraping. The patterns that can be made by incising range from small depressions to positive and negative designs or even bas-relief.

STAMPING OR PRESSING

The potter can make patterns on the surface of the clay by stamping or pressing designs into it. Special stamps can be made from carved wood, linoleum, plaster, or even gum erasers. Stamps can also be made of clay, which is molded or carved and then fired. Stamps may be improvised from any number of common objects—spools, sucker sticks, screws, nail heads, and kitchen tools.

ADDING TO THE SURFACE

The potter can make raised designs by taking bits, small balls, or strips of clay and pressing them to the surface. A little slip or slight moistening will help secure them. Medallions or other designs may be made in a small press mold and attached to the surface with slip. A surprising variety of interesting surface designs and textures can be achieved with this method.

ENGOBE AND SLIP

Engobe or slip is liquid clay that is colored and applied for surface decoration. The application of engobe does not change the porosity of fired ceramics as glaze does. The simplest engobe can be prepared by adding more water to the same clay from which the piece is made. If dry clay is used, the engobe can be mixed directly from the powdered clay or pug-wet clay can be thinned with water. The consistency should be that of heavy cream. A little glycerine or gum tragacanth solution may be added to improve adhesion.

The original color of the clay can be changed by adding small quantities of the following colored oxides:

Iron oxide—Venetian red to brown
Cobalt oxide—Blue
Copper oxide—Green
Rutile—Yellow ochre

The intensity of the colors will vary according to the amount of colorant added. The colors may be mixed with each other for further variation. The widest range of color can be obtained by beginning with a white or light-gray clay. If the clay body is terra cotta or dark red, the engobe prepared from it can only be made darker. Iron oxide, cobalt, and manganese, when combined, make black, which provides a suitable colorant for engobes made of dark clays.

This simple engobe should be applied to the clay while it is still damp. Since plastic clay is about one-third water, considerable shrinkage occurs as the clay dries. If this engobe is applied to a piece that has partially dried, the ratio of shrinkage between the two will be different, and the engobe coat may peel away as further drying occurs. To provide greater flexibility in the application of engobes, special engobes can be made or purchased. There are engobes for decorating on damp, dry, or bisque pieces. In these special mixtures, ingredients have been added to compensate for the shrinkage at different levels of dryness and for varying clay bodies. A variety of engobes that will fit a clay body are usually obtainable from the same source as the clay. Formulas for the preparation of engobes may be found in the references provided for the clay section of this book. All engobes should be tested on sample tiles before being used on a finished piece to ensure compatibility with the clay being used.

After a suitable engobe has been obtained, it may be decoratively applied with brushing, spraying, dipping, slip trailing, stamping, sgraffito, or stencil. It may be used on clay, over other engobes, or in combination with other engobes, and under or over glazes. Each of these application techniques provides very different results. Each method should be tried on test pieces, to determine its possibilities.

GLAZING

A glaze is a layer of oxide material that when fired undergoes a chemical change and becomes a thin layer of glass over the surface of the piece. Like engobes, glazes must be perfectly adjusted to complement the clay body underneath. There is an endless variety of colors and textures, from transparent to opaque and from high gloss to dull mat. The greatest variety of color—oranges, reds, bright yellows, luminous blues—is achieved most easily in the low-fire range. The higher temperatures required for stoneware tend to limit the color range. Potters spend many years experimenting and perfecting glazes that complement the clay they use. If the beginner can get a few successful glazes to work with, and combine these with other methods of surface decoration, he immediately has at his disposal a number of elements for achieving variety in his designs.

Although commercial glazes are available, the beginning potter can easily obtain the materials from which to make his own glazes. Oxides that are used for making glazes can be purchased at ceramic supply houses. When making a glaze, it is essential to follow the proportions of the recipe, because each element serves a particular chemical function in the formation of the glaze. Once the principles of glazing are understood and the potter has had sufficient basic experience, he can experiment with the exciting and rewarding art of creating his own new glazes.

Glazes are categorized according to their cone or firing temperature. A pyrometric cone is a small pyramid of clay and glaze material designed to mature, or melt, at a specific temperature. Temperature ranges for glazes are most often indicated by cone numbers. Cone numbers range from low to high, starting with numbers such as .015. In numbers preceded by .0, the higher the number, the lower the temperature. Therefore .015 is a lower temperature cone than .01. On the other side of the scale the temperatures rise with the number. For example, cone 1 melts at about 2060° F. and cone 6 melts at about 2180° F.

Glazes are usually applied to bisque-fired ware. However, to save time and firing costs, they may be applied to raw clay. Experience will indicate when this is feasible. Cover glazes can be applied to pieces by brushing, dipping, pouring, or spraying. For decoration, glazes can be applied by brushing, stamping, trailing, or stenciling.

It is possible to combine some high- and low-fired glazes on the same surface. In this case it is necessary to fire the high-temperature glazes first, since they will not be disturbed by subsequent firings.

METHODS OF
APPLYING GLAZE

Brushing. *Apply glaze with a brush. When applying glaze over under-decoration, be careful not to disturb the surface.*

Dipping. *If a large quantity of glaze is available, pieces may be dipped.*

Pouring. *You may glaze the insides of pots by pouring the glaze into the pot. Pour the glaze into the pot.*

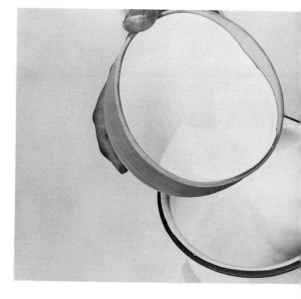

Swirl it around to cover the entire inside surface and pour out excess glaze.

Dry-Footing. *The foot of the pot can be dry-footed, or cleaned of glaze, so that it will not adhere to the kiln shelf during firing. If the pot is dry-footed, it can be stacked in the kiln on the unglazed surfaces of other ware. Remove the glaze from the foot with a wet sponge.*

Spraying. *Glaze may be applied by spraying. Thin glaze slightly with water, and spray.*

SURFACE DECORATION

The decorating techniques that follow may be done on raw or bisque-fired pieces. If the pieces have not been fired, care must be taken, for the pots are still in a very fragile state. One advantage in using bisqued ware, in addition to its strength, is that designs may be washed off and redone.

Experiment with different combinations of design materials and techniques, engobe or glaze alone, engobe under a transparent glaze, engobe over glaze, glaze over glaze. Engobe may be applied to raw ware and then bisque fired before glazing.

Each method will produce different results.

SURFACE TEXTURE

While the clay is plastic, the potter can make a design by adding or taking away from the surface. This, alone or combined with glazing, provides a rich means of decoration.

MATERIALS

1. Sample tiles of plastic clay
2. Tools—modeling tools, wooden sticks, combs, spools, tongue depressors, and other experimental tools

On the sample tiles experiment with any tools that can be used to incise or press designs into the clay. The motifs derived from the various tools can be used singly or in combination to make regular, ordered patterns. Try common household tools like the head of a meat pounder or the end of a bamboo brush. Many familiar items, when used as stamps, produce very handsome designs.

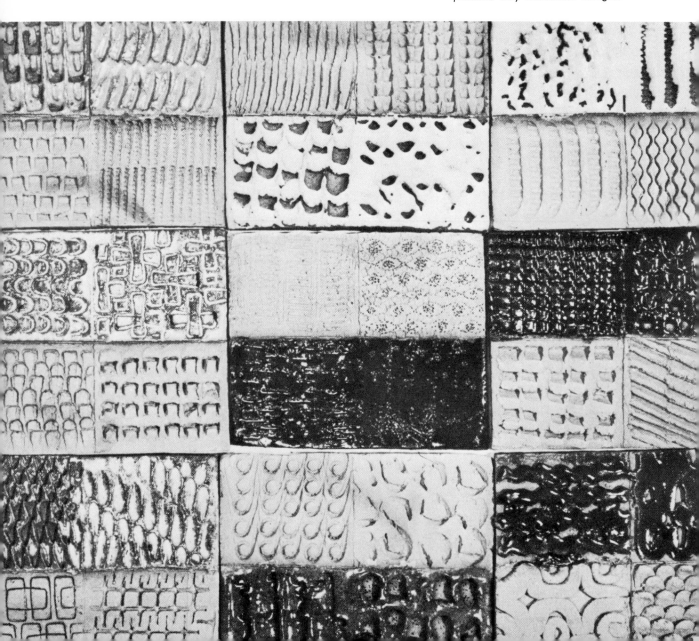

SGRAFFITO

A sgraffito design can be scratched in glaze or engobe on either an unfired or bisque-fired piece.

1 Apply the glaze or engobe by brushing, spraying, or dipping.

2 Draw the design on the pot.

3 Scratch out the design, using a knife or other suitable tool.

4 If the design is made in engobe, it may be given a coat of transparent glaze before or after a bisque firing.

PAINTING

Designs may be painted on raw clay or bisqued ware, on the clay itself or over engobe or glaze, using either glaze or engobe for the design.

WAX RESIST

Wax, which repels water, can be used to decorate clay surfaces. Glaze or engobe will not adhere to any area that has been painted with wax. When the clay is fired, the wax burns off, exposing the material beneath it. The design may be painted with wax on bisque-fired clay, either on the clay itself or over engobed or glazed surfaces. Thin glaze or engobe is painted over the wax design. Wax especially prepared for the wax resist process is available at ceramic supply houses.

MATERIALS

1. Wax
2. Bisque-fired ware to be decorated
3. Glaze or engobe
4. Brush

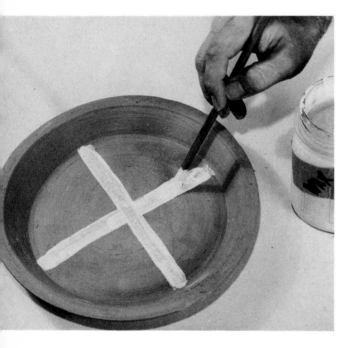

1 *On a bisque-fired piece, paint a design with wax. Allow wax to dry thoroughly.*

2 *Cover the design area with engobe or glaze.*

3 *Fire.*

STENCIL

Engobe or glaze designs can be stenciled on plates, bowls, tiles, and other ceramic ware. This method of decorating gives considerable control and permits the same design to be repeated many times easily. Designs may be applied over glazed or engobed surfaces.

MATERIALS

1. Stencil or blotting paper
2. Brush
3. Glaze or engobe
4. Water
5. Scissors or knife
6. Piece to be decorated

1 Cut a design from stencil paper.

2 Hold the stencil in place and dab on the glaze or engobe. Brush away from the edges of the cut design to avoid brushing the decorating material under the edges of the stencil.

3 Another way to stencil a design is to cut the stencil from blotting paper.

4 Wet the stencil with water and press it onto the piece.

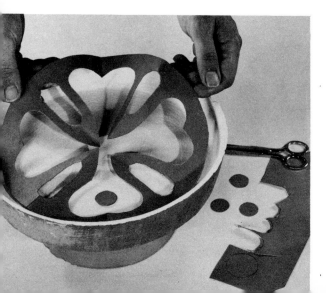

5 *Paint engobe or glaze through the stencil. When all the areas have been painted, carefully remove the stencil.*

SLIP TRAILING

In this process, design is made with slip or glaze squeezed onto the clay surface through a syringe. If the slip is of a heavy consistency, the design will be slightly raised on the finished piece. Slip trailing may be done with slip on leather-hard unfired ware, or with glaze on either unfired or bisque-fired pieces. A final coat of glaze may be added over either.

MATERIALS

1. Slip, engobe, or glaze mixed with water to the consistency of heavy cream
2. Slip trailer or syringe
3. Piece to be decorated

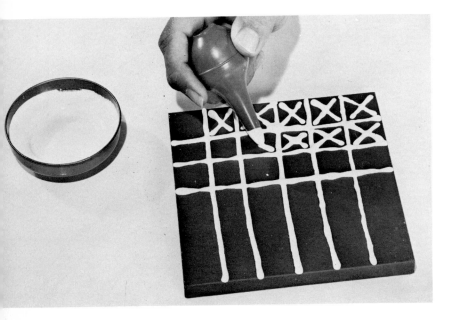

1 *Fill the syringe with engobe. Squeeze the syringe evenly while trailing the design on the surface.*

2 To slip trail stripes down the sides of a bowl, invert the bowl over some support, trail the glaze down the side by holding the syringe in one place, squeezing it, and letting the slip run down the side.

3 To slip trail a spiral design, put the piece to be decorated on a turntable. Rotate the piece slowly, moving the slip trailer from the center to the edge.

STAMPING

Stamps may be used to decorate clay with engobe or glaze. The piece to be stamped may be raw or bisque fired. Stamping may be done over an engobe or glaze ground, or done directly on the clay. A flat surface such as a tile takes stamping best, but with care, any shape of pot can be given a stamp design.

MATERIALS

1. Gum erasers
2. Razor blade or sharp knife
3. Glaze or engobe
4. Piece to be fired

1 *Cut a stamp design from the eraser.*

2 *Brush glaze or engobe on the stamp.*

3 *Press the stamp onto the surface to be decorated.*

FIRING THE KILN

To fire a pot is to subject it to a temperature that causes the components of the clay body to melt and mold together into a complete unit. The clay changes from its fragile raw state into a solid cohesive body. If the piece is glazed, the glaze must melt into glass and become one with the clay surface, which adds another factor to the process. Firing temperatures and timing vary with the contents of the clay bodies, the glazes, and the type of kiln being used.

KILN AND KILN FURNITURE

Kilns vary greatly in structure, size, and function. Many are heated by gas or electricity; for the beginner, the small electric kilns are the most suitable. Some considerations in the selection of a kiln are the initial cost, the method of heating, the size of the pieces to be fired, and the temperature range of the kiln. Some kilns have pyrometers or temperature gauges and automatic shutoffs, both of which are useful features. It is also possible to build a kiln, and if this is attempted, complete instructions should be obtained and carefully followed. Information about loading the kiln and setting heat controls accompanies each commercial kiln, and careful study of such information is valuable. Kiln accessories, called *kiln furniture,* are also necessary. They include many varieties of stilts, frames for holding pieces in place during firing, shelves, and shelf separators which increase the capacity of the kiln and permit the pots to be stacked in layers. A layer of sand or grog can be spread over the shelves as a protective coat for firing, if stilts are not appropriate.

The potter can determine the temperature of the kiln by placing a cone inside the kiln so that it is visible through the spyhole. Each cone melts and falls or drops at a specified temperature, thus indicating when the temperature has been reached. In some kilns with an automatic shutoff a cone is used to trigger the off-switch. Jewelry, usually made of very fine, low-firing clay, can sometimes be fired as low as cone .015, a very low heat which also allows for strong clear glaze colors. Most commercial glazes fire from .06 to .04 and can often be taken as high as cone 3 or 4. Earthenware firings are from .06 to 6 and stoneware from 6 to 10. Some of the newly designed small kilns will go up to cone 12, which is an adequate temperature for firing porcelain.

The time required for firing and the speed of increasing the temperature vary with the clay, the glaze, and the kiln itself. Test pieces can be fired and used as guides to better firing. Generally a long, slow, gradually increased firing will be more successful than a rapid one, and the clay pieces must be bone dry before firing. If they are not thoroughly dry they are likely to explode in the kiln. The drying of damp pieces may be completed in the kiln, if it is turned to a low temperature, and allowed to stand open for from about 8 to 24 hours or even longer, depending upon the size and thickness of the

pieces. After the firing is completed, a long period of cooling is necessary. A kiln should not be opened for 10 to 12 hours after the completion of a firing.

Loading or stacking a kiln must be done carefully. During a glaze firing there should be an adequate air space around each pot. Glazed pots may stick to each other or to the kiln wall if enough space has not been left. To economize on space, greenware pieces may be stacked together. When this is done, care should be taken to judge the weight of each piece so that a heavy piece does not stand on a fragile one. Pots are sometimes designed with unglazed rings in the bottom of the inside to allow the unglazed foot of the next pot to rest on it. This allows many similar pieces to be stacked together in a glaze firing.

Usually greenware and glazed pieces should not be included in the same kiln load.

FIRING FAULTS

If glazed pieces do not come out as expected, a refiring may be successful. The pieces can be reglazed and refired. This is a matter for experiment.

Crazing. If in the cooling process the glaze contracts more than the clay body, *crazing,* or fine cracks, appear in the glaze. These cracks prevent a piece from being watertight. The glaze is not compatible with the clay body and must be adjusted to fit, or a new glaze must be selected.

Peeling. Glazes that pull from the pot did not contract as much as the clay body, and the glaze has become an oversize garment around the pot. This also requires an adjustment of the glaze.

Crawling. If crawling occurs, the glaze crawls away from the clay body, leaving raw unglazed areas. Crawling is usually caused by glazing over greasy or dusty greenware or bisque ware. Avoid overhandling and improper storage. Another cause for crawling is using underglaze decoration that has a powdery or dusty surface. To avoid this, apply underglaze decoration thinly or mix a small quantity of gum solution with the engobe.

Flowing. If a glaze is fired at too high a temperature, it will tend to flow off the clay and not stick.

Firing Accidents. Explosions may occur in the kiln if greenware is not thoroughly dry, or if the thick-thin relationship of the piece is too great. This fault can usually be overcome by a long, thorough drying period before firing, or by preheating in the kiln preliminary to firing.

Broken Pieces. It is sometimes possible to repair a bisque or glazed fired piece that is broken in firing. Spread broken edges with slip, stick them together, and refire.

MATERIALS

1. Kiln
2. Kiln furniture—shelves, shelf supports, fire brick, stilts
3. Kiln wash
4. Sand or grog
5. Pyrometric cones
6. Thoroughly dry greenware to be fired

1 *Always read the instructions that accompany the kiln.*

2 *Shelves and kiln floor must be protected from glaze drippings and other firing accidents. Protect them by applying kiln wash, which facilitates cleaning. Mix kiln wash with water to the consistency of heavy cream. Brush it on the tops of shelves and the floor of the kiln. If kiln wash is applied to the underside of a shelf, it may peel off, fall, and damage the ware being fired below. Apply at least two coats, allowing time for drying between applications. A kiln-washed shelf may be placed on the bottom of the kiln for added protection to the kiln floor.*

3 *Select the correct cone for the firing. Place the cone at a slight angle in a small pillow of clay or in a piece of pumice. The cone has three faces and should be tilted on one of these faces, not on an edge. For greater accuracy, more than one cone may* be used. One cone just below the desired firing temperature may be added to permit the observer to gauge the approach of the correct firing temperature. The clay pillow that holds the cones should be dried before firing.

4 Pieces placed on the kiln shelves to illustrate the way the kiln is loaded. To load the kiln, plan the loading so that space is economically used. Place the small pieces on the lower shelves and tall objects above. Half-shelves may be used if required. Small pieces can be placed under projecting larger pieces. Space glazed pieces so they do not touch each other or the kiln wall. If pieces have glaze on the bottom, they must be elevated from the shelf with stilts. For additional protection from dripping or spattering glaze, a layer of grog or sand may be spread on the surface of the shelf. Shelves are supported with shelf separators.

5 After the kiln is loaded and the cone is in place where it can be seen through a spyhole, preheat the kiln. Leave the lid completely open during preheating. Partially close the lid before the first turn-up. To leave a small opening, prop the lid with a piece of fire brick or pumice block.

6 Bring the heat up slowly, allowing at least one hour between turn-ups. This slow raising of the temperature is essential to minimize accidents during the firing. After the last turn-up, close the lid completely and plug the air vents. Watch the cone at intervals. When the cone bends, the correct temperature has been reached. Turn off the elements and allow the kiln to cool.

7 Allow the kiln to cool slowly. A long cooling period is essential. Near the end of the cooling period the plugs may be removed and the lid of the kiln propped open slightly. When the kiln temperature is comfortable to the hand, the pots can be removed.

ADDITIONAL SUGGESTIONS FOR CLAY

Some schools purchase clay already mixed, and others have it prepared by someone designated to do this job. It can be kept in a moist state ready for use in a stoneware crock, a small garbage can, galvanized pail, large dishpan, or plastic sack. If it is rolled into balls about the size that a child can hold in both hands, distribution will be easier.

As a rule, the best tools for young children are their fingers; however, students in upper elementary grades will find such objects as wood meat skewers, Popsicle sticks, and old-fashioned hairpins helpful at times. Clay tools made of wood may also be purchased quite inexpensively. It should be remembered that tools are only a means to an end and in no way should be permitted to hinder personal expression.

There should be a prepared place to work, protected with newspapers, which later can be thrown away. Or individual mats can be made of a piece of heavy cardboard put inside a folded piece of material like oilcloth, which is then stitched or stapled on three sides. These mats can be easily wiped clean when the work period is over and stored by stacking. A 12-inch square of masonite or a wood board from the end of a box is also a good working surface.

If a "potting shed" were made available either in the school or in a simple structure on the school grounds, children would have a wider experience in working with this earthy material. Under most school conditions each student works in a very cramped area and with a small dab of material, hardly sufficient to test potential creative powers. To become wholly involved with the material is the most desirable objective. Some potters even prepare their clay directly on the floor where they can bend over it and have complete mastery of the medium. This enables them to use more force and freedom of movement. In a potting shed there is no fear of spoiling the appearance of the room. When the regular classroom is used for this work, care must be exercised to keep clay off the floor as it tracks very easily and creates a cleaning problem.

Young children usually complete what they are doing in one class period. If work is unfinished, however, it may be kept in any metal-lined container such as a cookie box or coffee can, and wrapped in a wet cloth. A label with the identifying name on it can be attached to each can with tape or paste. Small transparent plastic bags are also excellent for storage purposes. Both of these means provide simple ways to care for unfinished work as well as that being slowly dried.

Teachers should endeavor to provide form and texture experiences wherever possible in working with the clay medium. If children are introduced to these abstract qualities first, they will make application of them in the products they create. Texture experiments on a flattened piece of clay shaped like a tile will help develop a feeling for order and relationships. These may be incised marks made with such improvised

Christmas Display. 1954. Decorated Clay. Los Angeles Elementary Schools, Valley District. Katherine Dukes McAvoy, Art Supervisor. Courtesy, *Everyday Art* Magazine.

tools as the point of a pencil, a collar button, or any object that makes an interesting impression on the clay. Texture may also be produced by building up surfaces with clay pellets, raised "buttons," or small, wormlike coils in parallel groupings.

The making of a simple pinch pot from a ball of clay is a fine way to start young children working with the material, for it gives them a feeling for form. The pot, while being evolved from the ball, retains some of the form of the ball in the finished result.

The same can be true in building a form with coils of clay. If the sides of the pot are kept straight the structure will become a cylinder, and the child will respond to the geometric volume that is the basis of pots. Then he can try various modifications by building the coils outward and in to shape the pot. Head pots can be made this way. The child feels his face and shapes the coils to conform to his own features, which he tries to construct in this material. The results can be very original and expressive.

Tiles can be made in the classroom without too much equipment. A ball of clay is placed on a piece of paper or a board and flattened down carefully with the palms of the hands until it is smooth and even and about ½ inch thick. Or the clay may be rolled out with a rolling pin, a dowel, or broomstick, or even a bottle, in the manner of making a piecrust. Then it is trimmed with a knife or tongue depressor to the desired size.

After the clay has dried it may be left in its natural state, glazed and fired, or painted with opaque color and waxed. If possible, a child should have the experience of having and seeing a clay piece fired in a pottery kiln. It is very desirable that every school have a kiln available and that teachers be informed on how to operate it. When there is an art department the kiln should be under the supervision of the art teacher. If a potter's studio is nearby, a visit would be most valuable. Here one can see the production of pottery on the wheel and see how a kiln is loaded and fired. Pottery may be fired outdoors, on the ground, as primitive peoples have done in various places and cultures.

If teachers wish their students to have the experience of firing clay outdoors, they can find a protected space that is out of the way but that can still be supervised. Work can be fired on top of the ground, or in a circular hole 6 inches or more deep. In either case, a fire is started with chips or kindling, and a log, briquets, or coal is laid on the coals and kept burning. Clay work may be grouped over this before the fire is started, or placed on top after the log is heated through. An hour or two is needed to bake the objects; after the baking, they must cool off. A pole may be used to remove pots that are too hot to handle.

Many cultures used paint to embellish their ceramic ware. Many beautiful examples can be found among the folk art of Mexico and other countries where such products as ceramic sculpture, candlesticks, and similar clay objects have been decorated with paint. Even the Greeks painted their marble sculpture. Opaque color can be rubbed in while the clay is still moist or painted on with a brush when the clay is dry. If enamel color is used the surface will have a slight gloss, and if water paint is used the surface can be covered with floor wax, lacquer, clear varnish, or shellac, to give a finish and to prevent the color from rubbing off. Rubber-based paint may also be used and does not require additional protection.

Old clay that has dried, but that has not been fired or painted, may be returned to the container, broken, pulverized with a mallet or hammer, and used again when it is soaked in water. It takes a few days for the pieces to absorb the moisture and soften up. Clay pieces damaged in the firing can be broken into small pieces and used for mosaics.

Plate. Clay decorated with glaze and fired. Child age 8.

Necklace. Modeled with Egyptian paste. Adult student.

MOSAICS

Fernand Léger: *Soccer and Bicycling* (Detail). Completed 1960. Mosaic and
ceramic. 156′ length. Fernand Léger Museum, Biot, France.

MOSAICS

It is very probable that the art of making mosaics was introduced into the Western world from the Near East in Greek and Roman times, where it flourished and developed into an important art form. Because the materials used in mosaic making are quite permanent and sturdy, many early works still exist, even after many centuries; their original color and brilliance remain unaffected by time. Unless the craftsmanship is faulty, or the wall upon which it is laid should collapse, a well-constructed mosaic can withstand most accidents of nature, excepting human destruction. Many early examples were removed or plastered over because their beauty was not recognized, or because their subject matter was in disagreement with later customs or religious beliefs.

Traditionally, a mosaic is made of small pieces of material such as stone, glass, or glazed ceramic tile pressed into a bed of freshly laid concrete or plaster. These bits of material are called *tesserae*, from the Greek word for "square" or "four-sided." In ancient times these tesserae were usually made of many-colored stones, such as marble, alabaster, and porphyry. Sometimes semiprecious stones, nacre, and ivory were added for luster and variety. Later, glass cubes were used to increase the range of possible colors and add a new depth and richness to the design. These were cut from sheets of glass with hot chisels. Perhaps most exciting are the tesserae of gold, which provide a glittering light to the varied pattern of color and texture.

These were made by imbedding thin sheets of metal foil between two layers of glass, so the result is a small golden mirror.

In the ancient world, mosaics were important architectural features, brightening walls of stone with iridescent patterns of color. Egyptian, Greek, and Roman craftsmen improvised strong designs and charming, colorful scenes to enhance their temples, homes, walls, floors, and baths. Originally, the Eastern influence prevailed with its love of color and decorative pattern. But as developed by the Greeks and Romans, monumental mosaic art eventually became an imitation of painting, and lost much of its intrinsic quality. In Roman times, no rich man's villa was complete without its mosaic floors, both in and out of doors. Even the market places such as that at Ostia were decorated with mosaics, the designs often derived from the nature of the ware or produce offered at the shopkeeper's stalls.

From the beginning, the early Christians expressed their new beliefs in this art form. In the concealed worship places in the catacombs, many small mosaics were made. As in all primitive Christian art, the designs were bold and strong. Roman realism was abandoned in favor of the abstract forms that better represented their new concepts and spiritual values. And at the same time, the material became more expressive of itself; its rich hues and vital surface textures were explored anew. When Constantine legalized Christianity, the new churches that

Sumerian: *Standard of Ur, the King at Peaceful Pleasures.*
c. 2500 B.C. Shell, red limestone, and lapis lazuli in bitu-
men on a wooden base, 8″ x 18⅞″. Courtesy of the
British Museum.

Roman: *Tritons and Sea Gods, Floor from the Market at
Ostia.* Black and white marble mosaic. Alinari.

Greek and Roman mosaics second century A.D. (second
half) from Antioch. Courtesy of the Metropolitan Museum
of Art, Purchase, 1838, Joseph Pulitzer Bequest.

MOSAICS   **363**

were built offered many opportunities for the mosaic artist. Vast areas, like those in Hagia Sophia and in San Vitale in Ravenna, were left for mosaic murals to lend splendor and richness to interior walls. Into these monumental mosaics the Christian artists poured all their affection for the stories and legends of their faith, illustrating the Bible and the Apocrypha, and the lives of their saints, providing visible sermons for those that could not read. All their ability in design and composition went into these works, which remain the apogee of mosaic art.

The mosaics of San Vitale are excellent examples. Here the rhythmic patterns of the round arches, columns, and the encompassing vaults and dome are extravagantly overlaid and developed with rich mosaic designs. On either side of the apse are portraits of the donors, the Emperor Justinian and the Empress Theodora; he, accompanied by his courtiers, she, by her retinue. Here we see the work of an accomplished and sensitive designer. The composition is developed from a series of verticals and arcs, repeating the nature of the architecture. The design is strong in darks and lights, and is varied with many patterns. The figures are clearly outlined and boldly conceived, and each fits into its place in the total plan. Color and texture are used for design, not representation, and from the facets of the hundreds of golden tesserae the reflected light delights the eye with its almost mysterious coruscations.

The detail of Theodora's head and shoulders illustrates the simplicity of the technique, based upon the requirements of the material. Too much detail would be lost in the complicated surface texture, so the artist has kept to essentials. Strong contrasts of color and value maintain the surface and reveal the design. The nature of the material is not concealed, but is incorporated into the plan of the work.

In contemporary art there has been a reawakening of interest in this ancient medium.

Roman: *Pavement of Triclinium from the House of Cornelius Tayas.* First century B.C. Marble mosaic. Alinari.

Byzantine: *Detail of pavement.* Baptistry, Florence. C. 1200. Alinari.

364   CRAFTS DESIGN

Byzantine: *The Empress Theodora and her Retinue.* c. 547 A.D. San Vitale, Ravenna. Mosaic. Alinari.

Detail from the mosaic above.

Many modern artists and craftsmen have explored its possibilities. With the lessons of the primitive Christian and Byzantine artists to guide him, Fernand Léger planned the mosaics over the entrance façade of the Léger Museum at Biot, France, which re-create for our day the same splendor and richness for this contemporary structure that *Theodora* does for San Vitale.

As in every art and craft medium, the effect of the finished product is dependent upon the design ability of the artist. Whether it be a small table tile or a vast mosaic mural, the underlying design structure gives the meaning to the form.

The artist begins his work with a careful drawing, or cartoon, keeping in mind the limitations of his material, its colors, values, shapes, sizes, and the feeling of the space his finished work will occupy. If the work is to be successful, it must be well designed within itself, and if it is to be part of a church or a home or a market place, the patterns built into the work should echo and

harmonize with the architecture around it. When the artist is satisfied with his drawing, he enlarges it to the exact size of the area to be filled, carefully prepares the wall, and lays the plaster or concrete ground. Sometimes the artist lays the ground in sections over the drawing, which has previously been transferred to the wall; but often he prepares an area and transfers the drawing to the plaster by laying it on the ground and going over its outlines with a stylus, which makes a small indentation on the surface of the wet ground. No larger area is laid than the artist is able to work on at one time, for the ground sets up and becomes unworkable, and must be removed for a fresh start.

Before him the artist has all the variously colored tesserae separated in little bins, and, working from his drawings and color notes, he selects the color he needs for each area. If the tessera is not the right size, he cuts it with a chisel or nippers, so that it will fit into the space

Opposite page: Byzantine: *The Virgins Bearing their Crowns as Offerings to the Virgin,* Sant' Apollinare Nuovo, Ravenna. Sixth century. Mosaic. Alinari.

Byzantine: *Emperor John II Comnenos and Empress Irene and Alexios, their son and co-Emperor flanking the Mother of God and the Christ Child.* Mosaic panel from the South Gallery of the Church of Hagia Sophia, Istanbul (facsimile). 1118–1122 A.D. Painting on photographic paper simulating glass and stone tesserae, 58⅛" × 126". Seattle Art Museum, Donald E. Frederick Memorial Collection.

Byzantine: *The Birds in the Ark (Detail),* from the story of Noah in the Narthex of St. Mark's Cathedral in Venice. Eleventh century. Mosaic. Alinari.

required. Then he presses each tessera into place in the soft ground. After each section is laid, the artist levels the faces of the tesserae by pressing a straightedge against the surface. Or, if the artist wishes, he can tilt the tesserae to suggest volume or reflect the light in different ways to enhance his design.

The materials used in making mosaics have many qualities that make them especially suitable for design. Tesserae of stone, glass, or tile —rich in texture and color, opaque, transparent, and translucent—are exciting to touch and look at, even before they are incorporated into a design. These qualities can add greatly to the visual effect of the work if it has been planned to bring out and emphasize the nature of the materials. The materials also have limitations which the artist or craftsman must consider as he plans his design. The shape and size of the tesserae, even if very small, suggest broad treatment in simple areas, and require a carefully worked out dark-light pattern. If the basic design is not strong enough, the interest of the separate pieces and the surface texture will dominate the design or completely conceal it. Even on a very large mosaic panel, the design must be strong if it is to carry well.

When the artist begins his work, he should consider first the organization of dark-light and color to fill the space, create balance, and divide the area into interesting and satisfying relationships. Intricate shapes and small details are difficult to carry out without cutting the tesserae into very small pieces. Essential features of the design can be accentuated with value change or outline, as we have seen in the mosaic murals from San Vitale. Large areas can be made richer if slight color change is introduced by breaking areas of solid color with an occasional tessera of another hue, maintaining the value relationship. Even impressionistic effects are possible, building large color areas with differently colored tesserae, such as alternating blues and reds to make violets. The spaces between the

Persian: *Star Mosaic Medallion.* Fifteenth century. Ceramic tile, 23½″ square. Seattle Art Museum, Eugene Fuller Memorial Collection.

Juan O'Gorman: *Mural on the Library, National University.* Mexico City. Mosaic. Courtesy of Pan American Union and Coca-Cola Export Corporation.

368   CRAFTS DESIGN

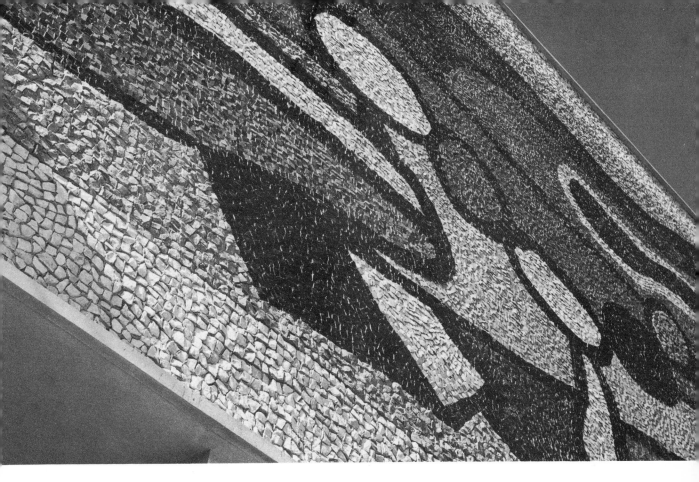

Fernand Léger: *Soccer and Bicycling* (Detail).

Fernand Léger: *Soccer and Bicycling*. Completed 1960. Mosaic and ceramic.
156′ length. Fernand Léger Museum, Biot, France.

tesserae also can add interest and variety to the design. The traditional white grout gives a crisp, clean edge to each tessera, accenting its color and texture. But if the designer wishes, he can color the grout by adding dry pigment to it, which greatly changes the visual appearance of the work and provides many possibilities for experimentation. If a level surface is not essential to the finished work, the tesserae may be pressed into the ground at different angles, catching the light to build form; or different levels, in the manner of a bas-relief, can add interest and variety to the surface. Mosaic lends itself easily to pattern building; and, as we have seen, when the total design is strong, many patterns can be combined as a source of richness. In mosaic, subject matter must be well integrated into the structure of the design and related to the space to be filled and the materials that are used. The quality of the spatial organization and the balance of dark-light and color are more important than naturalistic treatment of subject matter.

Some artists like to plan the design first with a charcoal, cut paper, or painted sketch, for these materials are very flexible and permit an easy working out of ideas. Then the sketch can be judged for balance, interest, space-filling qualities, and variety of sizes and shapes before the final work is begun. Two preliminary sketches, one of the dark-light plan, another of the color organization, are very helpful in developing the design, although as the work progresses in the actual materials, the designer may discover new possibilities that had not occurred to him before.

Antonio Gaudi: *Tower Finial from La Sagrada Familia.* Barcelona. Mosaic. Courtesy of *Course in Making Mosaics* by Joseph L. Young, published by Reinhold. Photography by Cecily Young.

Brazilian: *Mosaic Sidewalk in Rio de Janeiro.* Courtesy of Brazilian Government Trade Bureau.

Simon Rodia: *Section of Watts Towers*, southeast section of Los Angeles. 1919-1952. A construction of steel rods, mesh and mortar covered with mosaic incrustations of broken tiles, dishes, bottles, and seashells to form a unique work of folk art, 100' high. Courtesy of The Committee for Simon Rodia's Towers in Watts. Marvin Rand, Photographer.

Frances E. Simches: *White on White*. 1959. Mosaic wall panel, ceramic and concrete, 28" x 36". Courtesy of American Craftsmen's Council.

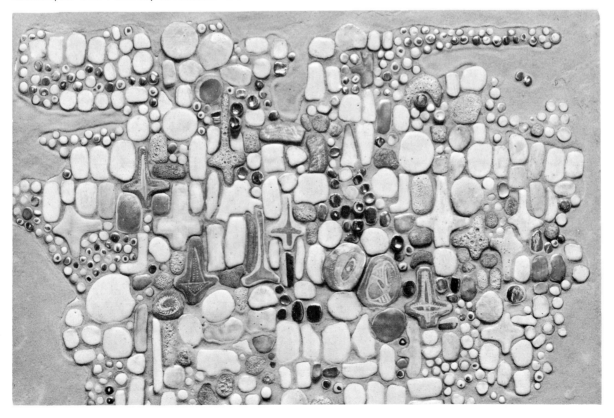

MATERIALS USED IN MAKING MOSAICS

TESSERAE

1. Glazed and unglazed tiles, commercial or handmade, imported or domestic
2. Broken ceramic dishes
3. Italian smalti (hand-chiseled glass tesserae)
4. Commercial machine-pressed Venetian or Mexican glass tesserae
5. Stones or pebbles
6. Shells and natural beach objects
7. Semiprecious stones
8. Discarded "junk" or costume jewelry
9. Broken colored glass bottles, dishes, windows
10. Brick

Many other materials are available that have interesting color and texture, and that can be cut or broken to usable sizes.

ADHESIVES AND FILLERS

1. Glues—commercial acetate and casein glues for sticking tiles to surfaces (such as Duco cement, Wilhold glue, and other tile and linoleum adhesives)
2. Grouts and fillers—grout and grout coloring (dry pigments), magnesite and magnesium chloride, alkali-proof cement colors to color mixtures (available at hardware and building supply stores), portland cement (more durable than magnesite in extreme exposure, but heavier when finished)

TOOLS

1. Tools for breaking tesserae or mosaic materials—tile cutters or nippers, wooden mallet or hammer, and additional materials: cloth sack, or newspapers to cover breakage area and flying pieces; glasses to protect eyes; small whetstone to file rough tile edges
2. Tools for cementing and grouting—trowel, spatula, putty knife or tongue depressors, tongs and tweezers, rolling pin or leveling board, and additional materials: brushes, bowls, cans or disposable mixing cups; rags or paper towels; newspapers

MOUNTING SURFACES

1. Masonite panels—small projects can be mounted on masonite
2. Plywood panels, ¼ to ¾ inch thickness: 3 feet square or less—¼ inch; 3 to 6 feet square—½ inch; larger—¾ inch
3. Framing—wood or metal moldings framing panel will facilitate the operation
4. Sealer—coating plywood on each side with a resin sealer will help prevent warping
5. Reinforcement—magnesite requires metal reinforcements on panels: metal meshing, chicken wire, hardcloth; these must be attached evenly over surface with evenly spaced brads

OTHER MOUNTING SURFACES

Mosaics can also be mounted on a variety of surfaces that are round and flat and dishlike, from can lids to garbage can lids and commercial flowerpot saucers.

DIRECT METHOD

In the direct method the mosaic tesserae are either glued directly to a prepared surface and grouted, or set into a mortar-bed of magnesite or cement. If the tiles are to be glued to the ground, a waterproofed plywood panel or a panel waterproofed with wood sealer should be used. Either mastic or glue may be used as an adhesive to attach the tiles to the panel. If the mosaic is to be a table top, it is much simpler to frame the panel before setting the tiles. The frame should be high enough to be flush with the top of the tesserae. If magnesite or cement is to be used, follow steps 4 and 5 in the Indirect Method (which follows this section). Spread small sections of the mortar-bed at one time and press each tessera into place.

MATERIALS

1. Prepared plywood panel
2. Tesserae
3. Tile cutters
4. Adhesive
5. Grout
6. Mixing pan
7. Water
8. Sponge or rags

1 *Plan the design, using paint, crayon, charcoal, or cut paper. If the design is composed of whole tiles only, you may plan the design by arranging the tiles.*

2 *Transfer the design to the prepared surface.*

3 *Cut tiles with nippers to fit the design shapes. To prevent splinters from flying, shield the tile with the hand, or place it inside a plastic bag when cutting. The cutter can be held on the edge or in the center of the tile.*

4 *To glue tiles in place, spread glue from the container evenly over an area to be tiled. If the layer of glue is too thick, it will ooze up between the tiles, fill the depressions, and make grouting difficult.*

5 If mastic is to be used, spread the mastic on the design area to be filled. Use a small spatula or palette knife and spread evenly. Butter only one outlined shape at a time.

6 Press the tiles into place, leaving a space from ⅟₁₆ to ⅛ inch between tiles for grout. Allow to dry long enough so the tiles do not slip when pressed. Liquid glue dries rapidly; mastic takes about three hours.

7 To mix grout, place a small amount of water in a pan, add powdered grout, and stir to a heavy cream consistency. The grout can be made thicker if desired. If the surface to be grouted is vertical or is not framed, thicker grout is necessary.

8 Pour or spread the grout over the surface.

MOSAICS   **375**

9 Rub the grout into the spaces between the tiles with the hand. A small putty knife, plastic grouting tool, palette knife, or tongue depressor may be used as an aid. If a great deal of grouting is to be done or large areas are to be covered, it is advisable to wear rubber gloves to protect the hands from the drying action of the grout and the sharp edges of the tile.

10 Allow the grout to set. Remove the excess grout from the surface with a sponge, damp cloth, or paper towels.

11 Give the tiles a final cleaning with a sponge or damp cloth before applying silicone, marble polish, or wax to protect the grout.

12 Finished table top.

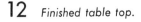

INDIRECT METHOD

In the indirect method the tesserae are first glued to a sheet of paper and then pressed into the adhesive-covered surface or mortar-bed.

The mortar-bed can be made of magnesite or concrete.

MATERIALS

1. Plywood panel
2. Wire screen
3. Staples or brads
4. Staple gun or hammer
5. Magnesite
6. Magnesium chloride solution 22° Baume
7. Mixing pan
8. Spatula
9. Paper
10. Library paste or water soluble glue
11. Tesserae
12. Nippers

1 *Plan the design, using crayon, cut paper, or paint. The design can also be planned with tiles. Arrange the tiles until a satisfactory design has been achieved.*

2 *Prepare the plywood panel. If the plywood is not waterproofed, it must be painted with a wood sealer. Cover the top of the panel with screen, using staples or brads.*

3 *The design will be in reverse when it is set in the mortar-bed. If it is necessary to keep the left-to-right order of the original design, as it would be in the case of lettering, the design must be drawn on the Kraft paper in reverse order. Glue the tiles in place on the pattern. Use library paste or water soluble glue. If the tesserae have a right and wrong side be sure to paste the right side down. Leave a small space between tesserae.*

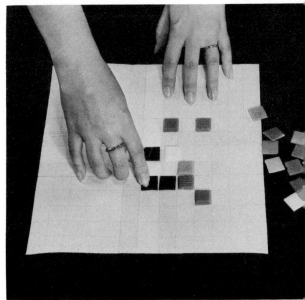

4 To mix the magnesite for the mortar-bed use a plastic, enamel, glass, or disposable paper container. Put some magnesite in the container and add enough magnesium chloride solution to make a thick paste. The paste can be thick or thin depending upon how it is to be used. A consistency of thin batter is needed for pouring. Mix only the quantity needed for immediate use because it sets up in about one hour. The mortar may be left its natural color or its color may be changed by adding alkali-proof cement color.

5 Butter the area with magnesite. The coat should be at least ¼ inch deep.

6 Invert the paper with the pasted tesserae and place over the mortar-bed.

7 Press the tesserae evenly into the mortar-bed.

8 Wet the paper backing and keep it wet for several hours until the mortar sets enough to hold the tiles. Then peel the paper off. Any paper that does not peel off easily can be removed with a wet sponge.

9 Add grout to fill the cracks if necessary.

MOSAICS 379

ADDITIONAL SUGGESTIONS FOR MOSAICS

The pieces for mosaics to be used by beginners or students can be segregated into small boxes, trays, or old plates, and arranged according to colors, values (dark and light, or dark, medium, and light), or by quality, texture, or size and shape.

Glue in tubes provides a convenient adhesive. Small, standardized, precut, waterproof plywood pieces are the easiest surface on which to glue tesserae. If grout or magnesite is to be used, it can be adequately mixed in cottage cheese cartons or shallow pans, and spread with spatulas, palette knives, or tongue depressors.

The working area, including the floor, should be covered with newspapers. Each student needs an allotted space to work, with either his own tile selection boxes or easy access to the master supply. If a predesigned plan is to be followed, tesserae may be selected before gluing begins. To get acquainted with the materials, children, especially young ones, may wish to use tesserae in the sizes or shapes already available, such as square tiles or pebbles from the beach. Gluing down the tiles in a random arrangement immediately as selected, working directly and experimentally, may help them to become familiar with the materials and method. For more advanced problems, sketches or plans can be utilized, as simple or complex as desired. They may be done with line, color, or limited value areas. Simple plans using stripes or straight lines, squares, or rectangular colored areas drawn with crayon or paint are suggested approaches. Large colored-paper shapes or even small squares of paper may be used.

If the tile is to be used whole, a simple, clear, uncomplicated sketch is easier to follow. If it is to be cut to suit suggested areas, almost any reasonable details can be followed. Tiles may be precut by the teacher into smaller pieces, giving the opportunity for detail in a selection type problem, without the confusion of cutting pieces in class. Children may then select the precut irregular shapes to fill their design plans as well as they can.

Teachers can devise many opportunities for experiences with this fascinating material, and whether the problem is a small, individual one or an extensive one for the group, such as a mural for a school building where cooperative effort of a whole class is needed, the excitement and pleasure can be shared by all.

SUGGESTED PROJECTS

Tiles done on wood panels or coffee can lids
Mosaic-topped boxes
Trays
Table tops
Wall decorations
Murals
Papier-mâché sculpture, covered with mosaic

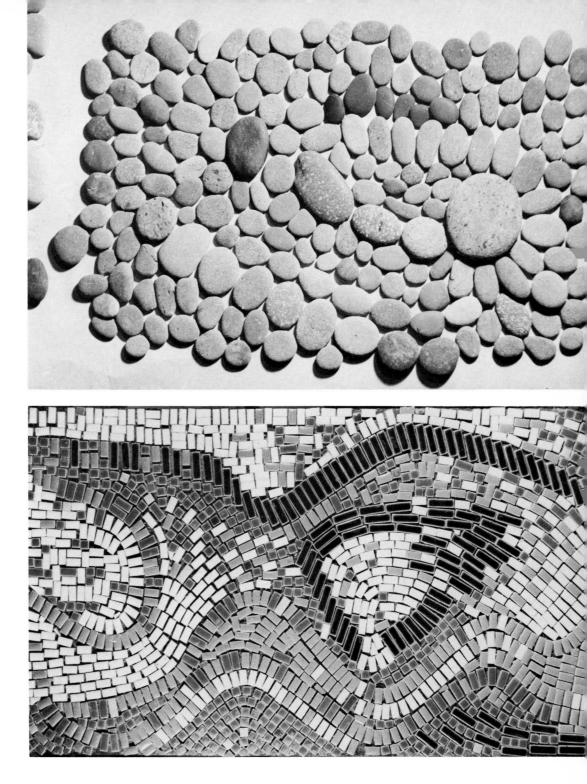

Laying Out the Design for a Pebble Mosaic. Courtesy of Reino Randall, from *Mosaics for Schools,* Bailey Films.

Ceramic Tile Mosaic Ready for Grouting. Courtesy of Reino Randall, from *Mosaics for Schools,* Bailey Films.

MOSAICS   381

Head. Cut paper mosaic, 18″ high. Jane Addams High School, Seattle. Mary Kutila, Instructor.

Butterflies. Table tiles. Mosaic, 9″ x 9″. Adult student.

Designing a Mosaic, Using the Direct Method.

Mural at Eastgate School (Detail). 1959. Mosaic, 6' x 30'. Elementary children, Eastgate School, Bellevue, Washington. Lucille Studebaker, Director of Art.

MOSAICS   383

ENAMELING

French, Limoges: *Reliquary Châsse.* About 1200. Champlevé enamel, 5½″ x 5⁷⁄₁₆″. Seattle Art Museum, Donald E. Frederick Memorial Collection.

ENAMELING

Enamel is glass ground to powder and fused with heat, usually on a metal surface. A vitreous glaze forms, which when cool may be opaque, translucent, or transparent. The surface quality of enamel can vary from a high gloss to a mat or dull finish. Color is added with metal oxides. The color quality is heightened because the light goes through the glaze material and reflects from the metal base out through the color. Copper, silver, gold, and steel are the metals most generally used with enamel, and of these, silver provides the highest degree of reflection and brilliance of color. Works of art covered or glazed with enamel are referred to as enamels.

The ancient Egyptians and Assyrians did their most magnificent enameling on clay and brick surfaces. The palace of Rameses III at Tell el-Yehudia and the palace of Nimrod in Babylon contained large walls of tiles decorated with enamels. Enameling is in this respect much like glazing clay.

The Greeks and Romans produced enameled jewelry with fine detail. Greek sculptors of the fourth and fifth centuries B.C. employed enamels for particular emphasis. They very often enameled the eyes of their sculptures. The gold drapery on the lost figure of Zeus made by Phidias for the temple at Olympia is said to have been elaborately enameled with figures and flowers.

The history of enameling generally falls into periods in which various methods of glazing were perfected. The major classifications of enamels are *cloisonné*, *champlevé*, *Limoges*, *plique-à-jour*, and *basse-taille*.

In *cloisonné*, recesses to contain the enamels are formed from narrow strips of metal, bent to shape and fastened to a metal ground with solder or enamel. These cloisons form little dykes that separate the enamel color areas and prevent them from running into each other when the enamel is fired. Cloisonné reached a high period of perfection in the hands of Byzantine craftsmen between the sixth and twelfth centuries. Nearly every church in Constantinople held a variety of treasures such as chalices, patens, cases for sacred relics, and bindings for gospel and service books. These highly ornate objects were made from rich combinations of metal, enamels, and precious stones. Work of the early Byzantine period was particularly characterized by the wide expanses of enamel held by bold, simple cloison designs.

The Beresford Hope Cross, a hinged repository for relics, is a fine example of this period. The cross-shaped container covered on each side with cloisonné enamel has the strong color and strong value contrasts characteristic of Byzantine enamels. On the front it has the crucifixion, and the central figure of the Christ is surrounded with early Christian symbols of the crucifixion. To the left and right of the Christ are half-length figures.

Byzantine craftsmen used combinations of simple colors, motifs, and values to create magnificently patterned pieces exceptionally strong in design quality.

Byzantine: *Beresford Hope Cross, in two parts, forming a reliquary.* Tenth or eleventh century. Silver, encrusted with transparent enamel in gold cloisons on a gold ground. 3⅜″ x 2¼″. Victoria and Albert Museum, London.

French: *A Saint.* End of eleventh century. Cloisonné enamel, 2¾″ high. Louvre, Paris.

Enamels were very often used to decorate the boxes or reliquaries used to contain holy early Christian relics. According to tradition the eighth- or ninth-century reliquary box was made to hold a piece of the true cross. The design on the cover depicts the crucifixion. The dominating cross makes a vertical and horizontal composition that repeats and strengthens the rectangular shape of the box. The space around the cross is filled with figures, inscriptions, and symbols. The central panel is bordered by a band of stylized heads that forms a strong dark and light pattern. The repetition of the heads on the top and the side of the box helps create a unified design.

The design and drawing used in Byzantine enamels are similar to that of Byzantine mosaics, and, because of their strong design quality and rich color, Byzantine enamels are classified as some of the most magnificent ever produced.

The cloisonné process was used extensively in China and later in Japan. In the Chinese dove-shaped altar wine vessel on wheels, simple pattern is combined with conventional and intricate symbols. Repetitive stripes decorate the body of the figure and there is a general repetition of circular shapes on the head, wheel, wings, and jar. The basic wing motif is altered into a key design and used as an allover pattern and also repeated along the back of the dove. The value contrasts are bold, and the negative shapes are an important part of the total design. There is a strong vertical and horizontal relationship between the parts. The tail and head are almost at right angles to the body. Each of these strong verticals is modified by the stripe feather pattern. In Chinese cloisonné, nearly every detail of design is outlined by metal bands so that it completely covers the whole surface to be decorated.

Champlevé is another technique used to fill recesses with enamel. The recesses, rather than being built up as in cloisonné, are chiseled, pounded, or etched into the surface of the metal

Opposite page: Chinese, Ch'ien Lung Reign: *Crane.* Cloisonné enamel on brass, stand of turquoise matrix, 4⅛" high. Seattle Art Museum, Eugene Fuller Memorial Collection.

Byzantine: *Reliquary for Wood of the True Cross* (top and side view). Eighth–ninth century. Silver gilt, cloisonné enamel, 4" x 2⅞". Courtesy of the Metropolitan Museum of Art, Gift of J. Pierpont Morgan, 1917.

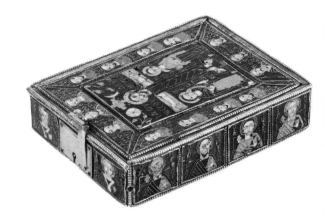

Chinese, Ch'ing Dynasty: *Dove-shaped Altar Wine Vessel.* Eighteenth century or earlier. Cloisonné enamel, 21⅝" high. In the Brooklyn Museum Collection, gift of Samuel P. Avery.

to create design areas. The expanse of metal left between the enameled areas may be great, or so narrow as to resemble cloisons.

The thirteenth-century French square box, or *châsse carrée,* is covered on the back with an allover pattern of rosette medallions. The cross formed by this rosette motif is repeated in a band or border around each side of the chasse. Secondary patterns appear through variations in the color and value of similar shapes. The design of the box is much enhanced by the attentions to detail achieved through the many subtle variations in shapes and sizes of the simple design elements used.

The twelfth-century plaque depicting the crucifixion is an example of champlevé used in conjunction with cloisonné details. This plaque from the Mosan school has a forceful symmetric design made by the vertical and horizontal placement of the enameled areas. The symmetry has been alleviated by rhythmic variations in the postures of the figures and the vitality of the

spaces left in the metal between the positive shapes. Lettering becomes an integral part of the design, taking its place in breaking the space around the dominant figures and the sun and the moon which so beautifully complete the arrangement of heads. The dark horizontal transept of the cross is repeated by the dark area at the base of the figures.

In this piece the positive shapes are enameled, and the metal or copper-gilt ground left as background. This technique was modified in the thirteenth century in France so that the figures were left in metal and the backgrounds enameled.

The bronze-gilt enameled *chasse* has figures of this type. The background areas are richly enameled with strong colors and a simple band of light turquoise against a dark blue; the negative spaces between the figures are nicely filled with rosettes. The figures are well designed and shaped to repeat the outside shape of the box.

French: *Châsse Carrée.* Thirteenth century. Champlevé enamel, height 10". Louvre, Paris.

Attr. to Godefroid de Claire: *Crucifixion.* Twelfth century. Mosan enamels, champlevé, 4" high. Courtesy of the Metropolitan Museum of Art, gift of J. Pierpont Morgan, 1917.

Basse-taille (low-cut) was another development of the cutaway or sculptured recess technique used to contain transparent enamel in which the recesses were chased or worked in low relief that is visible through the layer of enamel. This technique was first developed early in the fourteenth century in Italy. *The King's Cup,* made in France about 1380, is an excellent example of basse-taille. This elegant royal cup of the kings of France and England was shaped of hammered gold and the design applied in bands around the lid, bowl, and stem. The stem has twice been altered to increase the height, once during the time of Henry VII, when the band of Tudor roses was added.

Plique-à-jour (which means "light-of-day") developed as an enameling technique about the same time as basse-taille and is a process in which only the walls without backing hold the transparent enamel. This allows light to pass through the areas of colored glass. These enamels resemble small stained-glass windows when the cloisons are shaped and soldered together to form the partitions which separate and support the areas of enamel. Plique-à-jour may also be made by cutting or drilling openings in metal, in which case the metal is a more dominant part of the design than it would be if only cloisons are used.

Limoges is a surface technique in which none

G. Alpais (French): *Eucharist Cup with cover.* Thirteenth century. Champlevé enamel, 12″ x 6⅝″. Decorated with figures of apostles and angels. Louvre, Paris.

French: *Châsse.* Early thirteenth century. Bronze gilt plaques with champlevé enamel on wooden core, 6⅛″ x 5¼″ x 2¹¹⁄₁₆″. Chicago Art Institute, The Lucy Maud Buckingham Medieval Collection.

Japanese: *Bowl.* Early twentieth century. Plique-à-jour enamel. Courtesy of the Cooper Union Museum.

Fernand Thesmar (French): *Bowl.* 1903. Plique-à-jour enamel, 2″ x 2½″ diameter. Courtesy of the Metropolitan Museum of Art, gift of Mrs. Charles Inman Barnard, 1905, in memory of her mother-in-law, Susan Livingston Barnard.

French: *The King's Cup.* c. 1380. Basse-taille enamel on gold. British Museum.

French, Limoges: *Triptych, Center Panel, The Crucifixion.*
Fifteenth century. Limoges enamel. The Taft Museum.

ENAMELING 393

of the enamel goes below the level of the surface or is contained within walls. It gained its name from the city of Limoges, France, where the technique reached a high level of development. The entire surface of the metal is covered without interruption. The surface may be covered in a variety of ways but in Limoges the technique of painting became very important. Contrast the appearance of this painting technique with the examples of champlevé and cloisonné.

Today's enamelists employ all of the traditional techniques. The function of enamel is to add color and decoration to the metal on which it is fused, and its hard surface adds utility. It enhances and protects the metal surfaces on which it is fused.

Contemporary enamels include jewelry, bowls, trays, boxes, spoons and other utensils, plaques, and many more items. Decorative panels are being employed in building and architecture, and many architectural and furniture details are also made of enamel. Pieces for accent can be applied to or combined with other materials such as leather, wood, and metal for book covers, boxes, decorative wall hangings, and screens.

Commercial enameling techniques have permitted the use of enamels on pans, stoves, spoons and utensils, cups, and other familiar items.

John Paul Miller: *Flounder and Fossil.* Cloisonné enamel on gold pendant. 2⅛″ x 1⅝″. American Craftsmen's Council.

Ramona Solberg: *Necklace.* Basse-taille enamel on silver.

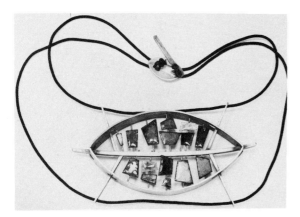

Russell Day: *Pendant Necklace.* Multicolored rectilinear enamel shapes and silver.

Jean Ames: *Adam and Eve.* 1959. Enamel panel.

Arthur Ames: *Triptych Number 2.* 1959. Painted enamel on copper, 11″ x 27″. Courtesy American Craftsmen's Council.

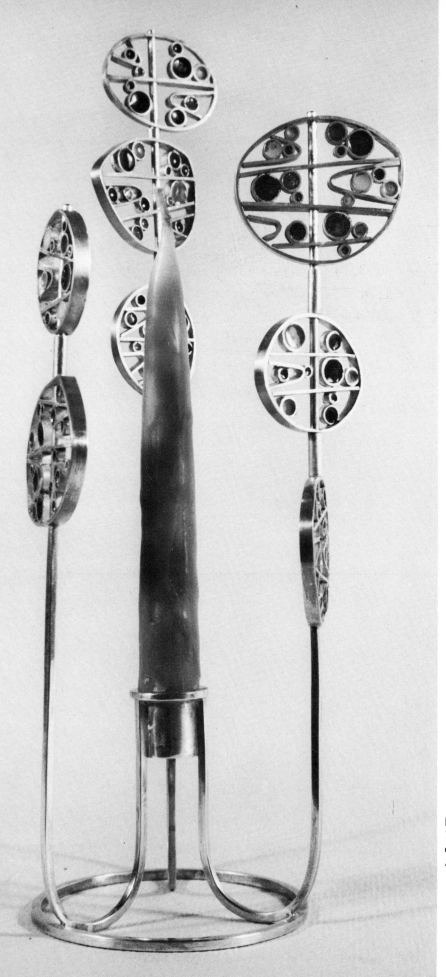

Ruth Penington: *Candlestick, Three Who Watch*. 1959. Plique-à-jour enamel on silver, 12″ high. Courtesy American Craftsmen's Council.

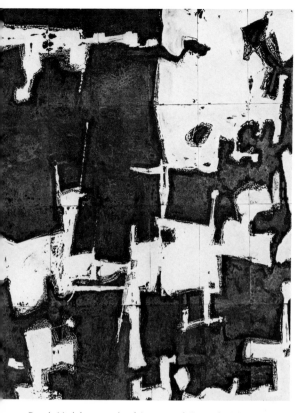

Paul Hultberg: *Architectural Panel*. 1959. Painted enamel on copper, oxidized, 48" x 42". Courtesy American Craftsmen's Council.

Harold Balazs: *Martian Martyr*. 1954. Enamel on copper, 15" x 15"

Stephen Oppenheim: *Kiln for Enos A. and Sarah DeWaters Art Center, Flint Community Junior College*. 1958. Porcelain enameled folded steel plate in bright red, aqua, and deep wine. 10' high.

Charles Smith: *Stove*. 1958. Porcelain enamel on steel, 36" high.

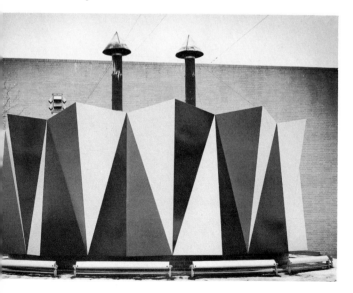

ENAMELING   397

ENAMELING

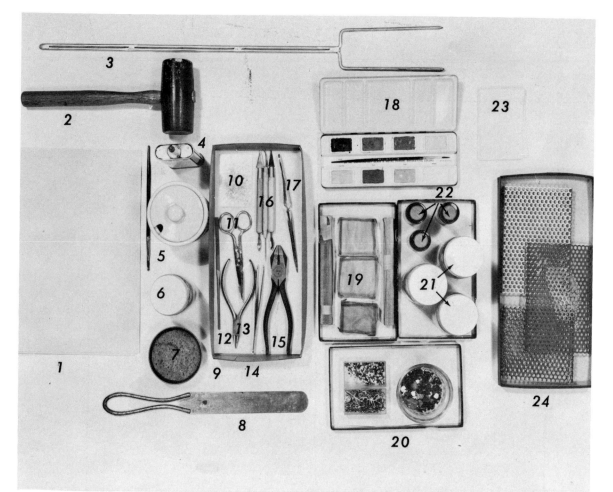

MATERIALS FOR ENAMELING

1. Sheets of paper
2. Mallet
3. Loading fork
4. Light machine oil
5. Brush and container for salt water (tablespoon salt to one cup water)
6. Junk jar for left-over enamel
7. Shallow dish with sponge
8. Spatula
9. Tool box
10. Sheet mica
11. Scissors
12. Hand file
13. Round-nosed pliers
14. Tweezers
15. Cutting pliers
16. Enamel tools and spatulas
17. Large tweezers
18. Box of cake enamels
19. 80-mesh screens: rolled, folded into sifters
20. Glass beads, threads, and chunks
21. Powdered enamel in jars
22. Powdered enamel in jars with sifter tops
23. Facial tissue
24. Nichrome fire screens

MATERIALS FOR ENAMELING

1. Pan of water
2. Glass container for nitric acid solution
3. Tweezers
4. Feathers
5. Hand drill
6. Hole punch
7. Bench vise
8. Asphaltum and brush
9. Box of jewelry findings
10. Box of precut copper blanks
11. Strip copper
12. Mallet
13. Bench pin and vise
14. Copper wire (20 gauge or smaller)
15. Soft solder
16. Steel wool
17. Carborundum stone
18. Jeweler's saw

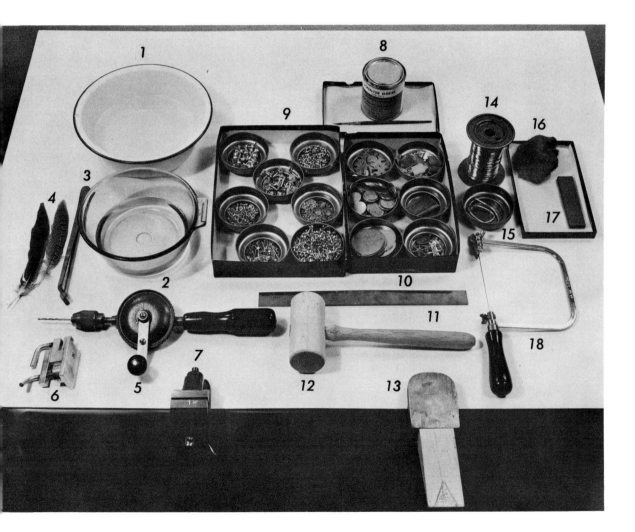

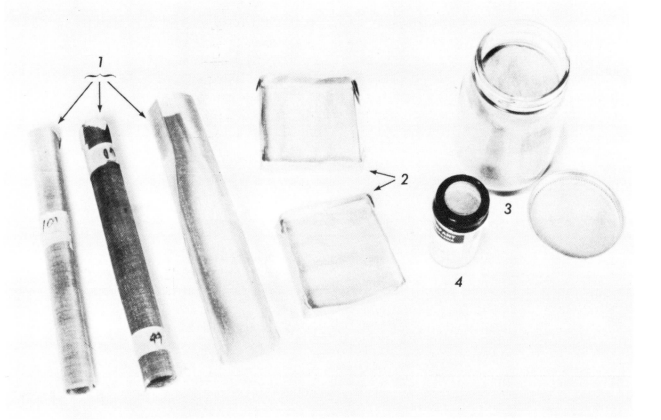

MATERIALS FOR ENAMELING

1. Rolls of 60-, 80-, 100-mesh screen
2. 80-mesh screen folded into sifters
3. Jar of powdered enamel
4. Jar of powdered enamel with sifter lid

SETTING UP A WORK AREA
FOR ENAMELING

A well-organized work area will simplify the enameling process. The enameling equipment and the kiln should be near one another to facilitate firing. A place for cleaning and soldering should be separate from the enameling area to prevent foreign particles from getting mixed with colors and other materials. The enamels must be kept pure to avoid undesirable contamination of color and other accidents which can easily spoil an otherwise perfect piece. It is convenient to keep the various tools and materials in small, labeled boxes for using and storing. The powdered enamels may be stored on a nearby shelf, each jar with a small, fired, sample piece attached to the label for easy recognition of its color and opacity. Such storage shelves should ideally be close to the work area. Access to a sink is desirable, but if this is not possible, a pan or crock of water is necessary.

DIAGRAM OF A WORKING AREA

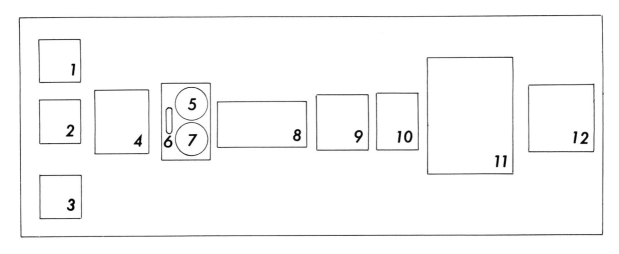

MATERIALS

1. Transparent enamels
2. Translucent enamels
3. Opaque enamels
4. Stack of clean paper
5. Salt water
6. Light machine oil
7. Leftover enamel jar
8. Tools
9. 80-mesh sift screens
10. Fire screens, 4 x 5 inches, nichrome
11. Kiln
12. Asbestos sheet

ENAMELING KILNS

There are many varieties and sizes of enameling kilns, commercial and homemade. A small kiln is adequate for simple jewelry projects, but a larger kiln is required for larger pieces such as bowls, boxes, or plaques. Many commercial kilns are equipped with a pyrometer, or temperature gauge, which affords greater control over the firing process. A kiln can be easily and inexpensively made with two firebricks, a nichrome wire screen, and a small torch. While lacking the fine control of a commercial this kiln is satisfactory for many projects, can also serve as a supplementary kiln or dou as soldering equipment.

Since the firing of enamel requires extr heats, the kiln should be located with regar safety and convenience. The firebrick kiln sh be placed on an asbestos sheet to avoid bur the work surface beneath with the torch molten drops from the piece being fired.

Enamel Kilns

Small commercial kiln with Pyrex top and asbestos sheet

A commercial front-opening kiln

Kiln made with firebricks, nichrome wire screen, and torch

FIRING ENAMEL ON AN OPEN KILN

Place the prepared piece on the screen. Fire from below or above with the torch by bringing the tip of the flame in contact with the piece until the enamel fuses. The surface should appear shiny and smooth as glass. Try both methods with sample pieces to compare results. Firing from above tends to alter the color, give a lustrous surface, and create accidental effects.

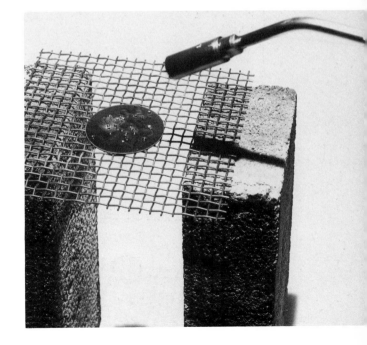

ENAMELING 403

PREPARING THE KILN FOR FIRING

The floor of the kiln should be protected with a coat of kiln wash. Kiln wash may be purchased in either liquid or powdered form. The powder is mixed with water to a consistency of heavy cream. Dampen the floor of the kiln with water. With a brush, apply a fairly heavy coat of kiln wash. One coat should last two months with normal use. When necessary, recoat. Brush or scrape used kiln wash out of the kiln before applying a fresh coat. If the floor of the kiln develops pits or cracks with use, these may be repaired with firebrick that is ground to a powder in a mortar and pestle and mixed with kiln wash to a heavy paste, then put into the cracks.

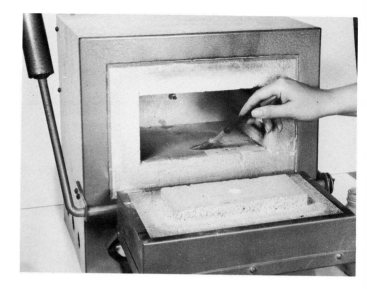

FIRING ENAMEL IN A FRONT-OPENING KILN

1 Before using a commercial kiln, carefully read the accompanying instructions.

2 Preheat the kiln to 1500° F. The temperature drops about 150° each time the door is opened and if the kiln is preheated about 45 minutes before use, lost heat is more easily regained. When loading and unloading the kiln it is advisable to wear an asbestos glove to protect the hand.

3 To load the kiln, lower the door and quickly insert the loaded fire screen with a loading fork.

4 Close the door as quickly and gently as possible to prevent heat loss, and leave piece inside for about 1½ minutes. Open and close the door slightly to examine and re-examine the piece during the firing.

5 Remove the fired piece with the loading fork as soon as the enamel has fused. The surface should appear as smooth and shiny as glass.

6 Place the fire screen with its load on an asbestos sheet or some other fireproof, level surface to cool. The asbestos sheet may be conveniently placed on top or to the side of the kiln, where the piece can cool slowly, out of strong drafts. Sudden cooling may crack the enamel. The colors on the fiery surface of the piece appear altered, but as the piece cools, the color regains its brilliance.

7 It is best to fire enamel pieces one at a time, because variation in size and color require different timing. Since it is difficult to duplicate a firing, paired pieces such as earrings should be fired together if possible.

PREPARING THE COPPER FOR ENAMELING

1 Cleaning the copper. Copper must be cleaned thoroughly before enamel is applied. Surface impurities may prevent the enamel from adhering to the metal. Clean the copper with steel wool, emery cloth, a file, or dip it in a 5 per cent nitric acid solution or a commercial metal cleaning solution. To clean with steel wool, hold the piece in the fingers by the edges, and brush the surface of the copper with a rotary motion. Once the copper is clean, it is important to keep fingerprints off the surface. Keep steel wool and cleaning process away from the central work area because steel wool fragments will cause small black hooks to appear in the fired enamel.

2 Protection from fire scale. Fire scale occurs when copper is heated. To prevent this black scale from sticking, the surface of the metal may be protected with a thin coat of salt water, which, when dry, will facilitate removal of any scale. The salt water (one tablespoon of salt to a cup of water) may be kept in any convenient container and applied to the metal with a brush. Commercial masking preparations may also be used for this purpose.

LIMOGES

In the Limoges processes, the metal surface is completely covered with enamels. No dividers separate the areas of enamel from each other as in the cloisonné and champlevé techniques.

The enamels may be applied by dusting, painting, sgraffito, or stencil. Glass threads, beads, and chunks may be used to vary the quality of the surface.

MATERIALS

1. Copper blank
2. Enamels
3. Glass threads, beads, and chunks
4. Sheets of paper
5. 80-mesh screen folded into shaker boxes
6. Spatula
7. Supporting disc
8. Fire screen
9. Pointed tools such as enameling tools, scribers, stylus, leather modeling tool, crochet hook, heavy darning needle
10. Light machine oil or glycerine
11. Gum tragacanth solution

DUSTING OR SPRINKLING PROCESS

The simplest method of application is to dust or sprinkle powdered enamel directly on the clean surface of the metal. To ensure adhesion, an undercoat of gum arabic solution can be painted or sprayed on the surface. This is not necessary for simple projects, however, especially if the piece is flat. Enamel powders are dusted through an 80-mesh screen which is folded into a boxlike container. Commercial sifter jars with screen tops are also available. Two separately fired thin coats of enamel are preferable to one thick coat. If the piece is placed on clean paper while dusting, extra powder can be returned to the container after sprinkling. Powder mixed with other colors or remnants contaminated with fire scale can be collected in a junk jar to be used for counter-enameling.

1 *Prepare the metal piece for enameling.*

2 *Brush or spray the surface of the piece with a thin coat of gum, if desired.*

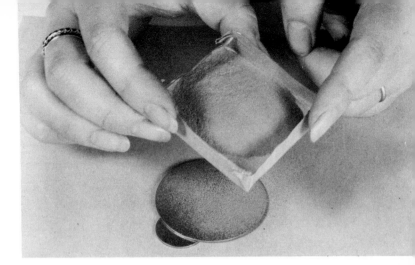

3 Place the copper on a clean piece of smooth paper. It is helpful to prop up one edge of the copper blank so there is enough space under it to insert the spatula. A coin, a small copper blank, button, or other small object will serve as a prop. Sprinkle carefully. Apply the enamel by gently tapping with the finger the jar or screen containing the powder so that it falls evenly on the surface of the metal. Moving the screen first around the outside edge of the piece and then into the center helps distribute the enamel evenly. When all the metal appears to be evenly covered with powder, the coat is complete.

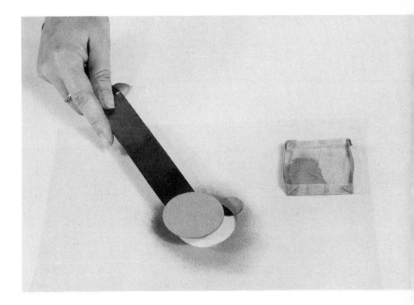

4 Lift the sprinkled piece carefully with a spatula, and place it on the fire screen.

5 Place screen in kiln with loading fork.

6 Fire the piece until the enamel begins to flow evenly together and appears smooth and shiny.

7 Remove the piece from the kiln and place the screen on the asbestos to cool.

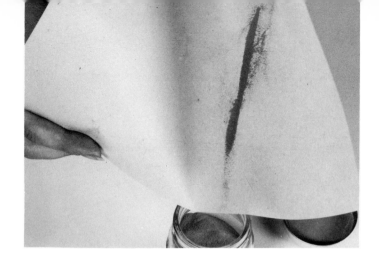

8 *Return leftover enamel collected on the paper sheet to its jar.*

COUNTERENAMELING

Since the expansion rates of metal and enamel differ, tensions are set up between the two as the fired pieces cool, which may result in warping the metal and cracking or crazing the enamel. To avoid these possibilities, the back surface of the piece can be given a coat of enamel or counterenamel. This counterenamel can be any color, even scrap enamel from the junk jar. Scrap enamel works especially well, because a mixture of colors does not flow easily during firing. However, if the back of the piece is to be visible in the finished product, as it would be in a bowl, the color of the back should be carefully selected to fit in with the over-all design. To counterenamel, follow the procedure outlined in the Dusting or Sprinkling Process. If the piece is to have an attachment soldered on later, such as the clasp on a pin, the area that will receive the clasp should be masked off or cleaned off before firing. The counterenameling should be done before the surface is decorated. When firing the counterenamel, remove it from the kiln just before it matures, while the surface is still slightly granular. The counterenamel coat will mature in subsequent firings.

Once the bottom is counterenameled, the piece must be supported on a steel stilt or trivet. If the trivet were not used, the counterenameled bottom of the piece would stick to the kiln floor when the top was being fired. The trivet will leave three small scars in the enamel where it has come in contact with the piece. These marks are a characteristic part of any counterenameled piece.

SGRAFFITO

1 Prepare the metal blank.

2 Apply and fire a base coat of enamel, as described on p. 407.

3 After firing and cooling the piece, sprinkle with a second color. Gum may be used to hold the powder in place, but is not necessary on a flat piece. If gum is used, allow it to dry thoroughly before proceeding.

4 Scratch the design through to the base color with any pointed tool. A brush may be used to remove unwanted specks and to clean uncontrolled edges.

5 Fire.

6 An alternate method is to mix enamel powder with gum tragacanth to make a thick, creamy paste to be applied to the piece with a modeling tool or small spatula. Place the piece on top of the kiln until the paste is dry and then scratch the design.

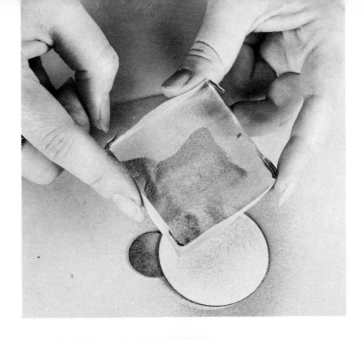

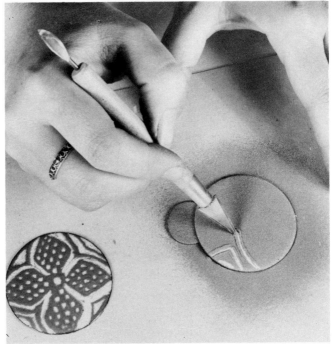

PAINTING A DESIGN WITH OIL OR GLYCERINE

Designs can be made by painting over a first coat of enamel with oil or glycerine. Light machine oil or a glycerine slightly diluted with water is used. The glycerine may be tinted with colored ink if desired to make the lines visible. The color of the ink will burn out in the firing. If the glycerine is sufficiently diluted, a pen may be used for an especially fine line. When sprinkled on the painted design, the enamel powder adheres only to the oil or glycerine.

1 Prepare a metal blank; apply and fire a base coat of enamel.

2 Paint the design with a small brush, using light machine oil or glycerine.

3 Dust evenly with powder.

4 Tap gently to remove excess enamel. Spots may be gently blown away or removed with a clean brush.

5 Fire.

STENCIL PROCESS

1 Prepare a metal blank; apply and fire a base coat of enamel.

2 Cut a stencil design from paper; moisten with a damp sponge.

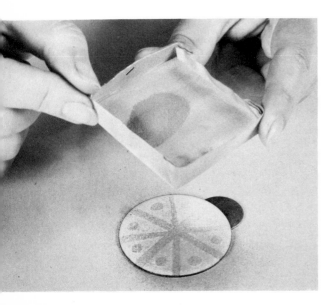

3 *Lay in place on the enameled blank.*

4 *Dust with powdered enamel.*

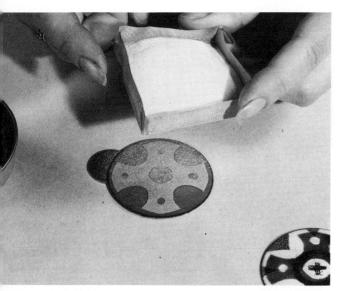

5 *Carefully lift the stencil, using tweezers, so the design remains undisturbed. Remove clinging remnants of powder with a clean brush.*

6 *Fire.*

7 *Repeat the process with a second stencil if a more complex design is desired. Several stencils can be used or variations made by placing the first stencil in different positions.*

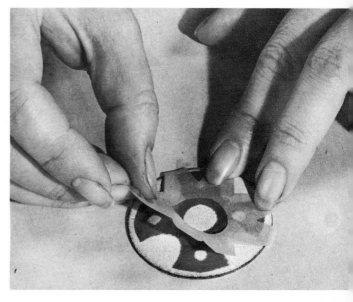

USING GLASS BEADS, GLASS FRAGMENTS, OR GLASS THREADS

1 Prepare a metal blank; apply and fire a base coat of enamel.

2 Place threads, beads, or chunks in a pattern and fire until they melt in place. These raised variations may be used in combination with other processes. Beads, threads, and chunks of glass may also be placed in unfired powdered enamel that has been dusted over gum, and then fired at the same time.

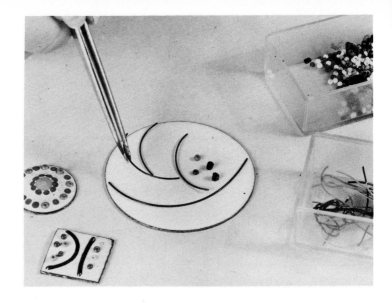

OVERGLAZE PAINTING

Colors for painting designs over a base coat can be purchased in pans, or powdered enamels may be ground in a mortar and pestle to a consistency suitable for application with a brush. Mix the hand-ground colors with a drop of oil of lavender, which serves as medium and binder. Pan colors such as those illustrated in step 6, which are already finely ground, are mixed with water to a desirable consistency.

1 Prepare a design.

2 Clean the copper blank; apply and fire a base coat of enamel. A light color may be preferable since it will permit the design to show more clearly.

3 Transfer the design to the piece. Use a china marking pencil or carbon paper. Scratch the design into the base coat with a steel point and remove the carbon or grease pencil lines with carbon tetrachloride.

4 Paint the design with the overglaze enamels.

5 Fire.

6 To vary the color, glazing colors over one another is preferable to mixing them together. Glazing enriches the color while mixing tends to muddy it. If pan colors are used, they must be fired at a lower temperature. A final coat of clear flux may be dusted over the surface and fired to prevent peeling and oxidation.

CLOISONNÉ

Cloisonné design is based on areas that can easily be enclosed with the cloisons or wire separators. The cloisons serve as walls that prevent color areas from running together.

MATERIALS

1. Copper blank
2. Enamels
3. Copper wire for cloisons (20-gauge or less)
4. Clear flux
5. Pliers
6. Hammer
7. Small spatula

1 *Plan the design.*

2 *Bend the wire into desired shapes. Use pliers or a nail for bending the wire.*

3 *Flatten the bent wire design with a mallet on a hard surface.*

4 *Lay in place on the cleaned piece of copper.*

5 *Flatten against the back piece so they fit together as closely as possible.*

6 *Place on sheet of paper and dust with flux.*

7 *Fire.*

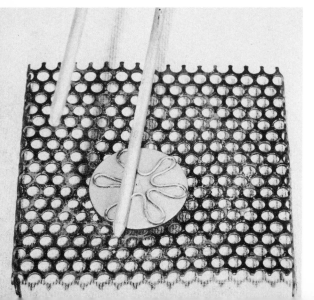

8 *After firing, push any raised wire against the back piece instantly, while the piece is still hot. The loading fork is good for this. If the wire is not securely held in place by the flux, the surface can be refluxed and the piece refired.*

9 *Mix the enamel powder with water to a pastelike consistency in a shallow dish. Tip the dish slightly to allow excess water to collect on the lower side. Dip enamel from upper side.*

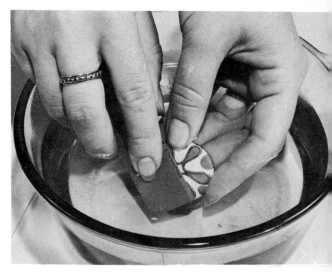

10 Charge or fill the cloisons with enamel paste. A small tool, such as an enameling spatula or an old dental tool, is good for scooping up wet paste.

11 Tamp color into place with the tool. Remove any smears on the wire with a clean brush and take up excess moisture from the enamel paste with the tip of a folded facial tissue. Allow to dry thoroughly.

12 Fire.

13 Recharge and refire, until the cloisons are filled to the top.

14 Clean the surface of the wire and the edge of the piece with a carborundum stone under running water or in a pan of water. In cleaning the edge, stroke away from the surface or the enamel may chip.

15 Finished example.

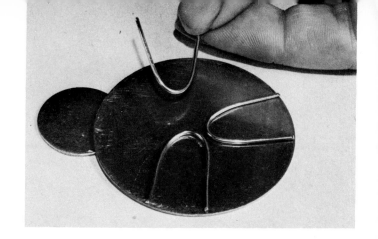

16 *Cioisons may be placed on the piece separately, rather than in one continuous shape. The separate shapes must be placed to create closed areas that can be charged with enamel paste.*

CHAMPLEVÉ

Champlevé enameling is based on etched-out hollows charged with enamel paste with areas of bare metal between.

1 *Plan the design.*

2 *Transfer the design to the metal with carbon paper or grease pencil.*

3 *Paint the design with asphaltum. The asphaltum is applied to the areas which are to be left unetched, including sides and back. As an alternative to this, the entire surface can be painted with an even coat of asphaltum, the design transferred onto this and then scratched out with a sharp tool.*

4 *Prepare the etching bath by adding one part nitric acid to seven parts water. For safety, pour the acid into the water. Avoid inhaling the acid fumes. Work in a well-ventilated area. Use rubber gloves when handling the acid and etching bath. Always mix etching bath in a glass container and store in a glass bottle that can be tightly stopped. This fluid is useful until it turns dark blue. To discard, wash down the drain with running water in order to dilute the acid and prevent damage to the drain.*

MATERIALS

1. Enamels
2. Copper blank
3. Nitric acid solution
4. Glass bowl
5. Carborundum stone
6. Small spatula
7. Brush
8. Asphaltum
9. Soap and water
10. Turpentine or kerosene

5   Immerse the piece in the etching bath. With the tip of a feather, occasionally brush away bubbles that appear on the surface of the metal. Leave the metal in the etching bath until the design has been etched to a depth of about 1/32 of an inch. Check the progress of the etch frequently.

6   When the etching is complete, rinse the piece with water to remove excess etching bath. Then clean the asphaltum from the metal: let it sit in a dish of turpentine or kerosene for about ten minutes, then clean it with a cloth. Wash with soap, brush, and water. Finish the cleaning with steel wool and cleanser if necessary.

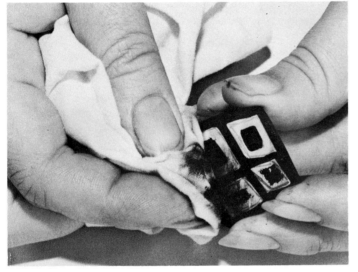

7   Fill or wet-charge the etched-out areas with enamel-water mixture. Apply the enamel with a small spatula. Fill the etched out areas to the level of the surface.

8   Absorb any excess moisture from the enamel with a soft cloth or facial tissue. Allow the enamel to dry thoroughly. To speed the drying, place on the kiln top, or in the kiln for a few seconds.

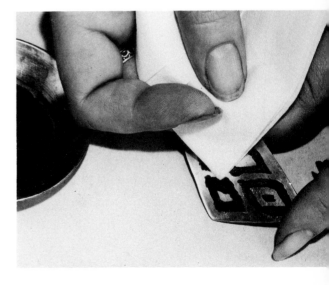

9 *Fire.*

10 *When the piece is cool, wash with soap and water. Recharge any low areas and refire.*

11 *Stone or grind the fired piece under water with a carborundum stone to make the enamel surface flush with the metal. If any enameled areas remain low, recharge and refire. Between each stoning and refiring, cleanse the piece thoroughly with soap and water. The stoning makes the surface dull. If a shiny surface is desired, give the piece a final firing to restore gloss.*

PLIQUE-À-JOUR

In the plique-à-jour process, openings cut or drilled in the metal are filled with enamel to form the design. Unlike the other enameling processes, plique-à-jour has no backing for the enamel, and the color quality is enhanced by light coming through the transparent or translucent enameled areas from the back. Plique-à-jour enameling can also be done on a framework of wire or metal strips, bent and soldered into place, much like a cloisonné piece without a back. Since the design is composed largely of these enamel-filled negative shapes, great care must be taken in their design.

MATERIALS

1. Transparent enamels
2. Silver or copper blank
3. Mica sheet
4. Small spatula
5. Drill
6. Vise
7. Soap and water
8. Carborundum stone
9. Steel wool
10. Facial tissue

1   *Drill holes in the copper or silver blank to form the design. Various sizes of drills may be used. Openings larger than ¼ inch are difficult to fill, because the unsupported enamel tends to pull from the edges or crack.*

2   *Clean the metal thoroughly.*

3   *Place the metal piece on a sheet of mica.*

4   *Wet-charge the openings with enamel powder and water mixed to a pastelike consistency, using a small spatula. A little gum solution added to the wet-charged enamel will help hold it in place while it is drying. Mix the enamel in a shallow dish and tip the dish slightly to allow excess moisture to collect on lower side. Dip enamel from the upper side. Light, transparent enamels are best suited to this technique.*

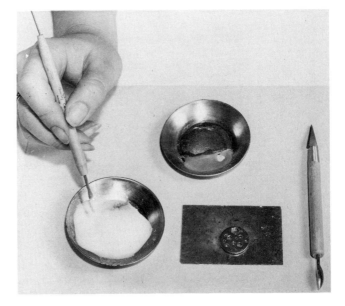

5   *Absorb excess moisture from the wet-charged enamel with a facial tissue. Allow to dry thoroughly.*

6 *Fire. Fire only until enamel turns glassy. Overfiring will cause the liquid enamel to pull away from the edges of the openings. The pieces must cool slowly and completely away from drafts.*

7 *Wash with soap and water. Recharge openings if necessary and refire.*

8 *After piece has cooled, remove mica sheet. Stone off under water to remove excess enamel and mica bits. Clean with steel wool.*

9 *Refire to restore glass. Take great care not to overfire.*

10 *Buff or polish.*

SOLDERING

To attach jeweler's findings to finished enamel pieces, soft solder must be used, since it flows at temperatures below the fusing point of enamel. Soft solder flux should be applied to all areas to be soldered. Flux in paste form is most convenient. Some soft solders, such as rosin core or acid core, contain their own flux. Of these, the rosin core soft solder is preferable, since the acid core solder reacts with the copper, making it difficult to clean. If soldering is used to attach the cloisons in the cloisonné process, extra hard solder should be used, since its high melting point permits of sufficient heat to fuse the enamel without disturbing the position of the cloisons.

MATERIALS

1. Rosin core soft solder or soft solder and soft solder flux
2. Blowtorch
3. Asbestos sheet
4. Hammer
5. Wire cutters
6. Jeweler's findings—cuff link backs, earring backs, pin backs, tie clasps, clips
7. Tweezers
8. Steel wool
9. Carborundum

1 Thoroughly clean the surfaces to be soldered, both the finding and the piece, with steel wool. If the counter-enamel has covered or partially covered the area to be soldered, it may be stoned away. Use a carborundum stone, under water, with a rotary motion.

2 If flux is to be used, apply it to the areas to be soldered with a matchstick.

3 Place the piece to be soldered, enamel side down, on an asbestos sheet.

4 Cut small pieces of solder, flatten slightly with a hammer, and place either under or along the edge of the finding, which has been put in place on the piece.

5 Apply the torch carefully and withdraw as soon as the solder flows. Overheating will spoil the finding and may damage the enamel.

6 Leave the piece in place on the asbestos until it is thoroughly cool.

7 Gently scrape off excess solder with a scraper or thick-bladed knife, as if you were peeling apples. Polish with steel wool.

ENAMELING   **421**

SAWING METAL SHAPES

For the beginner, precut metal blanks are very convenient and serve nicely as experimental pieces. A great variety of shapes and sizes is available commercially. Other shapes may be cut from metal strips or sheets. With a metal-cutting saw, openings may be cut in the interior of a piece where they are needed as negative shapes in the design, or in plique-à-jour, where openings are basic to the process.

1 *Transfer the design to the piece of metal with carbon paper. Lightly scratch the design into the metal with a scriber or steel point. For simpler shapes, a paper pattern may be glued to the metal.*

2 *The saw is held in a vertical position with the handle down while sawing. Insert the saw blade with the teeth down so that the cutting will be done on the downstroke. The blade should be taut.*

3 *The metal must be held steady while sawing. It may be clamped or held firmly against a bench pin.*

4 *Saw vertically by moving the saw up and down with slight forward pressure along the pattern line.*

5 *To saw interior openings, first drill a small hole in the metal large enough to admit the saw blade near the edge of the opening to be cut out. To drill the hole, either place the metal on a piece of scrap wood and clamp both to a solid surface, or clamp the metal in a vise. Protect the metal surface from vise or clamp marks with a padding of paper. Drill.*

6 *Insert the saw blade through the drilled hole. Then attach the blade to the saw, teeth down. Saw.*

7 *Rough saw edges may be finished with a file or carborundum stone. For plique-à-jour, the rough edge should be left as a tooth to hold the enamel.*

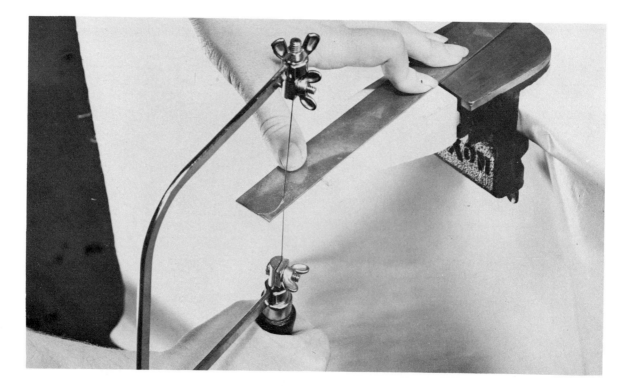

PUNCHING HOLES

Holes can be punched as well as drilled. A hole-punching machine is convenient for making an opening with which to attach a small piece to a chain or other support. The other end of this punch has a device for shaping small metal pieces.

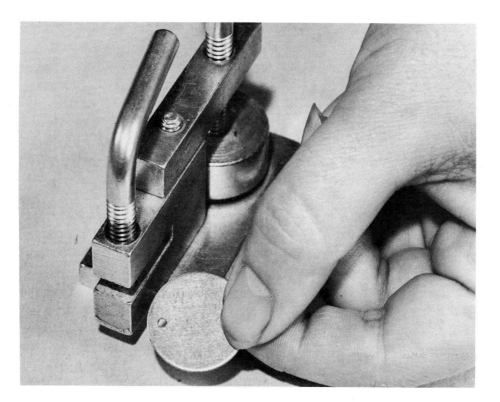

POLISHING

After thorough cleaning, the metal surfaces of an enamel piece may be brought to a fine finish by polishing with tripoli, jeweler's rouge, and a buffer. Rough edges should first be smoothed with a file, carborundum, or emery cloth. When working on the edge of an enameled surface, always file away from the enamel to avoid chipping. After the piece has been cleaned and polished, any exposed metal areas can be protected with a coat of clear lacquer.

MATERIALS

1. Buffing cloth or electric buffing wheel
2. Tripoli
3. Jeweler's rouge
4. File
5. Emery cloth
6. Carborundum
7. Lacquer

ADDITIONAL SUGGESTIONS FOR ENAMELING

Because of the technical abilities and skills involved and the special equipment and material that it requires, enameling is not generally recommended for younger students. Small groups of younger children can work successfully with enamels only if they can be carefully supervised by an instructor who fires their pieces for them. As a group or class project, enameling can best be presented on the junior or senior high school level.

The classroom should be highly organized to facilitate movement from one work area to another. The use of the kiln requires careful safety precautions and rules if the students are to fire their work themselves. A monitor system is helpful to regulate class firings.

Class work should begin with making test pieces for single colors, combinations of colors, and the basic techniques such as Limoges, sgraffito, wax resist and stencil, cloisonné, champlevé, and plique-à-jour. Later, these test pieces might be arranged and mounted on wood for a decorative panel.

Copper blanks or precut pieces are the most practical base material for beginning problems. Blanks may also be used for more complicated techniques such as cloisonné and plique-à-jour or special pieces can be designed and sawed from metal sheets.

SUGGESTED PROJECTS

Small enameled pieces are excellent for jewelry and can be made into necklaces, earrings, pins, tie clasps, or cuff links, with findings glued or soldered into place. Pieces may also be combined with other materials to make more elaborate problems such as panels, screens, boxes, book covers, belts, and many other items.

After the simple techniques of enameling are learned, larger and more expensive pieces such as bowls, boxes, trays, or panels might be attempted. These offer a larger surface for decoration.

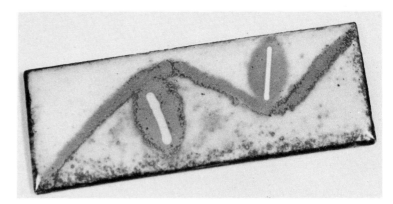

Enamel Pin. Sgraffito with Glass Threads. Child, age 10.

Enamel Pins with Glass Threads and Lumps. Child, age 9.

Enamel Pin and Earrings, Stencil Process. Child, age 11.

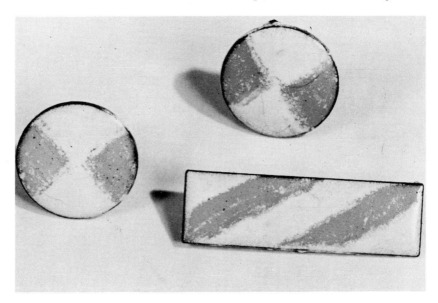

ADDITIONAL   SUGGESTIONS

India: *Textile (Detail)*. Cotton appliqué. Courtesy of Elizabeth Bayley Willis.

ADDITIONAL SUGGESTIONS FOR CRAFTS

Teachers have wonderful opportunities to enrich the learning experiences of their students in the classroom with the wealth of material available from the world's great art forms. From the culture of the ages can be found understandings of man's great creative efforts of the past as well as the best that the contemporary artist has to offer. In being introduced to the various forms of art, the student shares in the worthwhile experiences that have accumulated through this rich heritage. He has available to him a vast amount of source material to contribute to the inspiration of his own expressions and to add to his visual pleasure.

RELATIONSHIP OF ART TO OTHER UNITS OF WORK

Art as a subject has its own identity and is not a subordinate field created to serve other subject areas. It can, however, derive inspiration and motivation from other fields of study and in return offer enrichment to other subjects, making them more vital and meaningful. Any such relationship should be natural and not forced, so there will be complete freedom in developing art ideas. Subject matter can be drawn from every phase of the curriculum; it may be inspired by shapes seen in nature, or by history, literature, mathematics, and science lessons, or it may be created from personal experience. It is up to the teacher to supply the needed guidance for making such an experience a vital one.

For instance, a teacher may wish to initiate a unit on weaving while the class is studying primitive peoples or life in early America. A unit on the home or clothing may center attention on fabrics and a desire to know how cloth is made. Here various types of looms are available for experiencing the weaving process and studying the effects of combining different fibers. If students in a class do mosaic problems as the outgrowth of a study in history, they can be shown excellent examples of where this art occurs. These may be in the form of good pictorial reproductions of tile mosaics found in pavements or walls in countries such as Mexico, Spain, Greece, Italy, Turkey, Thailand, those in South America, and others being studied. Attention can be called to art values, technical aspects, and the character of the subject—whether the design is geometric, stylized, or pictorial in nature.

A study of bookbinding can derive much rich source material from the medieval period, when the making of books was a great art, and from this can come fascinating discoveries about the construction and use of books historically. This study will also enable the student better to understand the remarkable effect of the printing press upon our culture.

MATERIALS AND EQUIPMENT

Beginners do not need a great deal of material or expensive equipment for work in the crafts. They can learn to improvise and make substitutions in many instances, and often make use of things in their immediate environment.

Very beautiful and worthwhile objects such as scarves and mats can be made on box looms if they are thoughtfully planned and carefully executed. It is valuable training for students to learn that they can produce something of worth by such simple means.

Some crafts by their natures require more to work with than do others. This is true in enameling, where a kiln and enamel powders are essential to the process; however, even here, simpler means can be employed when necessary or when trying out the procedures.

As students become more experienced in the crafts and interested in their complexities, they may wish to secure additional tools with which to work.

ADJUSTMENT TO AGE LEVELS

Students of all ages can experience work in the crafts through a wide range of problems. The extent of the problems, however, will depend upon the stage of development and readiness for the work. Anything tedious that involves fine materials and intricate processes is undesirable for young children, whereas older children are challenged by more complicated procedures and impressed with a variety of tools and equipment. It is necessary to keep in mind the levels of difficulty in planning experiences so that the complications of the materials will not prove too overwhelming for the particular age group. There are different degrees of complexity involved in the various processes and these will need to be adjusted to the levels of maturity.

Simple processes are not just limited to children, for anyone can use the elementary techniques described for each craft. The important consideration is the amount of thought and personal sensitivity involved, and the quality of the design experience. The richness of the experience is revealed in the product.

The limitations imposed by materials and

methods do not hinder creative work but provide the necessary discipline needed in any craft.

CLASS ORGANIZATION FOR WORK

Most crafts lend themselves well to the classroom, for whether the class is large or small, when he is directed step by step, each student can get satisfying results. By presenting demonstrations on basic procedures to the entire group, the teacher can keep the work moving while giving individual help in working out the designs. Simple loom or braid projects can be handled well with groups, for once started most students can proceed alone with only occasional aid. Such activities carry themselves and provide opportunity for quiet absorption in the task of producing something of worth that gives personal pleasure.

With some crafts where considerable planning and a number of activities are involved it may be necessary to organize the class into groups. For instance, in block printing, some students can be completing their designs while others are cutting, and those who finish cutting first will be printing. The printing process can be demonstrated to a small group at a time as students are ready to print, or it can be presented to the whole class at once. Those who become proficient can teach or assist the others when their turn comes. If a large piece of drapery is being printed, several students can work together by dividing responsibilities. One can ink the block, one can place it in the correct position on the cloth, and another can hammer it to make the print.

Cleanup groups have to be organized also, and their duties must be assigned, for students are often careless about working habits. The necessary procedures for this should be demonstrated and carefully explained. Using plenty of newspapers on work areas and the surrounding floor will facilitate this work.

Sometimes teachers hesitate to use materials,

like clay, that require some preparation and are more difficult to handle in the classroom. With a little planning, however, these materials can be controlled so that each student knows how to take care of them. The values derived far outweigh any inconvenience experienced.

WORKING PROCEDURES

The crafts are based upon design with materials, and it is very essential at first to become acquainted with the material as it is used and to discover its possibilities. Students should be encouraged to do a great deal of experimenting and to try out various ideas, because experimentation is essential to any creative work. They can make test samples of colors and techniques in enameling; they can try modeling and stamping tools and dyes on scraps of leather; they can experiment with various weaving patterns and combinations of threads. The results of these discoveries can often be used in making articles. For instance, decorative papers made by experimenting with various processes can be kept and used later in bookbinding projects.

The young child will continue to explore and play with a material for a considerable period of time, depending upon his level of development. The teacher needs to be alert in providing him with opportunities at the proper time, which will permit the child to sense the art possibilities of the medium. He will work directly with the material, selecting and planning as he goes.

After the student has had plenty of opportunity to find out what he can do with the material, he can then learn to preplan his designs by using the elements and principles of art. By starting with simple forms he can gradually progress to more complex ones. His designing can then be directed to a particular purpose, for all crafts should serve some function. They are not activities done for their own sakes, but a means by which products are formed. A piece of weaving becomes a bag or belt, or mosaic tesserae are used for a tile.

STEPS IN WORKING WITH A CRAFT

1. Introduction to the materials used in the craft.
2. Introduction to the tools and the purposes for which they are used.
3. Demonstration of the processes involved in working with the materials and tools.
4. Experimentation with materials and tools to become acquainted with their qualities and the possibilities of their use in design.
5. Evaluation of the discoveries and their utilization where possible in the construction of objects for a particular purpose.
6. Application of methods of preplanning in which the elements and principles of art are used.
7. Starting with simple designs first, then later working toward more complex ones.
8. Consideration of whether designs should be abstract in character or whether pictorial units could be used.

Children have a natural sense of pattern, which can be developed through experiences with design. They should be encouraged to criticize their work and to try to improve it along with their design understanding.

Rich learning experiences are possible only when articles made are thoughtfully planned. Craft work from the kindergarten to college level has little educational value if the experience is limited to therapeutic or technical activity without consideration for the aesthetic pleasures, satisfactions, and growth resulting from planning and design.

Even very young children can learn the principles of organization and good design. They can best acquire the knowledge and skill needed for their age level through a balanced program of demonstration and experimentation. Demonstration provides the visual stimulus of seeing good design examples, such as natural objects and well-designed works from other cultures, the work of other children, and simple basic methods or techniques to establish working standards.

Space filling and space breaking are most important factors in design presentation. Students learn the value of combining elements into organized patterns that can be successfully applied to almost any surface. Basic stripes provide an endless variety of combinations in which the width, length, direction, color, value, and texture can be limited or added to, to suit the use or function. Stripes held in simple patterns may be enriched with geometric additions, circles or dots, squares and triangular shapes; or geometric and other shapes may be organized into stripe patterns.

Checkerboard patterns offer another endless variety of design possibilities that may be varied with the addition of geometric or pictorial shapes.

A single motif or a combination or variation of motifs may be used for an allover pattern. For instance, the feather motif that is often used in primitive and folk art is found in infinite variations, and yet the basic motifs are similar.

Patterns and motifs can be derived from observing natural objects. It is possible for children to learn a great deal by examining a bird's feather, a stone, a flower, or a shell if the design qualities are pointed out to them.

The balance of dark and light is very important to good design and can be learned through the study of positive and negative shapes. Simple geometric shapes, drawings of birds, butterflies, fish, and many other subjects, lend themselves to such plans. Through alternation patterns made with cut paper, it is possible for beginners to learn a great deal about positive and negative shape relationships. Alternation is a valuable technique for simple space breaking.

This design material is adaptable to any age level and may be simplified or made more complex to meet the ability of the student.

Acquaintance with materials will demonstrate to students how each material plays a determining role in the kinds of designs or forms that will result. What is learned in working with one material should be carried over to design experiences with other materials. A progression of design experience can and should be evolved. These concepts then should be integrated into all craft experiences and other art work, such as painting and sculpture.

Many parts of this book, such as Decorated Papers, Textiles, and Mosaics for flat designs, or Clay, Paper, and Bookbinding for three-dimensional designs, are especially suited for the presentation of beginning design problems. In many of these craft areas both two- and three-dimensional designs are combined. In bookbinding, the flat decorative papers become a part of the three-dimensional form.

Problems could include singly or in combination such principles as the recognition and use of:

1. Large, medium, and small;
2. Dark, medium, and light;
3. The names of colors and color mixing;
4. Shape;
5. Textural contrasts;
6. Rhythm and balance.

Each student should be encouraged to work at the peak of his capacity, and a knowledge of design will give him pride in his accomplishment. His work should also be evaluated according to his abilities, and he should be encouraged and helped to judge his results.

Appreciation of the techniques and design used in the crafts can be furthered by the study of fine examples in museums and reproductions. Rich sources of color and design will be found in the work of modern painters such as Matisse and Klee, in the works of ancient peoples such as the Persians, and in the primitive and folk arts of many lands. Children will observe good source materials by looking to animal and other nature forms for inspiration.

BIBLIOGRAPHY

Attic Greek (Geometric Period): *Vase, Dipylon.* Eighth century B.C. Ceramic, 26½" high. Courtesy of The Metropolitan Museum of Art, Rogers Fund, 1914.

BIBLIOGRAPHY

DESIGN AND RESOURCE

Best-Maugard, Adolfo. *A Method for Creative Design.* New York: Knopf, 1926.

Boas, Franz. *Primitive Art.* New York: Dover Publications, 1955.

Bossert, Helmuth T. *Decorative Arts of Asia and Egypt.* New York: Frederick A. Praeger, 1956.

———. *Folk Art of Europe.* New York: Frederick A. Praeger, 1953.

———. *Folk Art of Primitive Peoples.* New York: Frederick A. Praeger.

Christensen, Erwin O. *Index of American Design.* New York: National Gallery of Art. Macmillan Co., 1950.

———. *Primitive Art.* Bonanza Books, Viking Press, 1955.

Douglas, Frederick Huntington, and René d'Harnocourt. *Indian Art of the United States.* New York: Museum of Modern Art, 1941.

Gardner, Helen. *Art Through the Ages,* Third Edition. New York: Harcourt, Brace and Company, 1948.

Kepes, Gyorgy. *Language of Vision.* Chicago: Paul Theobald, 1947.

Lehner, Ernst. *Alphabets and Ornaments.* Cleveland, New York: World Publishing Co., 1952.

———. *Symbols, Signs, and Signets.* Cleveland, New York: World Publishing Co., 1950.

Lewis, Albert B. *Decorative Art of New Guinea.* Chicago: Field Museum of Natural History, 1925.

Linton, Ralph, and Paul S. Wingert. *Arts of the South Seas.* New York: Museum of Modern Art, 1946.

Lipman, Jean. *American Folk Art.* Pantheon, 1948.

Moholy-Nagy. *Vision in Motion.* Chicago: Paul Theobald, 1947.

Munsterberg, Hugo. *The Folk Arts of Japan.* Rutland, Vermont and Tokyo, Japan: Charles E. Tuttle Co., 1958.

Poulik, Josef, and others. *Prehistoric Art.* New York: Tudor Publishing Co.

Riis, P. J., *Etruscan Art.* New York: Philosophical Library, 1954.

Sourek, Karel. *Folk Art in Pictures.* London: Spring Books.

Trowell, Margaret. *African Design.* New York: Frederick A. Praeger, 1960.

PAPER

Betts, Victoria. *Exploring Papier-Mâché.* Worcester, Mass.: Davis Press, 1955.

Cizek, Franz. *Children's Colored Paper Work.* New York: G. E. Stechert and Co., 1927.

Hobson, A. F. *Paper Sculpture.* Leicester, England: Dryad, Ltd., 1956.

Hughes, Toni. *How to Make Shapes in Space.* New York: E. P. Dutton and Co., 1955.

Johnson, Pauline. *Creating with Paper: Basic Forms and Variations.* Seattle: University of Washington Press, 1958.

Johnston, Mary Grace. *Paper Sculpture* (portfolio). Worcester, Mass.: Davis Press, Inc., 1952.

Lipski, Tadeusz. *Paper Sculpture.* New York: Thomas Y. Crowell Co., 1948.

McPharlin, Paul. *Cutting Paper Sculpture.* New York: X-acto Crescent Products Co., 1946.

———. *Paper Sculpture—Its Construction and Uses for Display and Decoration.* New York: Hastings House, 1944.

Martin, Marie Gibert. *Pasteless Construction with Paper.* New York: Pageant Press, 1951.

Palestrant, Simon S. *Practical Papercraft.* New York: Homecrafts, 1950.

Sadler, Arthur. *Paper Sculpture.* London: Blanford Press, Ltd., 1955.

Sarasas, Claude. *Folding Paper for Children.* Tokyo: Dainippon Yubenkai Kodansha, 1951.

Schott, Otto and Hans. *Es Glantz und Glitzert.* Winterthur: Verlag Franz Schubiger, n.d.

BOOKBINDING

Banister, Manly. *Pictorial Manual of Bookbinding*. New York: The Ronald Press, 1958.

Chiera, Edward. *They Wrote on Clay*. Chicago: University of Chicago Press, 1938.

Cockerell, Douglas. *Bookbinding and the Care of Books*. London: Pitman, 1931.

Diehl, Edith. *The Art of Bookbinding* (2 vol.). New York: Holt, Rinehart and Winston, Inc., 1946.

Groneman, Chris H. *General Bookbinding*. Bloomington, Ill.: McKnight and McKnight, 1946.

Johnson, Pauline. *The Design and Making of Books*. Seattle: University of Washington Press, 1961.

Kitson, Edward. *Bookbinding*. New York: Dover Publications, 1954.

Klinefelter, Lee M. *Bookbinding Made Easy*. Milwaukee, Wisconsin: Bruce Publishing Co., 1934.

Lewis, Arthur William. *Basic Bookbinding* (paperback). New York: Dover Publications, Inc., 1955.

McMurtrie, Douglas C. *The Book: The Story of Printing and Bookmaking* (Third edition). Fair Lawn, N. J.: Oxford University Press, 1943.

Meyer, Peter. *The Book of Kells*. Berne, Switzerland: Urs Graf Verlag, 1950.

Woodcock, John. *Binding Your Own Books* (Puffin Picture Book 104). Great Britain: Penguin Books, Ltd., 1956.

WEAVING

Albers, Anni. *On Designing*. New Haven, Conn.: Pellango Press.

Alexander, Marthann. *15 Simple Ways to Weave*. Bloomington, Ill.: McKnight and McKnight, 1954.

Aller, Doris. *Handmade Rugs*. Menlo Park, California: Lane Publishing Co., 1953.

Amsdem, Charles Avery. *Navajo Weaving*. Albuquerque, N. M.: University of New Mexico Press, 1949.

Atwater, Mary Meigs. *Byways in Hand-weaving*. New York: The Macmillan Co., 1954.

Becher, Lotte. *Handweaving*. New York: Thomas Y. Crowell Co., 1954.

Birrell, Verla. *The Textile Arts*. New York: Harper and Brothers, 1959.

Blumenau, Lili. *The Art and Craft of Handweaving*. New York: Crown Publishing Co., 1955.

Christopher, F. J. *Hand Loom Weaving* (paperback). New York: Dover Publications, Inc., 1954.

Lurçat, Jean. *Designing Tapestry*. London: Rockliff Publishing Corp., 1950.

Overman, Ruth, and Lula Smith. *Contemporary Handweaving*. Ames, Iowa: Iowa State College Press, 1955.

Simpson, L. E., and M. Weir. *The Weaver's Craft*. Peoria, Ill.: Chas. A. Bennett Co., Inc., 1957.

Weibel, Adèle Coulin. *Two Thousand Years of Textiles*. New York: Pantheon Books, 1952.

DECORATED TEXTILES

Birrell, Verla. *The Textile Arts*. New York: Harper and Brothers, 1959.

Karasz, Mariska. *Adventures in Stitches and More Adventures, Fewer Stitches*. New York: Funk and Wagnalls Co., 1959.

Tanner, Robin. *Children's Work in Block Printing*. Peoria, Ill.: Chas. A. Bennett Co., Inc., 1948.

Zweybruck, Emmy. *The New Stencil Book*. Sandusky, Ohio: Prang Publishing Co.

LEATHER

Aller, Doris. *Sunset Leathercraft Book*. Menlo Park, Calif.: Lane Publishing Co., 1952.

Cherry, Raymond. *General Leathercraft*. Bloomington, Illinois: McKnight and McKnight, 1955.

Cox, Doris, and Barbara Warren. *Creative Hands*. New York: John Wiley and Sons, 1951.

Dougherty, Betty. *Your Leather Book*. Peoria, Illinois: Chas. A. Bennett Co., Inc., 1951.

Groneman, Chris. *Applied Leathercraft* (revised). Peoria, Ill.: Chas. A. Bennett Co., Inc., 1952.

CLAY

Duncan, Julia Hamlin, and Victor D'Amico. *How to Make Pottery and Ceramic Sculpture*. New York: Museum of Modern Art. Distributed by Simon and Schuster, 1947.

Ellis, Clifford and Rosemary. *Modeling for Amateurs*. New York: Thomas Y. Crowell Co.

Leach, Bernard. *A Potter's Portfolio*. New York: Pitman Publishing Corp., 1951.

Norton, F. H. *Ceramics for the Artist Potter*. Cambridge, Mass.: Addison-Wesley Publishing Co., Inc., 1956.

Rhodes, Daniel. *Clay and Glazes for the Potter*. Philadelphia and New York: Chilton Company, Book Division, 1957.

————. *Stoneware and Porcelain*. Philadelphia and New York: Chilton Company, Book Division, 1959.

MOSAICS

Aller, Doris, and Diane Lee Aller. *Sunset Mosaics*. Menlo Park, Calif.: Lane Book Co., 1959.

Jenkins, Louisa, and Barbara Mills. *The Art of Making Mosaics*. Princeton, N. J.: D. Van Nostrand Co., Inc., 1957.

Meyer, Peter. *Byzantine Mosaics*. New York, Toronto: Iris Books, Oxford University Press, 1952.

Sister Magdalen Mary, I.H.M. *Mosaics for Everyone*. Los Angeles: Immaculate Heart College, 1958.

Young, Joseph L. *Course in Making Mosaics*. New York: Reinhold Publishing Corp., 1957.

ENAMELING

Bates, Kenneth F. *Enameling, Principles and Practice*. Cleveland and New York: The World Publishing Co. 1951.

Coleman, Gerry. *Copper Enameling* (pictorial instructions). Inglewood, Calif.: Gick Enterprise, 1957.

Enamel, an Historical Survey to the Present Day. New York: The Cooper Union Museum for the Arts of Decoration, 1954.

Gauthier, Marie-Madeleine S. *Emaux Limousins Champlevés des XII, XIII et XIV Siècles*, 268 Blvd. Saint Germain, Paris: Gerard Le Prat, 1950.

Martin, Charles J. *How to Make Modern Jewelry*. New York: Museum of Modern Art. Distributed by Simon and Schuster, 1949.

Maryon, Herbert. *Metalwork and Enameling*. New York: Dover Publications, Inc., 1955.

Pack, Greta. *Jewelry and Enameling*. Princeton, N. J.: D. Van Nostrand Co., 1945.

GENERAL CRAFTS

Cox, Doris, and Barbara Warren. *Creative Hands*. New York: John Wiley and Sons, 1951.

Fearing, Kelly, and Evelyn Beard. *Our Expanding Vision*. Austin, Texas: Bennett Publishing Co., 1960.

Payant, Felix. *Create Something—A Handbook for Beginners*. Columbus, Ohio: Design Publishing Co., 1939.

Robertson, Seonaid. *Creative Crafts in Education*. Cambridge, Mass.: Robert Bentley, Inc., 1953.

Wankelman, Willard, Karl Richards, and Maretta Wigg. *Arts and Crafts for Elementary Teachers*. Dubuque, Iowa: William C. Brown Co., 1954.

Zechlin, Ruth. *Complete Book of Handcrafts*. Amsterdam, Netherlands: Internationale Uitgevery Duphare, 1959.

PERIODICALS

American Fabrics
Arts and Architecture
Craft Horizons
Creative Crafts
Design
Domus
Everyday Art (American Crayon Co.)
Everyday Art Design Quarterly
Graphis
Sunset
School Arts
Woman's Day

Mexican: *Banks in the shape of a head.* Twentieth century. Fired clay with painted decoration. Approx. 6½″ high.